Contents

Contents

Structures of Memory

You must be able to:

- Explain the differences between short-term memory and long-term memory
- Identify and give examples of different types of long-term memory.

Short-term and Long-term Memory

- Memory is a psychological ability that everybody uses on a daily basis. It is used to store information such as the names of people and places, facts for exams, as well as remembering skills and life events.
- People would be unable to function without their memories.
- There are several different memory **stores**, which work in different ways.
- The two most important ones are a brief temporary store called **short-term memory (STM)** and a permanent store called **long-term memory (LTM)**.
  - Short-term memory (also called 'working memory') has a limited **duration** – it can only store information for a short time. It also has a limited **capacity**, as it can only take in and process a small number of items.
  - The duration of STM has been estimated at 30 seconds, and in terms of capacity, it can hold around seven words or numbers at a time.
  - Long-term memory lasts much longer – memories that have been well understood and practised are essentially permanent. It also stores an unlimited amount of information.

> I would forget my friends' phone numbers very quickly unless I saved them or wrote them down. This shows the limited duration of short-term memory.

> It can be hard to learn new information, but once you fully understand it, you can remember it for many years. This is because it needs to be encoded to long-term memory.

Types of Long-term Memory

- Long-term memory itself is not a single store but has different structures that encode and store different types of information.

Type of Memory	What is Remembered	Example
Episodic memory	Memory for life events	Remembering a family holiday
Semantic memory	Memory for facts	Remembering that a penguin is a type of bird
Procedural memory	Memory for skills	Remembering how to insert a SIM card into a phone

- An episodic memory means remembering an event from a person's own life. This form of LTM is like a mental diary or journal.

- The term 'semantic' means *meaning*; semantic memories are understood and can be explained to other people, but do not necessarily relate to specific life events.
- A procedural memory is the memory for a skill or action. These are unusual in that the memory is often hard to explain in words.

Forgetting

- It's possible to successfully remember one type of long-term memory and not another.
  - Some people suffer from amnesia – memory loss – which can result from a blow to the head or from brain damage.
  - These individuals tend to forget episodic memories rather than procedural memories (skills) or facts about the world.
- Long-term memory is also subject to forgetting. One major cause of forgetting is that two similar events or pieces of information get mixed up. This is called **interference**.
- The passage of time can lead to gradual forgetting in LTM. It can be hard to retrieve old memories, especially out of context.
- Memories can be triggered by a **cue**, i.e. the presentation of related information, or part of the memory such as the first letter of a word or name. A question can also act as a cue. Reviewing and self-testing can help information to be consolidated in LTM.

	Key Point

The two main types of memory – short-term and long-term – have fundamentally different features.

Brain Areas Involved in Memory

- As well as having separate functions, LTM and STM functions are processed by different areas of the brain. The frontal lobe of the cerebral cortex is essential for STM and for related cognitive processes.
- Several brain areas are important for LTM. Most notably, the **hippocampus** – an area of the limbic system in the brain – is involved in the formation of new semantic and episodic long-term memories.
- Case studies of people with brain damage demonstrate that long- and short-term memory are separate.
- For example, Henry Molaison (HM), had his hippocampus removed during brain surgery.
  - His STM was unaffected but he was unable to form new semantic or episodic long-term memories (Scoville & Milner, 1957).
  - HM was still able to form new procedural memories, showing that these are processed by different structures of the brain.

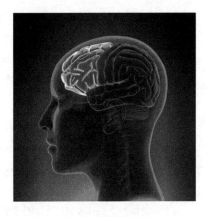

	Key Words

store
short-term memory (STM)
long-term memory (LTM)
duration
capacity
episodic memory
semantic memory
procedural memory
interference
cue
hippocampus

	Quick Test

1. Which memory store is involved if you walk into another room and then realise that you have forgotten why you came there?
2. Anna is trying to remember the names of the different types of cells that occur in plants. What type of long-term memory is she using?

Processes in Memory

You must be able to:

- Explain how memories are encoded and stored
- Explain and give examples of how memories are retrieved
- Explain what is meant by active processing in the context of memory.

Memory in Everyday Life

- Problems with memory, such as forgetting facts or phone numbers, or missing an appointment, help to demonstrate how important memory is for everyday life.
- To function, people rely on holding things in STM as they work on them, and they must be able to put new information into LTM and later bring it back to mind.
- Memory is an **active process**. This means that it is not like a box in the head where things are stored, but a process (or set of processes) that people engage in constantly.

Three Key Processes

- An everyday example of using memory could involve a person reading a new fact on a website one morning (**encoding**), engaging in other activities for a period of time (**storage**), and later in the day telling somebody about what they had read (**retrieval**).

> **Key Point**
>
> Memory involves encoding information, storing it for a period of time, and then retrieving it at a later date. Memory is used to complete tasks, solve problems and make sense of new information.

- **Encoding** means taking new information into memory. To use a computer analogy, it is like saving the information to the hard drive. Encoding is therefore an **input process**.
- **Storage** is the process of maintaining information in temporary or permanent memory over time, avoiding forgetting or distortions. To maintain the memory in storage, it usually needs to be consolidated by regular revision. Sleep also helps information to be consolidated.
- **Retrieval** means accessing the stored information when you need it, and bringing it back to mind. It is therefore the **output process** of memory.

- These processes typically refer to LTM, but the same processes happen in STM over a much shorter timescale. Storage is very limited and information must be retrieved quickly.
- There are various ways that information can be retrieved.

> **Key Point**
>
> Retrieval can be difficult. It often involves effort, and there is no guarantee that information which is stored in a person's mind will be successfully retrieved when needed.

- One is via **recognition**, meaning that the information or stimulus is repeated and the person compares it to what is in their memory. A multiple choice test makes use of recognition memory.
- **Cued recall** means that the person gets a cue – a prompt or reminder of some kind. One example would be seeing someone's first initial and then remembering their name.

– **Free recall** means that the stimulus is not present and there is no cue – the person retrieves the information directly from memory. One example of this would be a student writing down a quotation in an English exam from memory. Typically, this is the most difficult form of retrieval.

An Active Process

- Memory is an active process, where a person is constantly trying to make sense of their surroundings and link them to prior memories.
- Information is only taken into memory if a person pays attention to it. This typically happens when they find things interesting or emotional in some way. Therefore, learning new information is also active.
- STM is often called 'working memory' because it is used for active processing of information in everyday tasks, e.g. following a series of instructions. It is not simply used for storage.
- LTM is sometimes compared to recording a video. However, this misleadingly suggests that it happens fairly automatically and is retrieved in the same form as it was remembered. In fact, both encoding and retrieval involve mental effort, and the processes involved can cause the information to be changed.
- The active nature of encoding and retrieving means things can be distorted depending on our expectations (see page 14).

One example of memory is remembering someone's name after you meet them. When you introduce yourself, they will usually tell you their name. However, perhaps you don't make much of an effort to retain the name and it quickly fades from your STM. For this reason, it will not be encoded to LTM.

How Memories are Formed

- Repetition is important for memory, as it provides more chances for information to be encoded. However, simply repeating things does not always cause them to be encoded to LTM, particularly if the information is hard to understand.
- The best way to build a new memory is to link the new item to what is already understood, and then repeatedly retrieve it from memory, preferably in a way that is spaced out over time. (This is the method that is used throughout this series of textbooks – helping you to learn via spaced retrieval!)

 Key Point

Memory is an active process which involves making sense of new information and linking it to what we know.

Key Words

active process
encoding
storage
retrieval
input process
output process
recognition
cued recall
free recall

 Quick Test

1. What term is used to mean taking new information in by converting it into a form that can be stored?
2. A person is asked for their postcode. After a moment's thought, they give the correct answer. Which process does this describe?

The Multi-Store Model of Memory 1

You must be able to:

- Describe the three stores of the multi-store model of memory
- Explain how information moves between the stores of the model.

Connections Between the Stores

- Memory can be divided into a temporary store called short-term memory (STM, also known as 'working memory') and a permanent store called long-term memory (LTM).
- The **multi-store model of memory** (Atkinson & Shiffrin, 1968) proposed that these two stores are connected together via a process called **rehearsal**. This means that holding information in the short-term store by repeating it again and again allows it to be encoded to LTM.
- According to the multi-store model, this is the only way that information can be permanently memorised. Unlike STM, the LTM has an unlimited capacity.
- Rehearsal also allows a person to hold information in their STM for longer, to prevent it being forgotten in the short-term, as the STM has a short duration.

Sensory Memory

- The multi-store model of memory also describes a third key memory store: **sensory memory**.
- Sensory memory is a very brief store, allowing sensations such as sounds and images to be retained for a moment even before we have time to think about or process them.
- The multi-store model states that this new sensory information can only be transferred from sensory to short-term memory if we pay **attention** to it.

> ### Key Point
>
> The multi-store model presents a simple overview of the architecture of memory.

Multi-store model

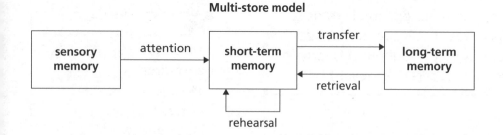

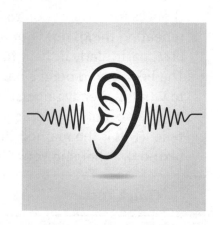

- In effect, there is a separate sensory store for each of the senses: visual, auditory, and so on.
  - The auditory store in sensory memory can hold spoken words for around two seconds, allowing people to focus their attention on something that has just been said to them.
  - Research by Sperling (1960) showed that the visual sensory store has a very brief duration – less than one second – but a large capacity. This suggests that most of the sensory information that is initially processed by the brain will fade without ever entering STM.

Types of Encoding

- As we have already seen, encoding means taking information into memory. Each store encodes information in its own way, according to the model. This means that each store can only take in and process a particular type of information.
  - The STM encodes information based on its sound. This is called **acoustic encoding**.
  - The LTM encodes information based on its meaning. This is called **semantic encoding**.
  - The sensory memory has a separate store for each sense, and therefore encodes information in several ways – visually, acoustically, and so on.
- Information can be converted to the appropriate type of encoding for each store. For example, when someone reads a sentence (a visual task), the STM converts the words on the page into sounds.
- The fact that the long-term memory encodes things semantically has important implications.
  - It suggests that when someone remembers something like a story or joke over a long period of time, they will remember the gist (i.e. the main meaningful ideas), but not the exact words used. The same applies to a concept learned at school.
  - It also means that people will tend to forget things over the long term unless they understand them.

Key Point

The three key stores of the multi-store model are viewed as being joined together via the processes of attention and rehearsal.

Key Words

multi-store model of memory
rehearsal
sensory memory
attention
acoustic encoding
semantic encoding

Quick Test

1. What process is required for information to be transferred from sensory memory to STM?
2. Which type of encoding depends on understanding the meaning of new information?

The Multi-Store Model of Memory 2

You must be able to:

- Explain supporting evidence for the multi-store model of memory (Murdock's serial position curve study)
- Evaluate the multi-store model of memory.

Supporting Evidence for the Multi-Store Model of Memory

The Serial Position Curve

- An experiment that appears to support the multi-store model was conducted by Murdock (1962).
- He gave participants lists of random words to remember, and compared the chance of each word being recalled with its position in the list.

Results of the Study

- The study found that words at the start of the list were better remembered than those in the middle. This is known as the primacy effect.
- Words at the end were better remembered too – this is called the recency effect.
- Overall, these effects can be shown on a U-shaped graph known as the serial position curve.

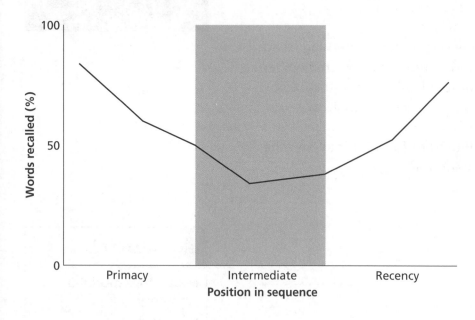

- According to the multi-store model, the primacy effect occurs because items at the start of a list are easier to rehearse, and therefore get encoded into long-term memory. By the middle of the list there are too many to rehearse.
- The recency effect occurs because the last few items are in short-term memory, but because of its limited capacity, the middle items are pushed out from short-term memory in a process known as **displacement**.
- This provides evidence that there is a distinction between STM and LTM.

Evaluation of the Multi-Store Model

- The multi-store model shows STM and LTM as separate stores, an idea which is supported by the serial position curve and by the fact that each store relies on different brain areas.
- A problem with the multi-store model is that it does not account for the use of **visual encoding** in either short-term or long-term memory. However, people are able to take in and store visual information such as faces and maps.
- The concept of rehearsal is also over-simplistic. People appear to be able to take in information without rehearsing it, and there are occasions where a lot of rehearsal fails to encode information to LTM.
- The multi-store model doesn't show the different types of LTM (see page 6) – another way in which the model is over-simplistic.

Quick Test

1. Why couldn't the whole list of words from Murdock's experiment be held in short-term memory?
2. Explain one strength or one weakness of the multi-store model of memory.
3. If a friend tells you a list of their favourite films, which ones are you most likely to forget about later on – those at the start of the list, in the middle or towards the end?

Key Words

primacy effect
recency effect
serial position curve
displacement
visual encoding

Factors Affecting Memory

You must be able to:

- Describe Bartlett's War of the Ghosts study
- Explain and evaluate the theory of reconstructive memory
- Identify and explain factors that affect the accuracy of memory.

Bartlett's Research into Memory

- **Bartlett** was the first professor of psychology in the UK. He was interested in how long-term memories can be forgotten and distorted, and how this process is affected by culture.
- In contrast to a lot of other memory research, Bartlett's research used realistic stimuli – he studied memory for stories and pictures.

Schemas

- As discussed earlier, memory is an active process which involves people interpreting stimuli and linking it to prior memories. This concept connects to Bartlett's memory research.
- According to Bartlett, LTM is based around clusters of related meaningful information. These are called **schemas** (or schemata). A schema is a concept that people derive from life experience and which is influenced by their culture, such as a person's mental concept of a school or of a relationship.
- When taking in new information to LTM, a person tries to make sense of it. This can be seen as making an effort to connect it to their existing schema for that concept. If the information is bizarre or unfamiliar, this process can cause it to be **distorted** by making it more similar to the existing schema.

The War of the Ghosts Study

- Bartlett's best-known study involved a native American folk story called the War of the Ghosts. He wanted to find out if a person's memory for stories was affected by their schemas.
- He told this story to his research participants and then analysed their responses when they were later asked to remember it.
- The story was unfamiliar to their culture, so participants found it hard to remember. Bartlett noted four types of mistakes.

> **Key Point**
>
> The process of remembering doesn't involve passively taking in information but is an active process of making connections with existing schemas.

Bartlett's best-known research study focused on a native American folk story.

Additions	Participants added new material to help it make more sense to them.
Subtractions	Participants forgot sections that they hadn't understood.
Transformation to familiar	Participants changed things to make them more similar to what they were used to.
Preservation of detached detail	Certain unusual details that had caught people's attention were recalled, but not always in the right order, and unconnected to their original context.

- Bartlett concluded that the ideas from the story were forgotten or distorted because participants didn't have the cultural schemas in their LTM to which to connect the new information.
- Additions demonstrated the use of the participants' own cultural schemas during the retrieval process.

Reconstructive Memory

- Bartlett saw encoding and retrieval as an active process of building up a memory, motivated by the desire to understand. In other words, he saw remembering as being more like building something new rather than taking something out of storage.
- Following on from this research, he developed a theory of reconstructive memory. Bartlett realised that memories often have gaps in them, and that people use their existing schema knowledge to fill these gaps when they are retrieving a memory.
- He used the term effort after meaning to describe the way people try to make sense of new information, distorting it if necessary.

Other Key Factors Affecting Memory

- As Bartlett showed, culture is a major factor that affects memory.
- Several other factors affect memory, making people more or less likely to remember something successfully and accurately.

State	It's easier for people to remember something when they are in the same physical state as when it was first learned. This applies to both mood and to the consumption of drugs such as caffeine and alcohol.
Timing	Information is forgotten over time. However, this is not always a bad thing – a time delay and a period of forgetting makes a later revision activity more effective (this is called the 'spacing effect').
Interference	Information is forgotten because it gets confused with other information. Events and concepts that are unusual and distinctive are better remembered.
Context	It's easier to remember things in the same context that we first learned them. Visiting the place where something was learned can act as a cue to retrieval.

- False memories occur when we think we remember something, but it didn't actually happen, as found in Bartlett's research.
- Researcher Elizabeth Loftus also studied false memories. She and colleagues showed participants pictures or told them stories that were supposedly about their own childhood. Many people later claimed that the events had actually happened.
- Loftus and her researchers also found that false memories can be generated via leading questions. When people viewed a car crash and were asked how fast the cars 'smashed' into each other, they were later much more likely to say (incorrectly) that the video had shown broken glass compared to a control group. They had developed a false memory (Loftus & Palmer, 1974).

> ### Key Point
>
> State, timing, interference and context all affect the success of memorisation, and certain situations can lead to false memories forming.

> ### Key Words
>
> Bartlett
> schema
> distortion
> reconstructive memory
> effort after meaning
> culture
> state
> timing
> interference
> context
> false memory
> Loftus
> leading question

> ### Quick Test
>
> 1. Why was the War of the Ghosts story hard for Bartlett's research participants to understand?
> 2. Besides culture, name two factors that affect memory.

Where space is not provided, write your answers on a separate piece of paper.

Structures of Memory

1 What is the name of the temporary memory store with which people can remember a few items for several seconds? Shade **one** box only. [1]

A Encoding memory ○ B Long-term memory ○

C Short-term memory ○ D Permanent memory ○

2 State **two** ways in which short-term memory is limited. [2]

3 Complete the following table. [3]

Example	Type of long-term memory
A Being able to ride a bike	
B Remembering your first day of school	
C Knowing that an MP is a type of politician	

Processes in Memory

1 Is memory best described as an active process or a passive process? [1]

2 Which of the following is true? Shade **one** box only. [1]

A Encoding new memories happens fairly automatically. ○

B Memories are retrieved in exactly the same form as they were remembered. ○

C Both encoding and retrieval often involve mental effort. ○

D Items always enter long-term memory even if the person is not paying attention. ○

3 Which of the following is an input process to memory? Shade **one** box only. [1]

A Encoding ○ B Storage ○ C Retrieval ○ D Forgetting ○

The Multi-Store Model of Memory 1 and 2

1 Murdock (1962) conducted an important experiment into memory.

a) What is the name for the graph showing the effects found in this study? [1]

b) Explain how the experiment can be used to evaluate the multi-store model. [3]

2 Complete the sentences by choosing the best words from the selection below. You do not have to use all the words. [4]

encoding	meaning	words	semantic	visual

According to the multi-store model of memory, short-term memory takes in information using acoustic _____. This means that it processes and stores the sounds of words or other items. In contrast, the long-term memory uses _____ encoding – it stores information based on its meaning. This means that people tend to remember the gist of a story over the long term, not the exact _____.

3 Is rehearsal a sufficient process to encode new information to long-term memory? [1]

Factors Affecting Memory

1 Complete the sentences by choosing the best words from the selection below. You do not have to use all of the words. [3]

interference	repression	short-term	harder	easier	distinctive

Information can be forgotten because it gets confused with other information – a process known as _____. This happens less with unusual events because they are more _____, and therefore better remembered. It's also _____ to remember things in the same physical location as where we first learned them.

2 Name **three** ways in which people may be in a different state when they try to retrieve a memory. [3]

3 Which of the following describes a schema? Shade **one** box only. [1]

A A visual memory technique that can be used when revising. ⬭

B A mental concept, influenced by life experience and culture. ⬭

C The process of encoding things to long-term memory. ⬭

D A belief that people have about other cultures. ⬭

Perception and Sensation

You must be able to:

- Define sensation and give an example of a sensory process
- Explain the difference between sensation and perception
- Describe perceptual constancy, with examples.

The Difference Between Sensation and Perception

- In order for a person to respond to what is happening in the outside world, the senses process external cues such as light and sound. These are detected by specialist **receptor cells** in the body.
- This process is called **sensation**, and is the basis of how all animals experience the world around them.
- An example of receptor cells involved in sensation are the rods and cones found in the human retina, at the back of the eye. These are sensitive to light, although only cones can sense colour.
- For each sense, these cells send messages to **neurons** (nerve cells), which connect directly to the brain. For vision, these neurons form a pathway called the optic nerve.
- **Perception** occurs when the brain uses this information from the outside world to build up a mental image of what is happening. In other words, it must interpret the information that reaches the senses.
- A person's perception is not the same as the sensation received. For example, the process of visual perception must adjust images received by the eyes and make sense of them.
- The visual system has to allow for the fact that images hit the retina reversed and upside down.
- Perception is a rapid and largely effortless process, allowing people and other animals to react very quickly to external events such as threats.

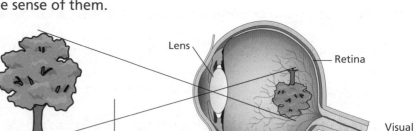

Perception involves adjusting sensory information.

The Role of the Brain in Perception

- Perception is possible because the brain builds up a picture of the world – using information from the senses and combining them with information from the memory.
- Many receptor cells must work together for perception to happen. A single rod cell can only detect how much light is hitting it. In order for an individual to see, a large network of these cells is required.

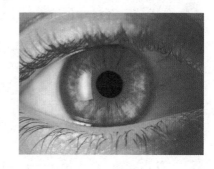

- If a stimulus in the world moves around, the **sensory cortex** of the brain can detect which way it is moving because of the changing pattern of light hitting the retinal cells. The shape of objects can be detected in a similar way.
- The perceptual systems of the brain therefore act like a computer, processing simple bits of information and building up a more complex picture that allows the individual to act – e.g. to pick up some food or to avoid something harmful.

Perceptual Constancy

- **Perceptual constancy** is the ability of the brain's perceptual system to make allowances for changes in the environment. Adjustments in visual perception are made to allow for the position and lighting conditions in four main ways.

Light constancy and colour constancy	An object is perceived as looking its normal (or expected) level of light/darkness even when lighting conditions change, as can be observed when reading a book in dim conditions – the paper still looks light, not dark grey. Similarly, people still perceive objects as having their usual colour, even when they are seen in darker or unusual lighting conditions. Grass still looks green after sunset, for example.
Size constancy and shape constancy	An object is perceived as having constant size even when it changes distance and therefore projects a different size of image onto the retina. For example, a train that pulls away in a station still looks the same size (it doesn't appear to shrink) as it gets further away and the image size changes on the retina. Likewise, an object which moves or rotates is perceived as being the same object, even though the image that is appearing to our retina may have changed radically.

- All of these constancies may seem obvious, but they require complex computation on the part of the brain. It is difficult to program a computer to recognise that objects remain the same through transformations of shape and light.

Stages in visual perception

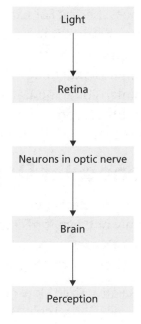

Light → Retina → Neurons in optic nerve → Brain → Perception

Key Words

receptor cells
sensation
neurons
perception
sensory cortex
perceptual constancy
light constancy
colour constancy
size constancy
shape constancy

Quick Test

1. What is the name of the process that occurs when receptor cells in the senses process external cues such as light and sound?
2. Perception depends on the brain interpreting the information that reaches the senses. Is this statement true or false?
3. Which perceptual constancy is involved when a blonde person's hair still looks blonde even when you see them at night?

Visual Cues and Depth Perception

You must be able to:

- Explain what is meant by depth perception
- Describe key monocular depth cues, and give example situations where they are used
- Explain the role of binocular depth cues.

Depth and Distance

- As the mind builds up a picture of the world by interpreting information from the senses, it needs to make sense of how close or far away objects are.
- This is known as **depth perception**, and is essential for survival in most species. For example, when a monkey or squirrel leaps for a tree branch, it must be able to calculate how close the branch is.
- **Depth cues** allow the brain to make sense of the two-dimensional image that hits the retina, converting it to a three-dimensional mental image of the world.
- In other words, depth cues are aspects of the visual scene that make it possible to work out how close or far away things are.

Monocular Depth Cues

- The simplest cues to depth and distance can be perceived using only one eye if necessary. These are therefore called **monocular** depth cues.
- Monocular depth cues include the following:

Relative size	More distant objects appear smaller than other similar objects. For example, the apparent size of a car on the road ahead allows a driver to perceive how close it is, given that most cars are roughly the same size.
Occlusion	If one object partially obscures another from where someone observes them, this shows that it must be the closer of the two.
Linear perspective	As things move further away, they appear closer together to the observer. This results in the perspective skills used by artists, where lines on a painting are drawn towards an imagined 'vanishing point', making the painting look much more realistic.
Texture gradient	When objects are more distant, the eye takes in less detail of their surface texture. This results in objects that are further away appearing to have a smoother and simpler blurry texture.
Height in plane	Compared to a horizon line, people or objects that are closer will appear lower down, while more distant objects appear higher up (although the opposite is true for objects in the sky, e.g. the clouds in a painting). This cue is similar in principle to linear perspective.

Example of texture gradient.

Binocular Depth Cues

- The mind can build on these basic depth cues by comparing the different visual sensations from the two eyes. This results in further cues known as **binocular** depth cues.

- Most predators have two forward-facing eyes, indicating that these cues play an important role in precise judgements of distance.

- The eyes are at two different positions on the head. Differences between the images from the two eyes (at least for people who have the use of both eyes) give a cue to distance known as **retinal disparity**:
  - If an object is closer, the discrepancy between the two eyes will be quite large.
  - If an object is further away, there will be a smaller difference between the two eyes.

- A further binocular cue is **convergence** (or 'eye convergence'). This cue comes primarily from the muscles that move the eyes rather than from the image itself. When an object is closer, both eyes have to rotate inwards slightly in order to bring it into focus in the centre of the retina. For a more distant object, less rotation is required.

Retinal disparity

Line up two fingers one in front of the other, close to your face. Look at them with your right eye, keeping your left eye closed. Now close your right eye, and look at them with the left. Do the images that you see with each eye look the same? You should notice quite a large difference between how your fingers appear to each eye.

Now try moving your fingers further away from your face by stretching your arm out. Again, close one eye, and then the other. What can you see now? The difference between what is seen by each eye should be less. This is because the things that they are seeing (your two fingers) are now further away, reducing the amount of retinal disparity.

Key Point

A range of monocular cues and a smaller number of binocular cues allow an individual to perceive distance.

Binocular cues rely on differences between images processed by the two eyes.

Quick Test

1. A hill that is closer to you partially blocks your view of another hill which is further away. Which monocular cue to distance does this demonstrate?
2. A tree looks closer if you are able to see the patterns of its leaves and bark. Which monocular cue is being used in this situation?
3. Which binocular cue relies on detecting how much the two eyes have to rotate in order to see an object?

Key Words

depth perception
depth cues
monocular
relative size
occlusion
linear perspective
vanishing point
texture gradient
height in plane
binocular
retinal disparity
convergence

Illusions

You must be able to:

- Identify and describe the Müller-Lyer, Rubin's vase, Ames Room and Ponzo illusions
- Identify and describe the Kanizsa triangle and Necker cube
- Explain major causes of visual illusions.

What are Illusions?

- Taking in information from the senses is not always simple or accurate. Sometimes, two people may experience the same stimulus via their senses but perceive it differently.
- An **illusion** is a stimulus that causes a person to see something different from what is actually there, or where there are two or more possible interpretations of the same image.
- There are several famous examples of illusions, all of which have been studied and debated by psychologists.

The **Müller-Lyer** illusion appears like a pair of arrowheads either pointing inwards towards a line, or outwards. Although the lines are the same length, most people perceive the line with the inward-pointing arrows as being longer.	
Rubin's vase is an illusion which can be interpreted as either two faces looking towards each other, or (using the space in between the faces) a vase.	
The **Ames Room** is a specially constructed room that appears ordinary when viewed from the front but is actually distorted, with one corner much further away than the other. If two people stand at the opposite corners, there is an illusion that one is much larger than the other.	
The **Kanizsa triangle** shows three circles with wedge-shaped sections removed like the corners of a triangle. People tend to see the sides of the triangle appearing faintly, especially towards the corner areas.	
The **Necker cube** is a 2D shape that tends to be interpreted as a cube – but there are two possible ways that it could be facing, making it possible for a person to 'flip' the way they perceive the shape.	

Explanations for Illusions

- Illusions show that some aspects of perception are fairly automatic. Even when you know about them, it is hard to avoid seeing the effect of the illusion.
- Illusions do not have a single explanation. Instead, they rely on several different factors that affect perception. All of them in some way cause us to perceive something inaccurately or lead to more than one possible interpretation that we struggle to reconcile.
- Two particular causes of illusion are ambiguity and fiction.

Ambiguity	There are two or more ways that a two-dimensional shape on the page or screen can be perceived. The Necker cube and Rubin's vase are examples of ambiguous figures.
Fiction	The person perceives something that is not actually there. The Kanizsa triangle is an example of a fiction – there is actually no triangle, yet people perceive one. According to the Gestalt approach to psychology, this is because of a tendency to perceive objects as wholes rather than many small parts, and to mentally connect objects that appear to belong together.

- Misinterpreted depth cues are another cause of illusions. Some illusions occur because the cues that guide us to depth and distance can also mislead the processes of perception.
- A key example of this is the Ponzo illusion. Here, the cue of linear perspective tricks the mind into thinking that the images closer to the vanishing point are larger.
- Depth cues are used in art with the aim of being misinterpreted, so that people perceive a flat, two-dimensional picture as a scene with depth and distance.
- Size constancy (see page 19) is another cause of illusions. When the context makes an object look closer or further away than it is, the process of size constancy causes it to appear larger or smaller than it really is. This occurs in the Ames Room illusion.

Key Point

Illusions are a much-studied group of stimuli that are either ambiguous or cause people to perceive things that are not actually there.

Ponzo illusion

This shows two identical lines on top of a pair of lines which are drawn towards a vanishing point.

Key Point

Illusions can be caused by errors in the processing of depth cues and size constancy.

Key Words

illusion
Müller-Lyer
Rubin's vase
Ames Room
Kanizsa triangle
Necker cube
ambiguity
fiction
Gestalt approach
Ponzo illusion

Quick Test

1. In which illusion do people tend to see a triangle that is not actually there?
2. What term is used to describe illusions where an image has more than one possible interpretation?
3. Why do people experience the Ponzo illusion?

Theories of Perception

You must be able to:

- Explain Gregory's constructivist theory of perception
- Explain Gibson's direct theory of perception
- Describe evidence in support of each theory.

Explanations of Perception

- Perception involves building up a coherent mental representation of the world that is accurate and makes sense, and allows us to function in the world.
- The previous sections have highlighted the potential role of both a person's sensations and their expectations in this process. But which of these two things plays the more important role?
- Researchers have tried to explain how perception works. Their ideas are known as theories of perception. There are two main theories, which both focus especially on visual perception.

The two perception theories

1.	Expectations and knowledge play a critical role in how people perceive the world.
2.	Perception mainly relies on information directly from the senses.

Gregory's Constructivist Theory

- A person's schemas can influence and distort what they remember. They can also affect what people perceive. This is the focus of the **constructivist theory** devised by **Richard Gregory**.
- The theory states that while perceptions are based partly on the information that comes into our senses, to a larger degree it depends on our expectations and experience, and therefore on nurture and our upbringing.
- This view states that perception depends on making **inferences** based on past experiences. In other words, the information hitting the senses is limited, so some degree of problem solving is necessary in order to work out what the world is like.
- **Top-down processing** is a term for perceptual processing that begins with thoughts and memories, rather than with sensation.

Evidence for Gregory's theory

- Illusions provide an important piece of evidence for Gregory's theory. In general, they suggest that the mind is trying to make sense of partial or ambiguous information, and using schema knowledge and expectations to do so.
- Gregory studied the Müller-Lyer illusion, finding that it was not perceived by people who had lived in round houses for most of their lives, such as the San hunter-gatherer people of the Kalahari. This suggests that illusions can occur because of our cultural experience.

Hollow face illusion

- The **hollow face illusion** also supports top-down processing. When people view an image of the back of a mask, they tend to perceive it as a face – the image 'pops out' and is not perceived as being hollow. Experience and expectations cause this to happen – people are used to seeing faces the correct way round and therefore (incorrectly) interpret the hollow mask as an outward-pointing face.

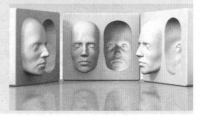

Gibson's Direct Theory

- The **direct theory** of perception takes the opposite view from the constructivist theory, assuming that perception is a matter of piecing sensory information together. It is based on the work of researcher **James Gibson**.
- The direct theory assumes two main things.

1. Expectations and knowledge do not play a major role in how perception operates.
2. The environment provides **affordances** to the perceiver. This means the information that it provides, helping its meaning to be understood, e.g. depth cues.

- **Bottom-up processing** is the term given to perceptual processes that are initiated by sensations from the world – in other words, processing based on affordances in the environment rather than cognitive processes.
- According to the direct theory, illusions are exceptions to normal perception. For the most part, people are able to perceive the world without distortions or ambiguity.
- Gibson thought that perception was largely innate. This means that people are born with the ability to do it – it's in their nature and they don't need to learn through experience how to make sense of sensory information.

Key Point

Gibson did not think that expectations and experience affect how we perceive the world, but Gregory thought that they play a major role and that perceptions are constructed by the mind.

Evidence for Gibson's Theory

- Gibson's view was that environmental affordances such as cues to depth are good evidence for direct processing. He believed that there is a single correct interpretation of sensations coming from the environment – it doesn't depend on who is looking at it.
- Gibson thought that all animals are able to perceive the world in similar ways. This view goes against the idea that perception depends strongly on memories and thought processes, because animals have simpler thought processes than humans.
- **Motion parallax** is the way that the visual world changes when a person or animal moves. Closer objects appear to move more, and more distant ones move less. According to Gibson, this usually allows illusions and ambiguities to be resolved.
- Gibson's colleagues supported the view that perception is innate by testing very young animals and babies on a perception test called the **visual cliff**, which involves a sheet of glass that is safe to walk on but looks like a cliff edge that they could fall over.
- The visual cliff experiment found that newborn animals and human babies are able to perceive depth, supporting the bottom-up theory.

Visual cliff

Quick Test

1. Which theory is supported by the role of depth cues in perception?
2. Which theory would predict that people in different cultures perceive the world differently because of their different experiences and beliefs?

Key Words

constructivist theory	direct theory
Gregory	Gibson
inferences	affordances
top-down processing	bottom-up processing
hollow face illusion	motion parallax
	visual cliff

Factors Affecting Perception

You must be able to:

- Describe the Gilchrist and Nesberg study of motivation, and the Minturn study of perceptual set
- Explain how perception can be affected by motivation, emotion and expectations
- Describe some of the ways that culture can affect perception.

Errors in Perception

- The processes involved in perception do not always produce an accurate impression of the world. Illusions demonstrate how information from the world can be ambiguous.
- The way that people perceive the world is affected by **individual differences**. Individual differences, in turn, are affected by life experience, meaning that people are more likely to perceive things the way they have in the past.
- Sometimes a person can see or hear things that aren't there at all, or feel tactile sensations such as pain without anything touching the skin. Things that we perceive in the absence of real sensations are called **hallucinations**.
- A dream is an everyday example of a hallucination – while people are asleep, they perceive things that are not actually there. Hallucinations can also occur as a reaction to drugs, or when a person is stressed or mentally ill.

Perceptual Set and Research Evidence

- What factors affect whether people perceive the world accurately? One is a person's **perceptual set**, which means a group of assumptions and emotions that affect perception. In other words, having a perceptual set means that people are biased in how they perceive the world.
- The perceptual set is affected by several factors, in particular **motivation**, **emotion** and a person's **expectations**.
- Evidence for the role of the perceptual set comes from two classic psychology experiments:

> **Key Point**
>
> Perception varies between individuals and is affected by a number of factors including motivation, emotion, expectations and cultural experience. Together, these factors are called the perceptual set.

- **Gilchrist and Nesberg (1952)** conducted a study where people were asked to judge the brightness of food colours, such as the red of a tomato. In one condition the research participants were hungry, and in another they had recently eaten.
- The researchers found that the colours of the foods were judged as being brighter and more vivid when people were hungry.

- **Bruner and Minturn (1955)** conducted a study that showed the role of expectations. Two groups of participants were shown the same ambiguous figure, which could either be perceived as a letter 'B' or the number '13'. One group were shown it alongside other letters such as 'A' or 'C', while the other group were shown it beside other numbers such as '12' and '14'.

– Participants' expectations led them to perceive the ambiguous figure in a way that fit with the other items. Even when the ambiguity was pointed out to them, the participants were still affected by their expectation – the letter condition, for example, stating that it looked more like a 'B' than a '13'.

Factors in Perceptual Set

- Several different factors affect the perceptual set. Whether these are present or absent can determine what a person perceives. These factors can operate in combination for an even stronger effect.

Factor	Explanation	Example
Motivation	To an extent, people are more likely to perceive what they want to perceive.	A football supporter is more likely to perceive their favourite team's play as skilful, while someone who is a fan of a band is more likely to listen to one of their new songs and enjoy it.
Emotion	Fears and worries can affect perception, such as a fearful child thinking that a shadow looks like a monster.	Hunger is an example of an emotional feeling that can affect perception. Gilchrist & Nesberg's study demonstrated how it can affect the way a person sees objects.
Expectations	Perception can be affected by expectations, with people more likely to see what they expect to see.	Ambiguous figure illusions are a good example of this factor, as is Bruner & Minturn's study into the role of context.

- A person's perceptual set is not fixed. Factors such as hunger and motivation can change, meaning that the same scene or object could be perceived differently by the same person on different occasions.
- Expectations can also change, as they are based on past experience. New and more recent experiences can have an effect on what a person expects to see.

Culture

- Culture can also be considered a factor in a person's perceptual set. The culture that a person has grown up in or lives in affects their expectations because of their cultural knowledge and beliefs.
- Culture affects how people choose to represent the world in art. The assumptions that have formed the basis of Western art for centuries are not shared by certain other cultures around the world.
  - In a study of villagers in Zambia by Hudson (1960), it was found that they couldn't easily perceive occlusion, suggesting that depth perception may depend on culture.
  - However, the way people interpret pictures can't easily be generalised to perception in everyday life.

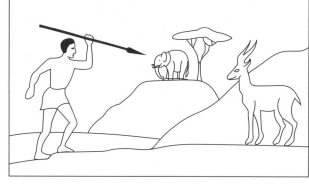

Cultures perceive depth cues in pictures in different ways, as shown by this image test of the relative distance of the animals.

Quick Test

1. What effect did hunger have on perception in the Gilchrist and Nesberg study?
2. Which concept can be defined as a group of assumptions and emotions that affect perception?

Key Words

individual differences
hallucinations
perceptual set
motivation
emotion
expectations
culture

Where space is not provided, write your answers on a separate piece of paper.

Structures of Memory

1 How long can items be held in short-term memory without making an effort to rehearse them? [1]

2 Is the short-term memory best described as a permanent store or a temporary store? [1]

3 How much information can long-term memory hold? [1]

4 What is most important for encoding semantic long-term memories – understanding the meaning, or seeing a visual image? [1]

5 Name **two** things that can act as a cue to retrieving a memory. [2]

6 Label the **two** brain areas shown below, and indicate whether they are essential for short-term or for long-term memory. [4]

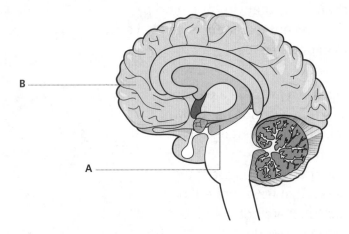

Processes in Memory

1 Which of the following is another term for short-term memory and emphasises that it is an active process? Shade **one** box only. [1]

A LTM	⭘	**B** Working memory	⭘
C Free recall	⭘	**D** Hard drive	⭘

2 Which of the following is **not** true of short-term memory? Shade **one** box only. [1]

A It is used for active processing of information in everyday tasks. ◯

B People can use it to follow a series of instructions. ◯

C It can rehearse items to store them for longer. ◯

D It is simply used for storage. ◯

3 Draw lines to match the terms. [3]

A Encoding   i) Output process

B Retrieval   ii) Loss of information

C Forgetting   iii) Input process

4 Complete the sentences by choosing the best words from the selection below.
You do not have to use all the words. [4]

| spaced | encode | repeating | understand | link | blocked |

Repetition is important for memory, but simply _____ things does not always

lead to them being encoded to long-term memory, particularly if the information is hard to

_____. The best way to build a new memory is to _____ the new

item to what is already understood, and then repeatedly retrieve it from memory, preferably in a

way that is _____ out over time.

5 Explain the role of attention in taking in new memories. [2]

6 Explain the different types of retrieval that are involved in the following example: [4]

Jana is sitting a psychology exam that has a set of multiple choice questions at the start.
She then tries a section of questions where a diagram of the brain is labelled and the
first letter of brain areas (e.g. 'C' for cerebellum) are given. Finally, she writes an essay
describing what she knows about theories of perception.

7 Explain the role of repetition in the process of encoding things to long-term memory. [4]

The Multi-Store Model of Memory 1 and 2

1 Draw a diagram of the multi-store model of memory. [2]

2 Complete the table, which summarises the multi-store model. [5]

Researchers who devised the model	
Names of the three stores	
Process by which information enters STM	
Process by which information is kept in STM for longer	
Process by which information is encoded to LTM	

3 Briefly describe a possible experiment that could be run to demonstrate the primacy and recency effect. [3]

4 Read the following example. Then explain how the **three** stores of the multi-store model are being used by the student. [3]

> A teacher reads out a question and then immediately calls the name of a student who was not paying attention. On hearing their name called out, the student takes a moment to recall the question and then gives a correct answer.

5 How long does sensory memory last, and what is its capacity? [3]

6 Complete the sentences by choosing the best words from the selection below. You do not have to use all the words. [4]

curve	list	STM	first	encoding	LTM

The serial position _____ can be used as supporting evidence for the multi-store

model. According to the model, the _____ few items from a list are repeatedly rehearsed and therefore enter LTM. By the middle of the _____, there are too many to rehearse and these items are therefore forgotten. The last few items can be retained because they are still held in the _____.

7 Draw lines to match the definitions with the terms they relate to. [4]

A	Research study into the primary and recency effects
B	Forgetting due to new information entering STM
C	Process essential for maintaining information in STM
D	The type of encoding used in LTM

i)	Displacement
ii)	Rehearsal
iii)	Murdock (1962)
iv)	Semantic

Factors Affecting Memory

1 An early British researcher studied distortions in memory using folk stories as materials.

   a) What was he called? [1]

   b) What **four** types of distortions did he find? [4]

2 Which of the following could result in a false memory? Shade **one** box only. [1]

   A Being asked a leading question ⭕   **B** Forgetting something ⭕

   C A blow to the head ⭕   **D** Consuming caffeine or drugs ⭕

3 Why was the story used in Bartlett's War of the Ghosts study hard for the research participants to understand and remember? [2]

4 Complete the table with the names of several factors that affect memory. [4]

....	Familiar concepts and stories are easier to remember than unfamiliar ones.
....	Information is gradually forgotten – although this can make a delayed revision session more effective.
....	Information can be forgotten because it gets confused with other information.
....	It's easier to remember things in the same surroundings as where they were learned.

Where space is not provided, write your answers on a separate piece of paper.

Perception and Sensation

1. What is the technical name for a nerve cell? [1]

2. Why can we perceive objects accurately even when it gets darker? [2]

3. What part of the brain processes visual information? [1]

Visual Cues and Depth Perception

1. Explain why depth perception is important to humans and other animals. [3]

2. Explain **two** depth cues that the artist has used when painting the picture below. [4]

3. Do textures that are further away look sharper and more detailed? [1]

Illusions

1. Is the process of perception always accurate? Explain your answer. [2]

2. Which illusion is shown in the following example? [1]

3 Tick (✓) or cross (✗) the statements about the perception of illusions to indicate whether they are true or false. [4]

Statements about the perception of illusions	True (✓) or false (✗)?
Some illusions occur because the stimulus is ambiguous.	
There is one basic explanation for all illusions.	
The Ponzo illusion is based on ambiguity.	
Illusions stop working when you know about them.	

Theories of Perception

1 What is the name of the researcher who is known for his work on the direct theory of perception? [1]

2 Complete the sentences by choosing the best words from the selection below. You do not have to use all the words. [3]

| illusions | perspective | affordances | visual | inferences | direct |

The _____ theory of perception states that the world provides enough

information to the senses for perception to happen. This view states that organisms are able

to piece sensory information together without using memories or _____.

The theory also states that the environment provides _____, i.e. information

that helps the person or animal make sense of the world, such as depth cues.

3 a) Which theory of perception states that inferences are a key aspect of perception? [1]

b) Define inference and give an example. [2]

Factors Affecting Perception

1 What term means the group of emotions and other factors that lead to a tendency to perceive things in a particular way due to assumptions and emotions? [1]

2 Give **two** examples of how people can sometimes fail to perceive the world accurately. [2]

3 The same person can perceive a scene differently on two different occasions. Explain why this is, mentioning at least **one** supporting research study. [4]

Brain Development

You must be able to:

- Identify and describe the main areas of the human brain
- Match brain areas to their psychological functions
- Explain the key stages of brain and nervous system development before and after birth.

- Developmental psychologists study how the mind and brain change across the lifespan, and particularly during childhood. They are interested in what causes an individual's personality and abilities to develop, and in the factors that can harm this process.

The Brain

- The human brain is part of the nervous system, i.e. the network of nerve cells throughout the body.
- The brain is composed of over 80 billion nerve cells (neurons) as well as other cells that support these neurons (the receptor cells of the retina are a specialist type of neuron that respond to light).
- Neurons are connected in a way that allows them to communicate and process information. This is what allows people to think, act and respond to the world.
- Each neuron is composed of a **cell body** with a nucleus, and has a fibre called an **axon** which connects it to other cells. The axon can carry an electrical signal to another area of the brain – sometimes a considerable distance.
- The axons of neurons also carry messages from the brain to the muscles, and from all parts of the body back to the brain as part of the senses.
- At the end of the axon is an axon terminal, which releases chemicals called **neurotransmitters**. These are picked up by other neurons, which can cause them to react and send out their own electrical signals.

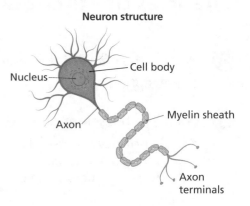

Neuron structure

Nucleus — Cell body
Axon — Myelin sheath
Axon terminals

Brain Development in the Womb

- The human brain begins to develop around the third week after a baby is conceived, early in the embryonic stage of pregnancy (the first 10 weeks).
- During the earliest development of the nervous system its cells are **stem cells**, which can later transform into any type of neuron. True neurons begin to form on day 42 of a pregnancy, and all of the main structures of the central nervous system have taken shape by day 56.
- The child's entire brain is largely complete by half-way through pregnancy. By this stage, the unborn child is able to move around and respond to sounds.
- The fully developed brain has several main areas, as the table on the next page shows.

> ### Key Point
>
> Development is a gradual process of change that is largely outside of our control and begins before we are born. The brain's key structures are complete by birth.

Area	Function
Brain stem	Autonomic functions such as breathing and heartbeat
Thalamus	Completes some basic sensory processing and then relays signals to the cerebral cortex
Cerebellum	Controls precise physical movement and helps to coordinate actions
Cerebral cortex	Cognition – thinking, perception and most memory processes; the visual cortex is part of the cerebral cortex

Brain Development After Birth

- A newborn baby has a much more complex level of interconnections in their brain than those of an adult, with more axons connecting its neurons together.
- As the child ages, most neural development occurs not by producing new cells or axons but by pruning unnecessary connections. This allows the brain to become more attuned to its environment.
- Other connections are strengthened, as the child learns rapidly.
- A child's environment plays a major role in how it develops after birth. Children require a stimulating environment, with opportunities to play in creative and challenging ways.
- Children who are in a **deprived** environment will be at a disadvantage, and this is likely to harm their intellectual development. However, the child's brain is very adaptable, and most early periods of deprivation can be overcome.
- Psychologists have studied Eastern European orphans who were kept in very poor quality orphanages in the 1980s, and later adopted by British families. They found:
  – There was generally a huge improvement in the physical and mental health of the infants after adoption.
  – Physical development caught up rapidly compared with that of other children, but brain development was slower to catch up.
- Important structural changes in brain development continue until a person's late adolescence, and a few changes are still occurring into the person's mid-20s. The human brain therefore develops for longer than that of any other species.
- Even once it is no longer changing its structure, the brain still shows **plasticity** throughout life. This means that new connections can be formed and unnecessary ones can wither away.

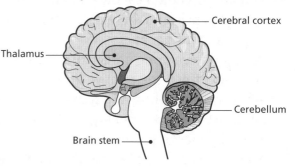

Anatomy and functional areas of the brain

Cerebral cortex

Thalamus

Cerebellum

Brain stem

Key Point

Unnecessary neural connections are pruned after birth as the baby attunes to its environment, and brain development continues until at least adolescence.

Key Words

cell body
axon
neurotransmitters
stem cell
brain stem
autonomic
thalamus
cerebellum
cerebral cortex
deprivation
plasticity

Quick Test

1. What is the name of a neuron's fibre that sends messages to other neurons?
2. Which brain areas are essential for the following functions?
   a) breathing b) perception c) precise physical movement
3. At birth, compared to later in life, are the interconnections between neurons more complex or less complex?

Nature and Nurture

You must be able to:

- Understand how the nature versus nurture debate relates to development
- Give arguments for the nature side of the debate
- Give arguments for the nurture side of the debate.

The 'Nature versus Nurture' Debate

- Human psychological development depends on both input from a child's environment, which includes their parenting, and the expression of genes.
- Although everyone agrees that both of these factors can have an effect, the relative importance of genes and of the environment in human psychological development is a matter of debate. Are personality, preferences, skills and flaws mainly due to genes or to life experiences?
- Some psychologists believe that genes are much more important than the environment, and that they largely determine what kind of personality and skills someone will develop. This is the **nature** side of the debate.
- Other psychologists think that upbringing and life experiences are more important. From this point of view, people are the way they are mainly because of what happens to them during their life. This is the **nurture** side of the debate.
- This debate impacts on a great many topics in psychology, such as:

    - Why are some people more intelligent than others? The nature side states that certain people are born with superior 'smart genes' while the nurture side focuses on upbringing and education.
    - Why are some people more friendly and outgoing than others? The nature side sees personality as innate, while the nurture side looks at life experiences.

Twin Studies

- The similarity of children to their parents is not useful evidence for the debate, because most children share both genes and an environment with their parents.
- One method used to get around this problem is the **twin study**.
    - Some of these studies compare the psychology of identical and non-identical twins within the same families.
    - Other twin studies look at the rare cases where identical twins have been adopted and raised by different families, allowing researchers to investigate how alike the twins are despite having different parenting and environmental conditions.
    - A limitation of adoption studies is that the adoptive families are often quite alike in terms of their culture and socio-economic status.

Key Point

The nature–nurture debate is the broad and ongoing argument over whether upbringing/ environment or genetics play the main role in human psychology.

The 'Nature' Side

- A strong emphasis on the role of genes. A gene is a sequence of DNA and is held within every cell in the body. The expression of a gene is a term meaning that it causes the body to produce a protein. This production of proteins in the body (including the brain) is essential for all aspects of development.
- As genes affect the development of the body, they control the growth of the brain.
- Twin studies have found that identical twins tend to be more similar in intelligence and mental health than non-identical (or 'fraternal') twins.
- However, it's not simple to link a psychological factor such as a mental illness or someone's personality to a single gene. Abilities generally link to a mixture of genes, and can change over time.

The 'Nurture' Side

- Although genes are important, what truly makes human beings unique is their life experiences. This includes the people we spend time with.
- One of a person's most important set of experiences, according to this view, is their upbringing, including the way their parents or guardians looked after them.
- Parenting seems to play a key role in a child's educational success. Some researchers have found that what parents do makes a bigger difference to education than what the child's teachers do!
- Culture is important in how people develop. Evidence comes from the fact that people in different cultures behave in different ways, e.g. they use different gestures and body language.

Combining the Sides

- It is important to realise that the two sides of the debate may both be correct on different occasions. Some psychological attributes such as personality might be largely genetic, while others such as criminal behaviour may be more to do with upbringing and culture.
- Any genetic influences on skills and personality could have an effect on later life experiences. For example, someone who was born with a more relaxed and outgoing personality might make friends more easily, and this would affect their life experiences. So genes and life experiences do not have separate effects on an individual, but work in combination.
- In addition, genes and the environment interact biologically. Genes can be switched off or on depending on life experiences. The study of this process is known as epigenetics.
- Epigenetics is one of the reasons why a gene might be expressed or not, along with other aspects such as developmental age.

Key Point

It is increasingly being understood how genes and the environment work together. Epigenetics is the study of how the environment impacts on whether genes are or are not expressed.

Quick Test

1. Name one psychological topic that the nature–nurture debate has impacted.
2. According to the nurture side of the debate, what major factors affect a person's personality and skills? Pick two of the following: parenting, biology, culture.
3. What term describes the situation where a gene is not switched on due to a lack of environmental stimulation?

Key Words

nature
nurture
twin study
genes
gene expression
upbringing
epigenetics

Piaget's Theories 1

You must be able to:

- Describe Piaget's theory, including the concepts of assimilation and accommodation
- Describe how Piaget's stage theory of cognitive development can be applied in education.

The Work of Jean Piaget

- **Jean Piaget** (1896–1980) was a developmental psychologist, and one of the most influential psychology researchers of all time.
- Piaget believed that children develop schemas (see Memory chapter, pages 14–15), which change and develop as they grow up. For example, a young child may have a schema for 'dog', but as they get older they learn about different breeds of dog.
- Piaget thought that schemas develop through two key processes.
  - **Assimilation** means fitting new information into an existing schema.
  - **Accommodation** means changing a schema, or developing a new one.
  - For example, a young child may at first think that a zebra is a 'stripy horse', but then realise that it is a different animal. This results in two separate schemas.

Jean Piaget

Logical Operations

- Piaget was interested in how children think and reason. He noticed that this differs with age – younger children are not just worse at thinking than adults, but they solve problems in different ways.
- One example that Piaget studied was **centration**, the tendency of young children to focus on one element of a problem and ignore others.

> **Key Point**
>
> Piaget thought that children's understanding of the world was based on schemas, which can change through assimilation and accommodation.

  - A demonstration of centration involves showing a child two glasses, one short and wide and the other tall and thin. Water is poured from the short glass into the taller one.
  - Younger children say that there is now more water. Because they centre on the height of the water and think 'bigger means more', they fail to judge its volume accurately.
  - Children who are around seven years old or above get the answer correct. They have developed the ability to make a **logical operation** in their mind. The logical operation here is to mentally reverse the process of pouring the water.

- The ability to complete logical operations allows older children to show **conservation** of volume, mass and other properties – realising that the appearance of an object can transform without it fundamentally changing.

Theory of Cognitive Development

- Cognitive development means the way that a person's thinking and understanding changes over time.
- Based on his experiments into children's logical operations, Piaget developed a **theory of cognitive development**, which stated that children's thinking goes through four main stages from birth to the age of 11 (see table). Each stage needed to be completed before the child could reach the next one.

> **Key Point**
>
> Piaget created a hugely influential theory of how children's cognitive processes develop through a series of stages.

Stage and Age	Features
Sensorimotor 0–2 years	Children's schemas are based on movements and they focus on learning how to interact with physical objects. By six months of age they develop object constancy – they understand that objects continue to exist even when out of sight.
Pre-operational 2–7 years	Children's thinking is highly **egocentric** – they can't understand how things look from another person's point of view. They also exhibit centration, leading to logical errors. They become able to use one object to represent another, e.g. in games.
Concrete operational 8–11 years	Children are able to make logical operations, and they no longer show centration. They can mentally reverse operations, e.g. the pouring of liquid into different-sized containers, allowing conservation of volume and other properties. However, children cannot yet solve abstract problems, meaning that their thinking is limited to concrete situations.
Formal operational 11+ years	A child cannot just solve concrete logical problems but can also think in the abstract, e.g. speculating logically about an object without it being present. They learn to process abstract mathematical symbols.

This teenager is in the formal operational stage, according to Piaget's theory.

> **Key Words**
>
> Piaget
> assimilation
> accommodation
> centration
> logical operation
> conservation
> theory of cognitive development
> sensorimotor stage
> pre-operational stage
> egocentric
> concrete operational stage
> formal operational stage

> **Quick Test**
>
> 1. What two processes can happen when people link information to a schema?
> 2. What term did Piaget use to mean focusing only on one aspect of a problem?
> 3. In which stage of Piaget's theory do children first learn to use one object to represent another?

Piaget's Theories 2

You must be able to:

- Evaluate Piaget's theory of cognitive development
- Explain research evidence relating to Piaget's theories.

Evaluation of Piaget's Stage Theory

- An important implication of Piaget's stage theory is that children will struggle to learn new concepts if they are not developmentally ready.

Strengths

- One strength of Piaget's work is that it can be applied in education. Piaget's stages closely match the way the school system is divided into different age groups, and is reflected in the methods of teaching and types of subjects covered. For example, subjects based on abstract reasoning such as algebra tend to be taught to children in the formal operational stage.
- Piaget's theory was one of the first to show that children's thinking is different from that of adults, and worth studying in its own right. It paved the way for future research.

Weaknesses

- Children develop at different rates. The stages can sometimes overlap and some people never reach the stage of abstract reasoning.
- The theory implies that children's thinking changes rapidly as they reach a new stage, when in fact cognitive development takes place slowly and gradually.
- Piaget's research focused on a small number of European children with professional parents, including his own children, and may therefore be culturally biased.

Research Evidence for Piaget's Theories

Three mountains problem

Three Mountains Problem

- Important evidence for Piaget's theory of cognitive development came from an experiment called the **three mountains problem**.

  - In this experiment, a child was shown a model with three mountains, each with something different at the top. Once the child had looked at the model, a doll was placed on it.
  - The child was then shown several photographs and asked to identify what the doll would be able to see. Older children tended to succeed, but those in the pre-operational stage chose a picture that was similar to what they themselves could see.

- The findings of the three mountains study supported the idea that younger children are egocentric – they can't picture the world from another person's point of view.
- However, critics of the study suggested that younger children only failed the three mountains problem because it was too difficult.
- Hughes (1975) created a simpler version of the experiment called the policeman doll study.

  - In this version, a policeman doll was placed on the mountains model, and the child was asked to place a second doll where the policeman couldn't see it. 90% of four-year-olds succeeded.
  - The policeman doll study suggests that young children are able to take another person's point of view, and are therefore less egocentric than Piaget believed.

Conservation of Number

- Piaget's concept of conservation includes thinking about number and quantity. He found that if a line of tokens are placed close together and then spread further apart, young children see that the line is longer and therefore assume that there are now more tokens.

- However, this experiment has also been criticised for being too complicated for young children to understand. McGarrigle and Donaldson's (1974) naughty teddy study simplified it by using a toy to mess up the tokens.

  - This time, the majority of children under the age of six correctly said that the number of tokens was unchanged.
  - This suggests that children can conserve number earlier than previously thought.

Quick Test

1. One strength of Piaget's stage theory is that it has been widely applied in a particular area of society. Which area?
2. Which research study suggested that Piaget had underestimated young children's ability to conserve number?

Key Words

three mountains problem
policeman doll study
naughty teddy study

Learning

You must be able to:

- Explain the concept of learning styles and its flaws
- Explain the role of praise and self-efficacy in development
- Describe the concepts of growth mindset and fixed mindset.

Learning Styles

- The theory of **learning styles** is a popular but controversial idea which suggests that everyone has a way of learning that suits them best – visual, auditory or kinaesthetic (i.e. movement-based).
- It suggests that educational activities are more effective if they match the person's learning style.

Evaluation of Learning Styles

- Although it has its supporters and is widely taught, several research reviews have concluded that there is no reliable scientific evidence for the learning styles theory.
- There is some evidence that having a preference for visual or verbal information is connected to biological differences, as described on the right.
- Learners with these preferences are sometimes called **verbalisers** and **visualisers**.

Key Point

The concept of learning styles is not supported by scientific evidence.

- People who prefer to learn via words showed increased activity in verbal areas of their brain. Those who prefer learning via images showed increased activity in visual areas (Kraemer *et al.*, 2009).
- However, neither group learned better when they used their preferred style. So different ways of learning may be just a matter of personal preference.

Willingham's Theory

- Psychologist **Daniel Willingham** has argued strongly that the entire concept of learning styles is inaccurate and harmful. He states that the best way to learn something depends on the type of information. For example, it makes no sense to learn a map verbally.
- It is helpful for all learners to use their senses together where possible. Combining both verbal and visual information improves the rate at which people later remember information – a concept called **dual coding**.
- Willingham also argues that factual knowledge is essential. If people have good knowledge, they are better able to understand new information. Therefore, learning should involve learning facts, not just skills.

Praise and Self-Efficacy

- A person's beliefs about themselves are not always accurate, and can be affected by a number of factors.
- One such belief is **self-efficacy** – a person's sense of whether they are good or bad at something.
- Getting negative messages from parents and teachers (e.g. parents saying, "She's not very clever") can affect self-efficacy. The message is **internalised** and becomes part of the person's self-efficacy beliefs. On the other hand, praise can have a positive effect.

Key Point

Praise can affect mindset and therefore learning.

- Praise and other feedback from teachers and parents can motivate learners and affect how they think about themselves, including their self-efficacy.

Mindset Theory

- Some genetic factors appear to affect intelligence and abilities, but many psychologists think that beliefs and attitude also play a key role in the development of abilities, and therefore in success at school and beyond.
- Psychologist **Carol Dweck** has studied learners' beliefs and developed a theory which states that there are two main mindsets that people can have: fixed or growth.
- A mindset is not the same as a self-efficacy belief – it is an explanation of why people tend to develop positive or negative self-efficacy. Some people believe that they are bad at something and there is nothing that can be done to improve. Others believe that they can improve with practice.
- Mindsets influence people's views on a range of their own abilities e.g. intelligence, sports proficiency and art ability.
- Praise can also affect mindset:
  - If a child is rewarded and praised for being clever and producing perfect work, they are less likely to try new challenges. This encourages a fixed mindset.
  - If a child is rewarded and praised for making their best effort and for trying challenging new tasks, this encourages a growth mindset. They are also more likely to learn new things.
- An important implication of mindset theory is that people with a fixed mindset tend to fear mistakes, as they see a mistake as reflecting low ability. In contrast, people with a growth mindset may see a mistake as helpful feedback.

Evaluation of Mindset Theory

- In support of Dweck's theory, Blackwell *et al.* (2007) studied maths attainment in students. They found that students with a growth mindset continually improved their grades, whereas those with a fixed mindset stayed at the same level.
- The theory has been accused of being over-simplistic, with students sometimes given the message that success is about working harder and that failure is due to having the wrong attitude.
- It is difficult to measure which mindset people have. Some people seem to have a mixture of the two mindsets, or show different mindsets on different occasions.

Fixed mindset	People think that ability levels are fixed, and that how well someone does at a task is largely due to factors outside of their control, e.g. genetics.
Growth mindset	People think that ability levels can be changed, and that how well someone does at a task is largely due to effort and learned skill.

Key Words

learning styles	self-efficacy
verbaliser	internalise
visualiser	Dweck
Willingham	fixed mindset
dual coding	growth mindset

Quick Test

1. Is there any sound scientific evidence for learning styles?
2. Isaac says "I'm not bad at tennis – I just haven't got the hang of it yet." Which type of mindset is shown in this example?

Where space is not provided, write your answers on a separate piece of paper.

Perception and Sensation

1 What general name is given to the cells that our senses use to gain information about the world, for example the rods and cones found in the retina? [1]

2 Label the diagram to show the processes and body areas involved in visual perception. [4]

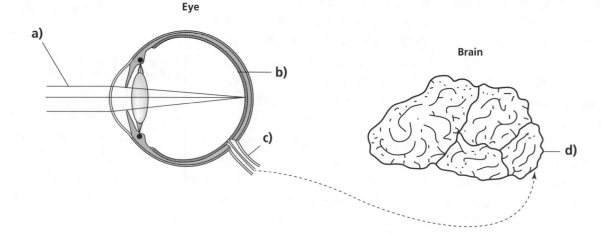

Eye

a)

b)

c)

Brain

d)

a) ....

b) ....

c) ....

d) ....

3 Briefly explain the difference between sensation and perception. [2]

4 Name **two** types of constancy which are features of visual perception. [2]

5 Is it easy to program a computer to perceive objects? Explain why / why not. [3]

Visual Cues and Depth Perception

1 Briefly explain what is meant by occlusion. [2]

2 The table shows **four** effects that people perceive as distance increases. Complete the relevant depth cues. [4]

Effect	Depth Cue
Lines appear to get closer together.	
Textures become less detailed.	
The difference between the images seen by the two eyes reduces.	
Objects appear closer to a horizon line.	

3 Sometimes predators such as cheetahs have to perceive the distance of one of their prey species such as a gazelle.

a) Why do many predators have two forward-facing eyes? [1]

b) What would happen if a cheetah failed to judge the distance of a gazelle that it was trying to catch? [1]

4 Complete the sentences by choosing the best words from the selection below. You do not have to use all the words. [4]

monocular	binocular	occlusion	relative	disparity	convergence

The simplest cues to depth and distance are the _____ depth cues, which

can be perceived using just one eye. These include _____ size, which means

that more distant objects appear smaller than other objects of the same type. Another cue

is _____, meaning that if one object partially obscures another from where

someone observes them, it must be the closer of the two.

5 In the renaissance, artists learned to portray depth and distance in their paintings.

a) What term is given for the point that lines converge on as they get further away, helping to demonstrate the cue of linear perspective? [1]

b) Why is it helpful to be able to use cues such as linear perspective in art? [1]

Illusions

1 Are illusions mainly linked to perception or to sensation? [1]

2 Describe the Necker cube illusion. [2]

3 Which illusion is shown in the following image? [1]

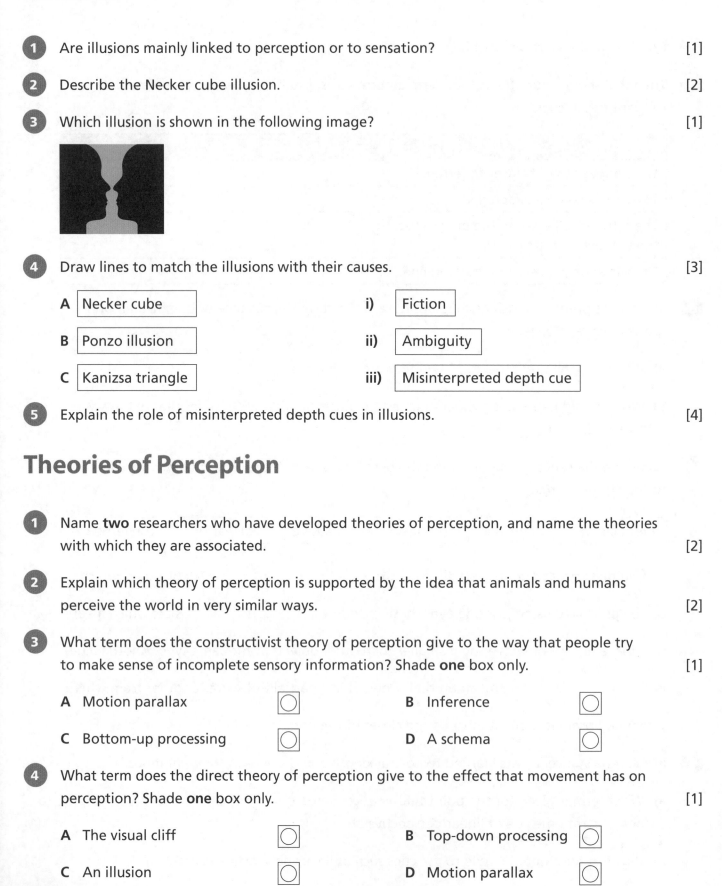

4 Draw lines to match the illusions with their causes. [3]

A	Necker cube	i)	Fiction
B	Ponzo illusion	ii)	Ambiguity
C	Kanizsa triangle	iii)	Misinterpreted depth cue

5 Explain the role of misinterpreted depth cues in illusions. [4]

Theories of Perception

1 Name **two** researchers who have developed theories of perception, and name the theories with which they are associated. [2]

2 Explain which theory of perception is supported by the idea that animals and humans perceive the world in very similar ways. [2]

3 What term does the constructivist theory of perception give to the way that people try to make sense of incomplete sensory information? Shade **one** box only. [1]

A Motion parallax ○   B Inference ○

C Bottom-up processing ○   D A schema ○

4 What term does the direct theory of perception give to the effect that movement has on perception? Shade **one** box only. [1]

A The visual cliff ○   B Top-down processing ○

C An illusion ○   D Motion parallax ○

5 Complete the following two sentences.   [2]

A demonstration of how babies are able to perceive depth involved an experiment called the

_____. An illusion that showed the importance of expectations when trying to

perceive faces is called the _____ illusion.

6 Explain what is meant by an affordance and which theory it supports.   [3]

Factors Affecting Perception

1 What general term do psychologists use to describe differences between people, including their age and culture?   [1]

2 Which researchers conducted a study into expectations in perception, showing that the context (other letters or other numbers) affected how an ambiguous figure was perceived? Shade **one** box only.   [1]

A Gilchrist and Nesberg   ◯   B Atkinson and Shiffrin ◯

C Gibson and Walk   ◯   D Bruner and Minturn   ◯

3 What term is used to describe the group of assumptions and emotions that affect and bias perception? Shade **one** box only.   [1]

A Light constancy   ◯   B Perceptual set   ◯

C Bottom-up processing   ◯   D Motion parallax   ◯

4 Explain what this picture can tell us about the role of culture in perception.   [4]

5 Briefly explain **two** classic research studies that demonstrated factors in the perceptual set.   [4]

Where space is not provided, write your answers on a separate piece of paper.

Brain Development

1 Name **two** parts of a neuron. [2]

2 An unborn baby's brain areas have developed by halfway through pregnancy. True or false? [1]

3 Define plasticity. [2]

4 What is the difference between the brain stem and a stem cell? [2]

Nature and Nurture

1 Which side of the nature versus nurture debate states that genes play a more important role in human development than the environment? [1]

2 Name a type of research study that can be done to help provide evidence about the role of genes in development. [1]

3 Tick (✓) or cross (✗) the statements to indicate whether they are true or false. [4]

Statements	True (✓) or false (✗)?
Identical twins tend to be more similar in intelligence than non-identical twins.	
If one identical twin has a mental illness, then the other twin will definitely get it too.	
If a gene is expressed, this means that it causes a protein to be produced, affecting development.	
Cases where twins are raised by different families are rare and difficult to study.	

4 Explain the nurture side of the nature versus nurture debate. [4]

Piaget's Theories 1 and 2

1 Complete the following sentence: [1]

Piaget believed children develop _____, which change and develop as they grow

up through the processes of assimilation and accommodation.

2 What term means that children can't picture the world from another person's point of view? [1]

3 Explain the features of the concrete operation stage of development. [3]

4 Read the following scenario. State what cognitive process is taking place, and why. [2]

> A young boy is visiting the zoo. He looks at an antelope – a type of animal that he has never seen before. It has long legs and is brown, so he decides it must be a strange kind of horse.

Learning

1 What terms are sometimes used for learners who prefer to process new information verbally or visually? [2]

2 Complete the sentences by choosing the best words from the selection below. You do not have to use all the words. [4]

coding	influencing	visual	shapes	styles	harming	tactile

Education involves supporting and .... people as they learn and develop,

and is fundamentally connected to developmental psychology. The theory of learning

.... is a popular but controversial idea, which suggests that everyone has a

way of learning that suits them: auditory, ..., or kinaesthetic. Reviews have

shown that this theory is not supported by reliable scientific evidence – educational activities are

not any more effective if they match the person's supposed learning style. However, people do

learn better if they use a combination of modalities to take in information; a concept known as

dual ....

3 State **one** thing that can affect self-efficacy. [1]

4 Does Willingham think it is important to learn facts? Why, or why not? [2]

Sampling

You must be able to:

- Explain what is meant by sampling from the target population
- Describe and evaluate different sampling methods
- Explain the issue of generalising research results from the sample to the population.

Populations and Samples

- Most psychology research involves a process where researchers formulate a hypothesis, then gather and analyse data to test their hypothesis.
- To conduct their study, the researcher(s) will need to select or recruit an appropriate group of research participants to test.
- The term target population refers to the group of people who the researcher is interested in studying. It is not necessarily the whole population of the country, but could be a more specific group such as school students.
- A sample is a group of people that take part in an experiment or other research study. The sample is selected from among the people in a target population.
- There are various ways of selecting a sample, and these are called sampling methods.

Generalising

- The way a sample has been selected is important when it comes to evaluating research.
- Ideally, the researcher wants to be able to generalise from the sample to the target population. This means concluding that the findings from the sample will also be true of the wider population.
- Generalising is only valid when a sample is representative of the target population as a whole – in other words, it has similar characteristics. For example, a representative sample would have the same percentage of people from each ethnic group and age group as the target population does.
- A good sample is also large – this reduces the impact of random variations among the members of the sample.

> **Key Point**
>
> There are many different ways to select a sample from the target population. Opportunity sampling is the most commonly used.

Sampling Methods

Opportunity Sampling

- The most commonly used sampling method is opportunity sampling. This means selecting a group of research participants on the basis of who is easily available, e.g. a lecturer selecting their own students.
- Many opportunity samples are biased – the people who are easily available may not be representative of the target population.

Opportunity Sampling Example 1: A researcher is interested in studying all adults, and she obtains an opportunity sample that consists of her own university students. This sample would not have the same variety of ages and backgrounds as all of the adults in the target population, and is therefore biased.

- To select an opportunity sample, the researcher approaches members of the target population that are conveniently available without taking any other characteristics into account. These people are then asked for their consent to participate in the study.

Random Sampling

- A **random sample** is one where every member of the target population has the same chance of being selected.
- It is often considered the best sampling method as it generally results in a representative and unbiased sample. However, it is more difficult and time-consuming than opportunity sampling.
- The best way to be sure that everyone has the same chance of being selected is to number every member of the population using a complete list, and then use a **random number** table or computer program to select the participants.

Systematic Sampling

- A **systematic sample** uses a procedure that avoids groups of people being selected together, e.g. by picking every tenth name on a school register or every fifth house on a street.
  - Systematic samples tend to be representative, but it's not possible to guarantee that they are unbiased – this depends on the characteristics of the target population. It may be that every fifth house on a street is more expensive than the others, with wealthier occupants, meaning that selecting these ones will not result in a representative sample.
  - The starting point has to be random. After that, the selection of participants at set intervals reduces bias by avoiding the selection groups of pre-existing groups (which is a major problem with opportunity sampling).

Stratified Sampling

- A **stratified sample** involves selecting people in order to maintain the overall proportions of the population in categories that the researcher considers to be important.
  - A true stratified sample has exactly the same proportions as the population. So if 30 per cent of the target population are elderly, then 30 per cent of the sample must be elderly.
  - A researcher may ensure a 50–50 proportion of males and females, or find people from every major career type so that the frequencies match those of society as a whole.
  - A stratified sample is representative, but only in the characteristics that have been stratified. It may be biased in other ways.

Opportunity Sampling Example 2: A student researcher approaches a group of people from his year in a school corridor and asks them to take part in his experiment; they agree. This sample is also biased – he is more likely to choose people who are approachable and/ or similar to himself.

Key Point

All sampling methods have their flaws, but random sampling is the least likely to obtain a biased sample.

Key Words

target population
sample
generalise
representative
opportunity sampling
bias
random sample
random number
systematic sampling
stratified sampling

Quick Test

1. Which type of sampling involves ensuring that every member of the target population has the same chance of being selected?
2. Opportunity sampling suffers from what flaw?

Variables and Hypotheses

You must be able to:

- Explain the role of the independent variable and the dependent variable in an experiment
- Explain what extraneous variables are and give examples
- Give examples of alternative and null hypotheses.

Experiments and Variables

- An experiment is one of the most important research methods used in psychology. It allows researchers to study human behaviour in a controlled and systematic way, by changing one variable and measuring the effect this has on another variable.
- A variable is any characteristic, attribute or environmental condition that can vary – in other words, it can have different values.
- Some example variables include:

how much you like your teacher

score on an IQ test

number of Facebook friends

how many hours someone revised for a maths exam

how many goals scored in one season

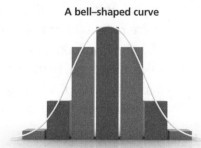

A bell–shaped curve

- A normal distribution is one in which the middle values are common while more extreme ones are progressively rarer, resulting in a graph that shows the frequency of values of the variable as a bell-shaped curve.
  - The normal distribution curve is symmetrical, and the frequency of scores declines the further they are from the area around the mean – rapidly at first, and then more slowly.
  - The mean, mode and median are all equal.
- Variables are often assumed to be normally distributed, unless researchers know otherwise.

The IV and DV

- In psychology experiments, a researcher manipulates or changes the value of one variable and measures the level of another.
- An experiment therefore looks for a cause-and-effect relationship between two variables – if one variable is changed, does the other variable also change?
  - The variable that is manipulated is called the independent variable, or IV for short.
  - The variable that is measured is called the dependent variable, or DV. The level of this variable forms the data that a researcher analyses.
- An experiment has two or more conditions which are compared. These relate to different values of the IV. For example, a research study into the effect of caffeine on sleep quality might have a caffeine condition and a no caffeine condition.

Extraneous Variables

- To determine whether the IV has an effect on the DV, the level of every other relevant variable needs to be kept constant. This is known as experimental control, i.e. it has to be a fair test.
- Any variable other than the IV which could potentially affect the DV is called an extraneous variable, or EV. For example, the *amount of time available* is a variable that may affect scores on a DV, and must be kept constant.

Writing a Hypothesis

- Every research study expresses a hypothesis (plural: hypotheses). This is a scientific prediction of what is expected to happen.
- Usually, the hypothesis predicts that the IV will have an effect on the DV, and also gives a rationale for this prediction based on past research.

> A hypothesis is typically phrased as follows: If (the IV) has an effect on (the DV), then there will be higher scores on (condition 1) than (condition 2).
>
> For example: *If having a nap boosts long-term memory, then students who take a short nap after revising for 30 minutes will remember more information than students who do not.*

- In experiments, the prediction that the IV will affect the DV is called the alternative hypothesis (or 'experimental hypothesis').
- Researchers must also have a clear idea of how their results will look if the IV does not affect the DV. This is known as a null hypothesis. In other words, this is a prediction of what will be found if the alternative hypothesis is not supported by the data. For the research study on caffeine, this would be stating that caffeine will not have an effect on sleep quality.

Non-experimental Research

- In non-experimental studies, there may not always be control over the key variables of the research study.
- Variables are just as important in non-experimental studies, but it may not be obvious which variable is having an effect on which.
- Many non-experimental studies lack control over EVs, too – only experiments control the IV and keep EVs constant. This is a major strength of the experimental method.

Key Point

In order to test the effect of the IV on the DV, any extraneous variables must be kept constant.

Key Point

An experimental hypothesis is typically expressed in terms of two variables: the independent variable (IV) and the dependent variable (DV).

Key Words

research methods
variable
normal distribution
cause-and-effect relationship
independent variable (IV)
dependent variable (DV)
conditions
control
extraneous variable (EV)
alternative hypothesis
null hypothesis

Quick Test

1. What term is used for the variable the researcher measures?
2. Write a suitable experimental hypothesis for the following variables: IV = quantity of caffeine consumed (500 mg versus 0 mg); DV is time taken to get to sleep.

Design of Experiments 1

You must be able to:

- Explain the use of laboratory, field and natural experiments
- Explain and evaluate independent groups design, repeated measures design and matched pairs design.

Location of Experiments

- As described in the previous section, it is necessary to control extraneous variables (EVs) in psychology experiments.

Laboratory Experiments
- One of the best ways to do this involves running the study in a controlled environment called a laboratory (or 'lab').
- An experiment based in a lab is called a **laboratory experiment**:
    - The lab can be any environment that allows the effects of distractions such as background noise to be reduced or preferably eliminated. An empty school room could function as a lab.
    - Usually participants are tested one at a time.
    - Lab experiments are very controlled but the setting is artificial, meaning that participants might not behave in the same ways that they would in everyday life.

Field Experiments
- To study behaviour in a more authentic setting, a researcher may use a **field experiment**:
    - A field experiment is any experiment that is conducted in a participant's natural environment, such as their workplace or somewhere that they typically study or socialise. This leads to more realistic behaviour, but extraneous variables such as distractions and background noise can affect results.
    - To keep the setting as realistic as possible, it may be necessary to test several participants simultaneously, resulting in more extraneous variables.

Field experiments can be done in group settings

Natural Experiments

- A third type of experiment is the **natural experiment**.
  - The key difference between this and other types of experiment is that it is not set up and run by the researcher – it occurs spontaneously in the real world, and the researcher records the outcome. For example, if some students used flash cards for revision and others did not, their exam results could be compared – to see if those who used flash cards got better grades. This would be a natural experiment.
  - From an ethical point of view, the experimenter is not responsible for the outcome of the study. This makes natural experiments ideal for studying harmful situations that could not be tested in other types of experiments, such as the effects of drug use or child neglect.
  - However, it is impossible to control extraneous variables in a natural experiment, and there is no random allocation to conditions. This makes it hard to be sure whether the IV has been the cause of any effects that are observed. For instance, using the example above, it could be that the students using flash cards were also more hard working and better at the subject, and the flash cards were not the reason that they did better.

Experimental Design

- Experiments always have two or more conditions that are compared, and the researcher needs to allocate the sample of participants to the various conditions. There are three main options, and which one is chosen depends on the specific details of the study:
  - Sometimes, all participants complete both/all conditions of the experiment. This is a **repeated measures** design.
  - Sometimes, the participants are randomly divided into groups, and each group takes part in a single condition. This is an **independent groups** design.
  - Two separate groups of participants could be created by matching participants up on important characteristics such as age or ability levels. This is a **matched pairs** design.
- A condition that is used simply for comparison is known as a **control condition**. This is used as a baseline.

> **Key Point**
>
> Experimental design means the way that participants are allocated to the conditions of the study.

> **Key Words**
>
> laboratory experiment
> field experiment
> natural experiment
> repeated measures
> independent groups
> matched pairs
> control condition

> **Quick Test**
>
> 1. Which experimental design is being used if a participant only completes one condition of an experiment?
> 2. State one extraneous variable which can affect results in a field experiment.

Design of Experiments 2

You must be able to:

- Describe how a laboratory experiment or field experiment could be set up using standardised procedures
- Explain the ethical issues that apply to psychological research.

Setting up a Study

- An experimenter must avoid any source of bias in their methodology. One important feature of a well-controlled experiment is the use of standardised instructions. These ensure that every participant is given exactly the same information at the start of the study (this also applies to non-experimental methods).
- Other aspects of the research procedure are also standardised, so that every participant experiences the same overall procedure.

Repeated Measures Design

- With a repeated measures design, order effects could bias the results. This is when participants improve or get worse at a task as they complete two or more conditions.
- To avoid order effects, the order of conditions is balanced so participants do not all complete the conditions in the same order as each other. This is known as counterbalancing.
- When counterbalancing, an equal proportion of the participants is divided among the conditions, each doing the conditions in a particular assigned order.

Independent Groups Design

- An independent groups design does not suffer from order effects because participants complete only one condition. However, they do suffer from participant variables – a type of EV. This is where differences between the participants, such as different ability levels, can affect the outcome.
- An important way to minimise the effect of participant variables and thereby avoid bias is to randomly allocate participants to the different conditions of the experiment.

Matched Pairs Design

- An advantage of matched pairs designs is that specific participant variables are controlled for by matching them up between participants. A limitation is that this does not control for all EVs, and it is more time-consuming to do than the other designs.

> **Key Point**
>
> In a repeated measures design, counterbalancing must be used.

Ethics

- Research must meet **ethical standards** for research, and follow a range of procedures to ensure that people are treated fairly. Overall, the participants must be treated with respect and should come to no **harm**. This can include psychological harm such as stress and embarrassment. In the UK, researchers follow the ethical guidelines set out by the British Psychological Society.

Ethical Procedures

- Key ethical procedures include:
  - Seeking **informed consent** from participants. People must know what they are consenting to, including the type of task and how long it will take. For research on children, parental consent is necessary.
  - Ensuring that participants are aware that they have a **right to withdraw** at any point during a study.
  - **Debriefing** participants at the end of the study, thanking them for their participation and giving them any information that it was not possible to give them at the beginning, such as the aim/hypothesis of the study.
- Researchers must seek ethical approval from their university or employer before proceeding.
- For the most part, research that involves **deception** is seen as unethical, because participants have not given their informed consent to take part.
- It is also essential for researchers to treat data **confidentially**, and not to release or publish the names of research participants.

Revise

Key Point

It is essential that ethical standards are upheld in all research, maintaining confidentiality, avoiding harm, and ensuring that participants are kept informed.

Quick Test

1. What problem could occur if every participant completed condition 1 of an experiment first, and then moved on to condition 2?
2. Why can't researchers publish the names of research participants in their studies?
3. What term means balancing the order in which participants compete experimental conditions?

Key Words

standardised instructions
order effects
counterbalancing
random allocation
ethical standards
harm
informed consent
right to withdraw
debriefing
deception
confidentiality

Non-experimental Methods

You must be able to:

- Explain the main types of data gathered in psychology research
- Describe non-experimental research methods – interviews, questionnaires, case studies and observation studies
- Evaluate non-experimental research methods.

Non-experimental Research

- Experiments are an essential part of psychology research, but sometimes other research methods are more appropriate.
- One advantage of certain non-experimental methods is that they get more in-depth results. There are two key types of data that psychology research obtains:
  - **Quantitative data**: data in the form of numbers
  - **Qualitative data**: data in the form of spoken/written words or some other non-numerical form.
- Ethical standards apply to non-experimental research. Additional considerations are explained below.

Observation

- **Observation** involves studying behaviour as it happens and recording data in the form of notes or videos. Often this involves a **naturalistic observation** – observing a participant in an everyday context such as their workplace.
- There are key design considerations in observation studies:

  - An observation study will typically set out **categories of behaviour** in advance. A checklist can then be used to record how often each behaviour occurs.
  - A single observer may make errors, reducing the reliability of their data, especially if they are untrained. For this reason, some studies use two or more observers. **Inter-observer reliability** means the extent to which different observers record the same data from the same observation.

- An additional ethical standard which must be upheld is avoiding any **invasion of privacy**. Participants should not be secretly recorded or their private conversations listened to, for example.
- Disclosing the observation will impact on the behaviour of participants, and this weakness should be considered when analysing the results of an observation study.
- A strength of observation studies is the ability to gather data on behaviour as it happens, but they lack the control of experimental research.

Interviews and Questionnaires

- **Interviews** and **questionnaires** are widely used research methods in psychology. Both involve asking people questions about their behaviour or thoughts.
- The main difference between these two methods is that interview questions are asked face-to-face, and questionnaires are completed on paper or via a computer.

> **Key Point**
>
> There are several non-experimental methods, each with their own strengths and weaknesses. The best choice of method depends on the aims of the research.

An observation schedule

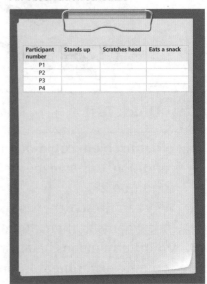

Participant number	Stands up	Scratches head	Eats a snack
P1			
P2			
P3			
P4			

- There are two main types of question.

Open questions	Allow the participant to answer in any way they want, e.g.: "What do you think of your teacher?". They provide qualitative data that is detailed but hard to analyse.
Closed questions	Give participants a pre-determined choice of possible answers, such as a multiple choice, e.g. "Are you going to take this subject next year? Yes/no." They provide quantitative data, e.g. the percentage of people who chose each answer. Responses are quick to analyse but less in-depth, as people do not have the opportunity to express their thoughts in full.

- Interviews generally use a lot of open questions and therefore obtain qualitative data. Questionnaires usually focus on closed questions, but a mixture of both types of question can be used.
- An interviewer can explain questions where necessary and can also follow up on questions if the answer is interesting or unclear. This is an advantage of the interview method.
- The main strength of questionnaires is that they can easily be distributed to a lot of people via email/the internet.
- An advantage of both methods is that they allow an insight into people's thoughts that is not possible by simply observing them. However, people may not tell the truth or may be unaware of the reasons behind their own behaviour.

Case Studies

- A **case study** is an in-depth study of one individual or a small group. It is not a single way of gathering data. It typically involves several techniques such as brain scans and ability tests.
- Observations and interviews can be used as part of a case study.

  – Some of these techniques/methods involve gathering **primary data**, which is where the researcher obtains and uses new data directly from the participant(s), e.g. using an interview.
  – Others involve obtaining **secondary data**, which has been generated before for a different purpose, e.g. government statistics or school tests, and the researcher obtains it and analyses it.

- Case studies are not an efficient way of studying a lot of people as they are time-consuming, but they are invaluable for studying unusual or unique cases, e.g. people with rare psychological disorders or brain damage. They gain in-depth findings.

Examples of types of data

	Primary Data	Secondary Data
Qualitative (verbal)	Open questions; descriptions taken during observations	Diaries; school reports
Quantitative (numerical)	Scores in experiments; numerical data from questionnaires, checklists and observations	Scores on school tests and exams; IQ tests taken for other purposes; government statistics

Key Words

quantitative data
qualitative data
observation
naturalistic observation
categories of behaviour
inter-observer reliability
invasion of privacy
interview
questionnaire
open questions
closed questions
case study
primary data
secondary data

Quick Test

1. "On a scale of 1–10, how much did you like primary school?" What type of data would be obtained from answers to this question?
2. Which research method is most suitable for studying an individual with an accidental brain injury?

Correlation and Data Handling

You must be able to:

- Explain and calculate descriptive statistics, using standard form and decimals
- Describe and evaluate the use of correlation studies
- Explain and interpret scatter graphs.

Average and Range Calculations

- An experiment or other research study generates data, e.g. a set of scores out of 20 on a memory test.
- **Statistics** are used to interpret and make sense of this data, as well as summarising it in a simplified form.
- It is important to be able to express an average score from a set of data, as well as how spread out the scores are.
  - The **range** shows the difference between the lowest and highest score, therefore giving an idea of how widely distributed scores are overall.
  - The **mean**, **median** and **mode** all express an average, central figure in different ways.

Mean: add up the sum of all scores in a set of data, and divide by the number of scores.

Median: place scores in order from low to high, and select the middle score. With even numbers of scores, the mean of the two middle scores is calculated.

Mode: the most common score in the distribution.

Calculations and Display of Data

- Researchers must not round any numbers until after the calculations are complete, at which point 3–4 significant figures will be shown.
- Standard form can also be used where appropriate to represent very large or small numbers, as can ratios, fractions and percentages.
- Frequency tables are used to count items in categories, such as the number of times behaviours occur during an observation study.
- One of the most common types of graph used for psychology experiments is the **bar chart**. They are helpful for displaying the results of two or more experimental conditions in a way that makes any difference between the mean scores clear to see.
- Another useful graph is the **histogram**. Rather than comparing two conditions, a histogram is used to display findings from a series of groups. For example, it could be constructed by using age categories (16–24; 25–34, etc.) along the x-axis, and percentage scores up the y-axis.

Frequency table

Class interval	Tally	Frequency
0–39			1
40–79	IIII I	6
80–119	IIII IIII III	13
120–159	IIII III	8
160–199	II	2
200–239	III	3
	Total =	33

Bar chart

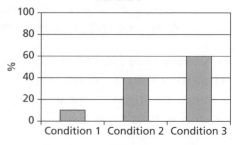

Histogram

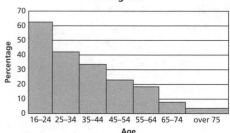

Source: Department of Health

Correlation

- **Correlation** studies could obtain data from any source, but it has to be quantitative data which shows a variable on a scale from high to low.
- Secondary data is often used, meaning that correlation can be used to study issues that would be impractical or unethical to study via an experiment. This is a strength of correlation.
- Two variables are studied; these are called **co-variables** (rather than IV and DV) because correlation studies do not demonstrate which variable is having an effect on which. In some cases, there will be no causal relationship at all.
- For this reason, researchers say that *correlation does not demonstrate causation*. This is the main weakness of correlation studies.
- Instead, correlation studies show whether two variables are related and, if so, how strong the relationship between the two co-variables is.
- Correlation studies typically display findings on a **scatter graph**.

Revise

Key Point

Correlation is used to analyse primary data gathered from a questionnaire study, or secondary data. It shows the direction and strength of a relationship between two co-variables.

- The scatter graph shows the **correlation strength** of the relationship between the two co-variables. The stronger the relationship, the closer the points are to forming a line on the graph, while weak correlations appear spread out.
- If there is no relationship at all, the dots will be scattered randomly. This is usually called a zero correlation.
- It also shows the direction of a relationship – as one variable increases, does the other increase or does it decrease? If the co-variables increase together, this is called a **positive correlation**. If one increases as the other decreases, this is called a **negative correlation**.
- A positive correlation will appear as a pattern on the graph which moves upwards from left to right, as in the example below.

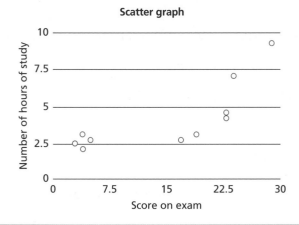

Scatter graph

Number of hours of study (y-axis) vs Score on exam (x-axis)

Key Words

statistics
range
mean
median
mode
bar chart
histogram
correlation
co-variables
scatter graph
correlation strength
positive correlation
negative correlation

Quick Test

1. What type of graph is most suitable for comparing the mean scores on two experimental conditions?
2. What type of correlation is shown if, on a scatter graph, the points rise upwards from left to right and are bunched close together, almost forming a line?

Where space is not provided, write your answers on a separate piece of paper.

Brain Development

1 For what type of functions is the brain stem responsible? Give an example. **[2]**

2 Label the figure with A, B and C using the statements below to show the key areas of a neuron. **[3]**

A Axon terminal, which can release neurotransmitters

B Axon, which can send a message elsewhere in the brain or body

C Cell body with nucleus

3 True neurons begin to form on day 42 of a pregnancy. Why is it unlikely that the unborn child can think and remember before this point? **[1]**

4 The visual cortex is part of the cerebral cortex. Which part of the brain acts as a relay between the senses and the visual cortex? **[1]**

5 How many neurons are there in the human brain? Shade **one** box only. **[1]**

   A Fewer than 1 billion ○   **B** Between 1–20 billion ○

   C Between 20–80 billion ○   **D** Over 80 billion ○

6 Which area of the brain controls precise physical movement and helps to coordinate actions? Shade **one** box only. **[1]**

   A The cerebral cortex ○   **B** The cerebellum ○

   C The brain stem ○   **D** The thalamus ○

7 Complete the sentences by choosing the best words from the selection below. You do not have to use all the words. [4]

| brain | pruning | nervous | newborn | neurotransmitters | axons |

The human _____ begins to develop soon after conception. Early cells called

stem cells can later transform into any type of neuron. The _____ of neurons

form a lot of connections with other neurons. A _____ baby has more of these

connections than an adult, and, after birth, _____ of connections occurs as the

child attunes to their environment.

8 Explain how a child's brain develops after birth. Include the role of the environment. [4]

Nature and Nurture

1 Which of the following explanations of personality development is **not** associated with the nurture side of the debate? Shade **one** box only. [1]

A Parenting ○ B Education ○

C Life experiences ○ D Genetics ○

2 Which of the following is **not** associated with biological development? Shade **one** box only. [1]

A DNA ○ B Education ○

C Genes ○ D Epigenetics ○

3 Complete the sentences by choosing the best words from the selection below. You do not have to use all the words. [3]

| nature | nurture | DNA | chromosome | upbringing | expression | cells |

The _____ side of the nature versus nurture debate places a strong emphasis on

the role of genes. A gene is a sequence of _____ and is held within every cell

in the body. The _____ of a gene is a term meaning that it causes the body to

produce a protein, a process which is essential for all aspects of development.

4   Which side of the nature versus nurture debate states that intelligence is largely innate?   [1]

5   Describe how genes and the environment interact during development.   [2]

6   Draw lines to match the terms with their definitions.   [3]

A	Epigenetics	**i)**	The study of how gene expression and the environment interact
B	Twin study	**ii)**	How a person is looked after and raised, e.g. by parents
C	Upbringing	**iii)**	Comparison of the psychological traits of one or more pairs of twins

7   Read the following example. Then explain some of the factors that could affect why Maryam is different from her sister.   [6]

> Maryam and Aneesa are twin sisters who have recently left school. Maryam is chatty and has an extroverted personality, while Aneesa is quiet and prefers to spend time alone. Maryam got really good A-Level grades and has gone to university to study psychology at one of the country's top university departments along with one of her best friends. Aneesa got lower grades, and decided to stop studying and look for a job. Both girls were always told to work hard by their parents, and given lots of support throughout school.

Piaget's Theories 1 and 2

1   What process means linking new information to an existing schema?   [1]

2   What is the name for the fourth stage of Piaget's theory?   [1]

3   Draw lines to match the terms with their definitions.   [4]

A	Accommodation	**i)**	Focusing only on one aspect of a problem
B	Centration	**ii)**	Thinking which focuses on the self
C	Egocentrism	**iii)**	Understanding that properties remain the same despite a superficial transformation
D	Conservation	**iv)**	Changing a schema or developing a new one

4   What is the name of the developmental stage where the child focuses on interacting with physical objects? Shade **one** box only.   [1]

A Sensorimotor ⭘   **B** Pre-operational ⭘

C Concrete operational ⭘   **D** Formal operational ⭘

5 What is the name of the developmental stage where the child becomes less egocentric? Shade **one** box only. [1]

A Sensorimotor ◯   B Pre-operational ◯

C Concrete operational ◯   D Formal operational ◯

6 Describe **one** experiment that has been used to criticise Piaget's theories. [4]

7 Discuss likely reasons behind the following situation, according to the theories of Piaget. [3]

> Stella is four years old. She has been playing with Fiona, who is the same age as herself, using colourful bricks to represent cars in a game. When Stella saw that her friend was playing with her favourite blue brick, she grabbed it. Her dad told her to apologise, but she cried and refused to do so.

Learning

1 What name is given to the controversial theory that everyone has their own most effective way of learning (verbal, visual or kinaesthetic)? [1]

2 An important developmental theory includes the concepts of growth and fixed mindsets.

   a) Explain the theory. [4]

   b) Briefly explain one piece of supporting evidence. [2]

3 Give **two** reasons why Willingham does not agree with learning styles theory. [2]

4 What term means a person's belief about how good or bad they are at something? [1]

5 Mehul says, "I'm not good at drawing, but I plan to take an art class and improve my skills." Which type of mindset is shown in this example? Give a reason for your answer. [2]

6 Read the following text. What factors or theories could help to explain Andy's study behaviour? [3]

> Andy is a Year 10 student. He has been told that he is a visual learner, and is therefore trying to learn a Shakespeare play using a flow chart on a large piece of paper. His psychology teacher has told him that while he might prefer visual information, using this alone will not help him to learn better. Instead, it would be best to combine his flow chart with verbal information such as quotations from the play. Andy replies that there is no point in trying too hard at it, because he's bad at English anyway.

Sampling

1. Which type of sampling involves selecting participants who are easily available? [1]

2. Read the text. Which sampling method is being used? [1]

> A researcher decides to select participants from a university corridor. She randomly chooses a starting point and time, and then selects every 20th person who walks along, asking them if they are willing to take part.

3. Complete the sentences by choosing the best words from the selection below. You do not have to use all the words. [3]

representative	generalising	small	large	inferring	reminiscent

It is important to be able to conclude that findings from a sample will also be true of the

target population. Researchers call this _____ the results from the sample to

the population. This is only valid when a sample is _____ of the target

population as whole – in other words, it has similar characteristics. A _____

sample helps to reduces the effect of variation within the sample.

4. What term is used to describe the group of people from which a sample is selected? [1]

5. Student researchers sometimes select a sample by asking their friends to take part in an experiment. Explain **two** ways in which such a sample might be biased. [2]

Variables and Hypotheses

1. What is the name of the prediction that a researcher makes at the outset of an experiment? [1]

2. Complete the following sentence. [1]

Researchers manipulate one variable – the _____ variable – and measure the

level of another variable, which is known as the _____ variable.

3. Explain what is meant by experimental control. [3]

4 Draw lines to match the terms with their definitions. [3]

A Normal distribution

i) Any variable that the researcher aims to keep constant/controlled

B Cause and effect

ii) Set of data where the middle values are common, while more extreme ones are rarer

C EV

iii) A relationship where changing one variable results in another variable changing

5 A researcher makes the prediction below at the start of an experiment. What term is used for this type of prediction? [1]

> If listening to classical music has a beneficial effect on memory, then participants who study with background classical music will remember more facts in a test than participants who do not.

Design of Experiments 1 and 2

1 Name the research design where all participants take part in every condition of the experiment. [1]

2 Tick (✓) or cross (✗) the statements about research ethics to indicate whether they are true or false. [4]

Statements about research ethics	True (✓) or false (✗)?
Participant data must be kept confidential.	
Once participants have given consent, they can't back out.	
Harm can include psychological harm, distress or embarrassment.	
The usual practice is to get informed consent at the end of a study.	

3 A researcher wishes to study the memory of university students, and carries out a memory experiment in a university library. What kind of experiment is this? [1]

4 Complete the sentences by choosing the best words from the selection below. You do not have to use all the words. [3]

order	conditions	experiments	control	counterbalancing	ethical

With a repeated measures design, _____ effects could bias the results. This is when participants improve or get worse at a task as they complete two or more conditions. To avoid this happening, the order of conditions is balanced so participants do not all complete the conditions in the same order as each other. This is known as _____. An equal proportion of the participants is divided among the _____, each doing them in a particular assigned order.

Non-experimental Methods

1 Which non-experimental research methods involve asking questions about people's thoughts and behaviour? [2]

2 Complete the sentences by choosing the best words from the selection below. You do not have to use all the words. [3]

reliability	naturalistic	validity	categories	examples	participant

Observation involves studying behaviour as it happens. Often this involves a _____ observation in an everyday context such as a participant's workplace. An observation study will typically set out _____ of behaviour in advance, and the observer will use a checklist to record these when they occur. However, a single observer may make errors, so studies often use two or more observers. Inter-observer _____ means the extent to which different observers record the same data from the same observation.

3 "What do you like to do in your free time?" What type of data would be obtained from answers to this question? [1]

4 Define the following types of data that are gathered in psychology research.   [4]

 a) Quantitative data   b) Qualitative data

 c) Primary data   d) Secondary data

5 Name the **two** types of questions that are used in interviews and questionnaires, and write an example of each.   [4]

Correlation and Data Handling

1 Briefly explain how the mean is calculated.   [1]

2 Describe how a bar chart might be used in psychology research.   [2]

3 Complete the sentences by choosing the best words from the selection below. You do not have to use all the words.   [4]

along	stronger	closed	upward	spread	direction

A scatter graph shows the strength of the correlation between two variables – the

_____ the relationship, the closer the points are to forming a line on the

graph, while weaker correlations appear _____ out. It also shows the

_____ of a relationship. If one co-variable increases as the other decreases, this is

called a negative correlation. A positive correlation will appear as a pattern on the graph which

moves _____ from left to right.

4 Describe the correlations shown in Graphs A–C.   [3]

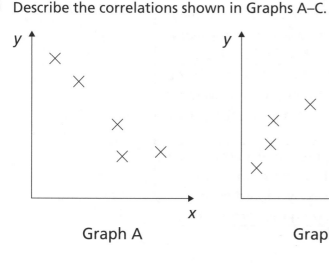

Graph A

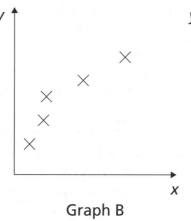

Graph B

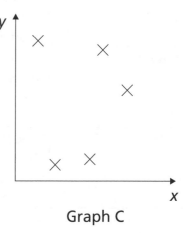

Graph C

Conformity

You must be able to:

- Explain social factors affecting conformity to majority influence
- Describe Asch's study of conformity
- Explain the strengths and weaknesses of Asch's study
- Describe dispositional factors affecting conformity.

Factors Affecting Conformity to Majority Influence

- Conformity is a type of social influence involving a change in belief or behaviour in order to fit in with a group.
- In the line study conducted by Asch (1951), it was discovered that people are likely to give the obviously wrong answer to a question if the majority also give the same wrong answer.
- However, a number of factors can affect levels of conformity.

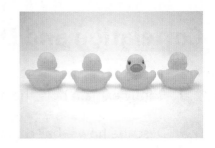

The presence of an ally	Asch found that it often took only one of the confederates to agree with the participant for them to go against the majority's inaccurate judgements. The more allies there were, the less likely the participant was to conform to the group. This lack of unanimity reduces the chances of the participant succumbing to normative conformity (seeking the approval of the group or the 'desire to be liked').
The size of the majority	The more confederates there were who made incorrect judgements, the more likely the participant was to conform.
Anonymity	If participants were allowed to give their answers in private, then they were less likely to conform to the majority.
Task difficulty	When a task becomes more difficult or the answer more ambiguous, levels of conformity increase because people are much more likely to adopt the views of others in the group.
Personality	People who were introduced to the concept of rebellion prior to the experiment were less likely to conform, indicating that personality might play a role.
Expertise	If people were considered an expert in the field relating to the task, conforming with the expert was more likely, regardless of whether they were giving the correct answer.

The Line Study

- **Aim:** The line study was conducted by Asch in order to investigate the extent to which social pressure from a majority could influence the likelihood that a person would conform.
- **Procedure:** Participants were required to look at a 'target' line drawn on a card and compare it to three lines drawn on another card. They had to say which line was the same length as the target line.
  - Two of the lines on the comparison card were obviously wrong and one was obviously right.
  - Only one of the participants was genuine; the others were confederates of the experimenter who had been told to give the wrong answer.
  - The genuine participant was usually one of the last to give their judgement so that they could hear the answers given by the confederates.
- **Results:** 75 per cent of participants gave the wrong answer at least once. If one or more of the confederates gave the same answer as the participant, the participant was less likely to give the wrong answer.
- **Conclusions:** Participants often conformed to the group's answers even though they were obviously wrong.

Strengths
• The study was highly controlled and was therefore able to establish a very clear pattern of conformity by most of the participants on one or more of the trials. • Results have been replicated several times, so the study is reliable.

Weaknesses
• The study can be criticised on ethical grounds because the participants often displayed stress reactions as they struggled to decide what answer they were going to give. • The study was carried out in a laboratory setting, in order to control variables. We cannot be sure that the behaviour displayed is typical of that seen in real life.

Key Point

Asch used deception in his study. This raises ethical issues.

 Quick Test

1. What is meant by conformity to majority influence?
2. Who conducted the 1951 study into conformity to majority influence?
3. What percentage of participants conformed at least once?

 Key Words

conformity
confederate
normative conformity

Obedience

You must be able to:

- Describe Milgram's agency theory of social factors affecting obedience
- Explain dispositional factors affecting obedience
- Describe Adorno's theory of authoritarian personality.

Social Factors Affecting Obedience

- Obedience to authority is defined as responding as instructed to a direct order.
- Milgram (1963) was interested in researching how far people would go to obey an instruction if it involved harming another person. He deceived participants into thinking that they were administering dangerous electric shocks to people because an authority figure told them to.
- Milgram found that the majority of people were willing to follow instructions given from an authority figure, even when those instructions involved inflicting harm on another. He found that 65% of participants were willing to administer the highest level of electric shock (450 volts) and all participants continued to 300 volts.
- There were, however, a number of factors that impacted this behaviour.

 Key Point

Obedience might involve doing something that you would prefer not to do, or even something you believe to be wrong.

Proximity	People are more likely to harm another person when given an instruction to do so if they cannot see the other person. For example, Milgram found that if a learner and the teacher were in separate rooms, the teacher was more likely to obey an instruction to shock the learner. However, if the learner was seated directly opposite them, obedience levels dropped.
Symbols of authority	People are more likely to inflict harm on another person if they believe the person giving the instruction is an authority figure. In the Milgram study, the teacher was much more likely to shock the learner if the researcher wore a lab coat.
Status of the situation	If the situation and the environment in which the instruction is given is believed to be legitimate and authoritative, the higher the likelihood that the instruction will be carried out. When the Milgram study took place at the university, the teacher was much more likely to shock the learner than if the study took place at an ordinary venue in the town.
Culture	Levels of obedience change between cultures. For example, studies have found higher levels of conformity in more authoritarian cultures (e.g. Japan) and lower levels in less authoritarian cultures (e.g. Australia).
Agency	Milgram suggests that people have two states of behaviour when they are in social situations: autonomous and agentic.

Autonomous and Agentic States

– When people are in an autonomous state, they direct their actions and feel personally responsible for them.

– When people are in an agentic state, they allow other people to direct their actions. Their actions are attributed to the person giving the instruction and not the responsibility of the person carrying out the instruction.

– In the Milgram experiment, many of the participants felt that they were simply carrying out the instructions given to them. In other words, they were only following orders.

Dispositional Factors Affecting Obedience

- Dispositional factors refer to factors about the individual that might lead to them being more or less obedient, such as personality.

- One theory developed by Adorno (1950) suggests that people who have an authoritarian personality display higher levels of obedience to authority.

  – Adorno developed a personality questionnaire to identify those with an authoritarian personality type. The questionnaire is known as the F-scale (F for fascist).

  – Adorno claimed that personality and attitudes stem from childhood influences, especially the actions of parents.

  – Parents who enforce high levels of discipline are more likely to raise children with an authoritarian personality.

- Elms and Milgram (1966) replicated Milgram's original study with participants who had completed the F-scale prior to taking part. They found a strong correlation between levels of obedience and authoritarian personality type.

  – Because this was a correlational study, we cannot be sure that the personality type was the cause of higher levels of obedience.

  – The questionnaire is easily manipulated and it's likely that many people will be able to second guess the questions to avoid being categorised as authoritarian.

  – The F-scale correlates highly with levels of education, so the results can also be explained on an educational level rather than a dispositional one.

Quick Test

1. What is meant by obedience to authority?
2. Who conducted the 1963 study into obedience?
3. Who developed the theory of the authoritarian personality?

Key Words

autonomous
agentic
Adorno
authoritarian

Prosocial and Antisocial Behaviour

You must be able to:

- Describe and explain factors affecting bystander intervention
- Describe the findings of the Piliavin *et al.* (1969) study on bystander intervention
- Explain what is meant by social loafing
- Describe how social and dispositional factors can affect crowd behaviour.

Prosocial Behaviour

- Prosocial behaviour refers to the positive impact of human actions.
- One particular form of prosocial behaviour is **bystander intervention**.

Factors Affecting Bystander Intervention

- People are more likely to help if there are fewer people present because they feel more responsible. This is called **diffusion of responsibility**.
- If other people present do not perceive the situation to be an emergency, people are less likely to help (**pluralistic ignorance**).
- People are more likely to help if the victim is similar in a number of ways to the helper (e.g. race, gender).
- People are more likely to help if they feel they have the expertise to deal with the situation (e.g. an off-duty medical professional).
- If the cost of helping outweighs the benefits, people are less likely to help (e.g. if helping is time-consuming or it could put the helper in danger).

The Subway Samaritan

- Piliavin *et al.* (1969) investigated bystander behaviour on the New York subway.
- Students acted out a scene where one of them (the 'victim') collapsed on a subway train.
- The victim was sometimes black and sometimes white, acted drunk, or used a cane, or appeared to be ill.
- In some versions, one of the team would go and help the victim.
- Two members of the team observed the reactions of the other passengers on the train.
- Piliavin found that people were more likely to help if the victim was ill or carried a cane and less likely to help if they were drunk.
- There was also a slight tendency to help those of the same race.

Bystander behaviour

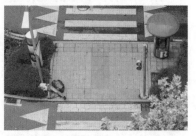

Crowd Psychology and Collective Behaviour

- **Deindividuation** is when the presence of a crowd or group leads to the loss of sense of individual identity.
- Deindividuation leads people to follow group norms rather than individual norms. It can lead to people acting more aggressively when they are part of a crowd.
- Zimbardo (1969) replicated Milgram's electric shock study into obedience but participants either wore a name badge or had their faces concealed with a hood. Those wearing the hoods gave more shocks than those with name badges, supporting the idea of deindividuation.
- The theory of deindividuation can also be used to reduce aggression, e.g. by installing CCTV cameras at football matches.
- Deindividuation in crowds can also lead to prosocial behaviour, for instance at religious gatherings.
- People might also exert less effort when part of a crowd than when they are acting as an individual, a process known as **social loafing**.
- Dispositional factors play a role in how people will behave.
  - For example, people with aggressive personalities are more likely to engage in acts of violence when in a group situation.
- Personal morality also influences group behaviour and can act to counter the aggressive acts of the group. For example, a person who believes that violence is morally wrong will be less likely to engage in violent acts perpetrated by the crowd.

> **Key Point**
>
> Crowds can act in both prosocial and antisocial ways, depending on the circumstances.

> **Quick Test**
>
> 1. What is meant by bystander behaviour?
> 2. Who conducted the subway study?
> 3. Define deindividuation.
> 4. Name one way a government might try to reduce the incidences of antisocial behaviour at football matches.

> **Key Words**
>
> bystander intervention
> diffusion of responsibility
> pluralistic ignorance
> deindividuation
> social loafing

Where space is not provided, write your answers on a separate piece of paper.

Sampling

1 Explain what is meant by a sample being biased. [2]

2 State **one** important principle that must be met in order for a sample to be truly random. [1]

3 Complete the following sentences. [2]

One flaw with systematic sampling is that there could be pre-existing biases in the target

population/list of names that stop the sample from being ....

To select a random sample from a numbered list of everyone in the target population,

a researcher might use a computer to pick ....

4 Explain what is meant by a stratified sample, and give a strength and a weakness of this sampling method. [4]

5 Which of the following sampling methods is likely to involve numbering members of the population? Shade **one** box only. [1]

A Random sampling ⭕ B Opportunity sampling ⭕

C Systematic sampling ⭕ D Stratified sampling ⭕

6 Which of the following sampling methods is simplest to carry out? Shade **one** box only. [1]

A Random sampling ⭕ B Opportunity sampling ⭕

C Systematic sampling ⭕ D Stratified sampling ⭕

7 Write down the terms that best match the statements. [4]

Statement	Term
a) Selecting participants to take part in a study	
b) The group of people who are studied	
c) Concluding that findings also apply to the target population	
d) Flaws in a sample, which mean some characteristics are not representative of the target population	

Variables and Hypotheses

1 What term is used to refer to different parts of an experiment, each of which links to a different value of the independent variable? [1]

2 What is the name of the variable that a researcher measures? Give an example. [2]

3 Complete the sentences by choosing the best words from the selection below. You do not have to use all the words. [4]

manipulates	blocks	IV	DV	cause-and-effect	bias	correlational

In psychology experiments, a researcher _____ or changes the value of the

independent variable and measures the value of the dependent variable. An experiment

therefore looks for a _____ relationship between these two variables. The values

of the _____ relate to the two or more conditions of the experiment. The scores

on the _____ form the data that a researcher gathers and analyses.

4 State **two** characteristics of a normally distributed variable. [2]

5 Read the text. Then state what the **three** conditions of the independent variable are. [3]

> In an experiment into the spacing effect in memory, 24 Year 8 students learn a set of French words on Monday. Eight of them revise the words later the same day, eight revise the words the following day, and the remaining eight pupils revise them the following Monday. All of them are tested later that month.

6 What is the name of the variable that a researcher manipulates in an experiment? Shade **one** box only. [1]

A Independent variable ◯ **B** Dependent variable ◯

C Extraneous variable ◯ **D** Controlled variable ◯

7 What is the name of the prediction of what will be found if the alternative hypothesis is **not** supported by the data in an experiment? Shade **one** box only. [1]

A Extraneous prediction ◯ **B** Cause-and-effect prediction ◯

C Null hypothesis ◯ **D** Experimental hypothesis ◯

8 Discuss the likely extraneous variables which could affect the following experiment. [4]

> A researcher is studying the effect of pictures on memory by giving students visual and verbal tasks. The experiment is carried out in the school cafeteria.
>
> Students are given a set of sentences to study. One group is given sentences only. The other is given the same sentences but each one has a picture that goes with it. Some sentences are about planets of the solar system, and others are about famous sports stars – the choice of sentences is random.
>
> Both groups are given as long as they like to study the items, and then given a short memory test.
>
> Some participants take part in the experiment when they first arrive at school in the morning, and others take part during their lunch hour.

Design of Experiments 1 and 2

1 What term is used in research to mean treating participants fairly and in accordance with their rights? [1]

2 Which ethical consideration means that participants cannot be given incomplete information at the start of a study? Shade **one** box only. [1]

A Informed consent ⃝ **B** Right to withdraw ⃝

C Avoiding harm ⃝ **D** Debriefing ⃝

3 Which of the following is **not** an ethical issue in research? Shade **one** box only. [1]

A Right to withdraw ⃝ **B** Avoiding harm ⃝

C Confidentiality ⃝ **D** Control ⃝

4 A researcher carries out a study into perception, where participants are asked to view an illusion with or without a backing colour. Everyone does condition 1 first and then condition 2. What problem could occur, and how could the researcher have avoided this? [2]

5 A researcher wishes to study the effects of caffeine on how well university students can concentrate when watching a lecture. Explain how this could be done either as a field experiment or as a lab experiment. Give your view on which experimental design should be used. [4]

6 Complete the table. [4]

Design	Description	Weakness
Repeated measures design		
Independent groups design		

7 Why is it important to randomly allocate participants to conditions in an independent groups design? [2]

8 What name is given to an experimental condition that is used purely for comparison? [1]

Non-experimental Methods

1 Explain what is meant by a closed question and state a research method that might use one. [2]

2 Researchers gather different types of data in psychology.

a) Name a research method that gathers primary data. [1]

b) Name a research method that gathers secondary data. [1]

3 Give a strength and a weakness of the observation method. [2]

4 Tick (✓) or cross (✗) the statements about non-experimental methods to indicate whether they are true or false. [4]

Statements about non-experimental methods	True (✓) or false (✗)?
Non-experimental methods always obtain qualitative data.	
For ethical reasons, it is important to inform and gain consent from participants who are being observed.	
Surveys only used closed questions.	
Case studies only use secondary data.	

5 Which of the following is an example of secondary data? Shade **one** box only. [1]

A School reports ⃝ **B** Observations ⃝

C Brain scans ⃝ **D** Ability tests ⃝

6 Which of the following research activities would obtain qualitative data? Shade **one** box only. [1]

A A survey with closed questions ⬡   **B** A checklist used in an observation ⬡

C An interview with open questions ⬡   **D** An IQ test ⬡

7 A researcher is studying an individual with an accidental brain injury. Discuss the different research methods or techniques that might be involved, and any other data that should be gathered. [3]

8 Explain why observation studies often use more than one observer. [2]

Correlation and Data Handling

1 How is the range calculated, and what does it show? [2]

2 A researcher placed all of the scores from one experimental condition in order. Then he identified which score was at the midpoint of this set of data. Which statistic was he calculating? Shade **one** box only. [1]

A The mean ⬡   **B** The mode ⬡

C The median ⬡   **D** The range ⬡

3 What term is used to describe the correlation that is shown when dots on a scatter graph are randomly spread out, with no discernible pattern? Shade **one** box only. [1]

A Strong correlation ⬡   **B** Zero correlation ⬡

C Weak correlation ⬡   **D** Negative correlation ⬡

4 Explain the difference between a bar chart and a histogram. [2]

5 Explain the difference between a weak correlation and a negative correlation. [2]

6 Read the following text. Explain the **two** types of data used and how they would be analysed. Give a possible hypothesis for the study. [5]

> A researcher is studying the relationship between the number of books read per year and a child's grades at school. After gaining parental consent, the research team surveys 50 school children about their reading habits. They also obtain school grades via the head teacher.

7 On the graph below, sketch a strong (but not perfect) positive correlation. Label the axes 'Study time' and 'Average grade'. [2]

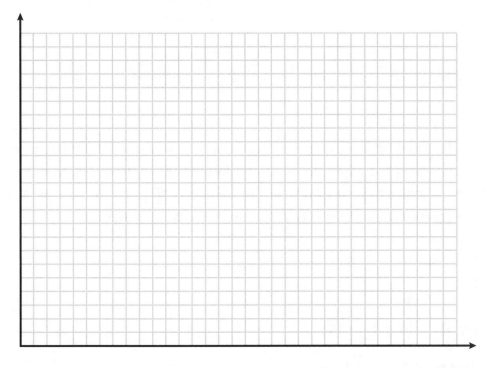

8 Complete the sentences by choosing the best words from the selection below. You do not have to use all the words. [5]

multiplying	middle	four	dividing	two	mean	common

It is important to be able to express an average score from a set of data. The

_____ is calculated by adding up the sum of all scores in a set of data and

then _____ by the number of scores. The median is calculated by placing all

the scores in order, from low to high, and then selecting the _____ score.

With even numbers of scores, the mean of the _____ middle scores is calculated.

Finally, the mode is obtained by identifying the most _____ score in a set

of data.

Where space is not provided, write your answers on a separate piece of paper.

Conformity

1 Why are people less likely to conform if they give their answers in private? [2]

2 Your maths teacher asks the class a difficult question. Susan, who is very good at maths, gives an answer that you know is wrong but when the teacher asks another student they give the same wrong answer. When it comes to your turn to answer, you give the same answer as Susan. Using your knowledge of conformity, explain why you gave the wrong answer. [4]

3 Asch conducted his study of conformity in 1951.

a) Describe the procedure of Asch's line study. [6]

b) The participants in the Asch study often displayed stress reactions as they struggled to decide what answer they were going to give. Why is this a weakness of the study? [2]

c) What was the advantage of carrying out the study in a laboratory setting? [1]

d) What was the conclusion of the Asch study? [2]

Obedience

1 A researcher ran an experiment about obedience. An actor asked people to pick up litter in a park: in Condition A the actor wore a uniform and in Condition B the actor wore casual clothes. Levels of obedience were higher in Condition A than in Condition B.

Use your knowledge of psychology to explain why the level of obedience was different in Condition A and Condition B. [2]

2 In Milgram's experiment, levels of obedience were higher when the study was conducted at the university than in a venue in town. Why might this be? [2]

3 What did Milgram discover about proximity? [1]

4 Describe what Milgram meant by agency. [2]

5 What does the F-scale measure? [1]

6 What did Elms and Milgram discover about the link between authoritarian personality and obedience? [1]

Prosocial and antisocial behaviour

1 Outline what is meant by the term bystander behaviour. [1]

2 Identify **one** factor that can influence bystander behaviour. [1]

3 Describe the procedure of Piliavin's subway study into bystander behaviour. [4]

4 Describe **one** study that investigated deindividuation. [4]

5 Deindividuation is universal. What is meant by this statement? [2]

The Possible Relationship Between Language and Thought

You must be able to:

- Explain Piaget's theory of language and thought
- Explain the Sapir-Whorf hypothesis
- Describe how language and thought affect our view of the world.

Language Depends on Thought (Piaget)

- We discussed Jean Piaget (1896–1980) in the Development chapter, pages 38–41. He indicated that development takes place in a number of stages and that language development is the result of cognitive (or thought) development.
- According to Piaget, a child must first be able to use ideas and concepts before being able to use language. A child might use and repeat words before understanding the concepts behind these words. Piaget called this egocentric speech.
- The purpose of adult communication is to convey ideas and information. A child must be able to understand what specific words are used for before applying them to communication.
- This can be seen in the link between impaired cognitive development in children and impaired language development.
- However, some children have severe learning difficulties but normal language development, suggesting that language development isn't dependent on cognitive development.
- Some studies have found that language development can accelerate cognitive development.

Thinking Depends on Language (Sapir-Whorf Hypothesis)

- Language influences the way people perceive and think about the world.
- There are two types of Sapir-Whorf hypothesis:
  - The strong version says that language determines thought.
  - The weak version says that language influences thought.
- Differences between languages determine the types of thoughts people are able to have.
- There are certain thoughts an individual has in one language that cannot be understood by those who live in a society that uses a different language.
- The way people think is strongly affected by their native language.

> **Key Point**
>
> There are two main theories concerned with the relationship between language and thought. Piaget's theory states that language determines thought, while the Sapir-Whorf hypothesis suggests that thinking is dependent on language.

Language and Memory

- The Sapir-Whorf hypothesis suggests that language influences the way in which people remember events.
- Carmichael (1932) showed a series of nonsense pictures to two groups of participants.
  - The pictures were paired with a label but the label was different for each group.
  - When asked to draw the picture from memory, it was found that the label had influenced the participants' memory of it.

Colour Recognition

Zuni Tribe

- The Zuni (a Native American tribe) only use one term for the yellow-orange region of the colour spectrum.
- When Zuni participants were shown a coloured chip and asked to locate the chip amongst other chips, they performed better if there was a simple colour name (e.g. red) rather than a mixture of red and blue.

Himba Tribe

- Goldstein studied the Himba tribe of northern Namibia, who have the same word for green and blue (bura).
- However, the Himba use different words to distinguish between shades of green (dambu for light green; zuzu for dark green).
- When members of the Himba were shown 11 green squares and 1 blue square, they had difficulty indicating which square was the odd one out.
- When they were shown 12 green squares, 1 of which was a lighter green, they had no problem identifying the odd one out.

- These studies add support to the Sapir-Whorf hypothesis.

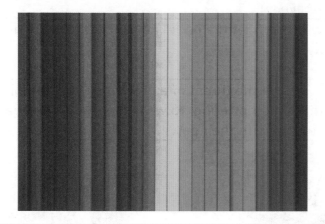

> **Quick Test**
>
> 1. What are the two main theories of language and thought?
> 2. What is meant by egocentric speech?
> 3. Who studied the Himba tribe?

Differences Between Human and Animal Communication

You must be able to:

- Describe the limited functions of animal communication
- Describe Von Frisch's bee study
- Explain the difference between animal and human communication.

Limited Functions of Animal Communication

- Non-human animals use communication as a survival tool, which results in greater simplicity of use.
- For non-human animals, communication is necessary for aspects of survival such as:
    - mate selection
    - defending or expanding territory
    - finding food
    - reporting their whereabouts to others
    - warning against danger.

Communication during contests	Communication is used to attract the attention of a future mate or to solidify pair-bonds. Many non-human male animals communicate their superiority over other males through their plumage (e.g. peacocks) or other attributes. Male birds of paradise engage in a complex dance in order to attract females.
Territorial	Signals are used to defend or to claim territory. Territorial signals include song in birds, leaving markings on trees (e.g. the wild boar) or scenting territory using urine (e.g. dogs).
Food-related communication	Food calls are used to inform the group that food has been found (e.g. the 'waggle dance' of the honeybee).
Reporting whereabouts to others	For example, wolves howl to both let the pack know where they are and to signal the pack to stay away.
Alarm calls	Signals are used to communicate the threat of a predator. One example is the magpie, who uses its distinctive 'chattering' to warn other magpies against predators, while rabbits thump with their paws.

Key Point

Non-human animals use communication for survival.

Von Frisch's Bee Study

- As mentioned earlier, honeybees communicate information about the location of pollen-rich flowers via what is known as the waggle dance.
- The movements involved in the waggle dance were first translated by Karl Von Frisch.

  - A bee finds a food source while exploring.
  - It returns to the hive to communicate its location.
  - Using the sun's position as a guide, it waggles its body in the direction of the food source.
  - The food's distance is communicated by adding extra shuffles.
  - The more plentiful the food source, the longer the duration of the dance.

Properties of Human Communication not Present in Animal Communication

- Human communication consists of both signals and symbols.
- Symbols are sounds, gestures, material objects or written words that have a specific meaning to a group of people.
- Key differences between human communication and that of other primates is that humans have an open vocal system and a larger bank of symbols to use in communication.
- Communication in non-human animals tends to occur within the present tense and is related to real-world information such as status, food, territory and mate availability.
- Human communication, on the other hand, generally uses past, present and future tense, allowing them to talk about past events, plan ahead and discuss future events.
- Human communication also allows for the discussion of possible future outcomes based on present situations and expected outcomes.

> **Key Point**
>
> Communication in both animals and humans consists of signals. Symbols are sounds or gestures that have meaning to those using them.

Quick Test

1. What is the main purpose of communication in non-human animals?
2. Who conducted the study into communication in honeybees?
3. What is the name of the behaviour honeybees use to communicate the location of food?

> **Key Words**
>
> symbols
> gestures
> open vocal system

Non-verbal Communication

You must be able to:

- Describe the differences between verbal and non-verbal communication
- Explain the importance of eye contact in non-verbal communication
- Describe other types of non-verbal communication, including open and closed postures, and personal space.

Verbal and Non-verbal Communication

- Verbal communication is a type of communication that uses words.
  - Words can be spoken, written or produced using sign language.
- Non-verbal communication is a type of communication that doesn't rely on spoken or written words.
  - It can include body posture or gestures.
  - It can also include certain aspects of language such as tone of voice (rather than the meaning of the words spoken). These are known as **paralinguistics**.

> **Key Point**
>
> Non-verbal communication doesn't rely on spoken or written words.

Functions of Eye Contact

- The functions of eye contact include regulating the flow of conversation, signalling attraction and expressing emotion.
- According to Argyle, eye contact regulates the flow of information in a number of ways.
- **Information seeking:** During a conversation, we obtain immediate feedback on the reactions of the listener by gazing at the face, and the eyes in particular.
  - Looking away can signal to the speaker that the listener isn't interested.
  - Breaking eye contact when listening can mean that the listener wishes to speak.
  - Looking away from the listener can help the speaker to filter out unnecessary information.
- **Providing feedback:** According to Argyle, the development of social skills is encouraged through feedback provided by eye contact.
  - People need to see how others are reacting so that they can decide if the listener approves with what they are saying.
  - Eye contact signals a positive reaction, while breaking eye contact signals disapproval.
- **Expressing emotions:** Eye contact is linked to emotional intimacy. Rubin found that couples who scored highly on measures of love also spent longer in mutual eye contact.

Body Language

- Body language involves a number of **postural** behaviours, including open and closed posture, postural echo and touch.

An **open posture**	Revealing and leaves sensitive areas vulnerable. The head is usually slightly back, the chin slightly raised, arms by the side and the legs uncrossed.
A **closed posture**	Often seen as defensive and protecting. Hands are held up to the chin or the head is lowered to protect the throat; arms and legs are crossed.
Postural echo	The mirroring or the adoption of the same posture as the person doing the talking. This encourages mutual positive feelings.
Touch	Communicates emotion. Studies have found that when nurses speak to patients they also touch them. This shows sympathy and understanding.

Personal Space

- Personal space is an imaginary area that people view as their own territory.
- When personal space is invaded, people react to it in a number of ways, including feeling uncomfortable and adjusting their own position in order to regain territory.
- Factors affecting personal space include cultural norms, gender, and status.

  - Hall (1914–2009) found that personal space differs between cultures (e.g. people in South America stand closer to each other than those in the United States).
  - Heshka and Nelson (1972) found that when they are strangers, females stand further apart than males.
  - People of a similar status tend to stand closer together, while those of a different status stand further way.

> **Key Point**
>
> Elements of non-verbal communication include eye contact, body language and the use of personal space.

> **Quick Test**
>
> 1. What is meant by non-verbal communication?
> 2. What are the main functions of eye contact?
> 3. What is meant by open posture?
> 4. What is meant by closed posture?

> **Key Words**
>
> paralinguistics
> posture
> open posture
> closed posture
> postural echo

Explanations of Non-verbal Behaviour

You must be able to:

- Understand Darwin's evolutionary theory of non-verbal communication
- Describe evidence that supports the view that non-verbal behaviour is innate
- Describe evidence that supports the view that non-verbal behaviour is learned.

Darwin's Evolutionary Theory of Non-verbal Communication

- Charles Darwin (1809–1882) believed that non-verbal communication was an **evolutionary** mechanism; in other words, it is evolved and **adaptive**.
- All mammals (both human and non-human) show emotions through facial expression. This behaviour is universal and, therefore, evolutionary.
- Types of non-verbal behaviour persist in humans because they have been acquired for their value throughout evolutionary history.
- Non-verbal behaviour is therefore **innate** – it is something that we are born with.
- Darwin's theory takes the side of nature in the nature–nurture debate because it argues that non-verbal behaviour is not learned from the environment.

> ### Key Point
>
> Charles Darwin suggested that all non-verbal communication is evolutionary, but other scientists believe that non-verbal communication is learned.

Evidence that Non-verbal Behaviour is Innate

- Some scientists believe that non-verbal behaviour is innate.
- Children who have been blind since birth still display the same facial expressions as sighted children.
- Matsumoto (2008) studied sighted and blind judo athletes and found that both groups produced the same facial expressions in certain emotional situations.
- This supports the evolutionary theory of non-verbal behaviour.

Evidence that Non-verbal Behaviour is Learned

- Other scientists believe that non-verbal behaviour is a learned response.
- In other words, non-verbal behaviour develops as a response to observing and imitating people within one's own culture (e.g. shaking hands, kissing on the cheek or bowing).
- Yuki *et al.* (2007) conducted a cross-cultural study using American and Japanese participants.

  - Each participant was shown a number of emoticons with different emotional expressions and asked to rate them from very sad to very happy.
  - Japanese participants gave higher ratings to those emoticons with happier eyes while Americans rated happy mouths higher.
  - This indicates that non-verbal communication is affected by cultural experience. In other words, it is learned.

- Yuki's results suggest a nurture orientation (rather than a nature one, as with Darwin), so it positions itself on the nurture side of the nature–nurture debate.
  - Yuki's study lacks ecological validity because the study used computer-generated faces and not real ones.
  - Yuki used students to test the hypothesis. Results might have been different if the study used older or younger participants.
  - Findings cannot be generalised to other emotions because Yuki only examined happy and sad faces.

Quick Test

1. What did Charles Darwin believe about non-verbal behaviour?
2. What did Matsumoto's study find?
3. Who conducted the study into non-verbal behaviour using American and Japanese participants?

Key Words

evolutionary
adaptive
innate

Where space is not provided, write your answers on a separate piece of paper.

Conformity

1 Describe what Asch discovered in his study of conformity. [2]

_____

_____

2 Explain why the presence of an ally might reduce levels of conformity. [2]

_____

_____

3 What did Asch discover about the size of the majority in his study? [2]

_____

_____

4 Name **one** other factor that might affect levels of conformity. [1]

_____

5 How did Asch use deception in his study? [2]

_____

_____

6 Suggest **one** strength and **one** weakness of Asch's study into conformity. [2]

_____

_____

Obedience

1 How does obedience differ from conformity? [2]

_____

_____

2 What was the aim of Milgram's study? [2]

3 Name **two** factors affecting obedience. [2]

4 Describe **one** factor that might lead to someone developing an authoritarian personality. [1]

5 Name **one** weakness of the F-scale. [1]

6 Why can't we be sure that an authoritarian personality is the cause of high levels of obedience in some people? [1]

Prosocial and Antisocial Behaviour

1 Fatima is doing her Christmas shopping. The town is really busy and she sees a man fall over in the street. Nobody tries to help him or ask him if he is okay. Fatima wonders why this might be, especially as there are so many people around. Fatima doesn't stop to help.

   a) Explain to Fatima, using your knowledge of psychology, why nobody stopped to help the man. [2]

   b) Under what circumstances might this have been different? [2]

2 In the subway Samaritan study, who were people more likely to help? [2]

3 Why might trick or treaters get more on Halloween if their faces are covered? [2]

4 **a)** Using your knowledge of crowd psychology, explain why violence often occurs at football matches. [4]

   b) How could we reduce violence at football matches? [1]

   c) Referring to your answer in **b)**, why might this strategy work? [1]

Where space is not provided, write your answers on a separate piece of paper.

The Possible Relationship Between Language and Thought

1 **a)** Briefly describe Piaget's theory of language and thought. [3]

....

....

....

b) According to Piaget, what is the purpose of human communication? [1]

....

2 Describe the weak Sapir-Whorf hypothesis. [1]

....

Differences Between Human and Animal Communication

1 Outline **one** difference in animal and human communication. Use an example to explain your answer. [2]

....

2 Give **one** example of food-related animal non-verbal communication. [1]

....

3 Describe **two** forms of non-verbal communication in animals, related to territory. [2]

....

4 How do bees tell the rest of the colony how far the food source is from the hive? [1]

....

5 What is meant by the word 'symbol' in relation to communication? [2]

....

6 What does human communication allow for that animal communication doesn't? [2]

....

Non-verbal Communication

1 Read the text and then answer the question that follows.

> Abi and Rebecca are best friends but their teacher doesn't allow them to sit together in class. When Abi enters the classroom, Rebecca smiles at her and Abi waves to her. When the teacher isn't looking, Rebecca passes a note to Abi and after Abi reads the note she laughs out loud. This annoys the teacher. The teacher tells both girls to stop being silly and to pay attention. Abi frowns at the teacher.

From the passage above, identify two examples of verbal behaviour and two examples of non-verbal behaviour. [4]

2 During a conversation, what can looking away indicate? [1]

3 Why might a person break eye contact during a conversation? [1]

4 Describe a closed posture. [3]

5 **a)** What is personal space? [1]

b) What can happen when someone invades your personal space? [1]

Explanations of Non-verbal Behaviour

1 Briefly describe Darwin's theory of non-verbal communication. [4]

2 Evaluate Yuki *et al.*'s study of emoticons. [4]

3 What is the difference between something being innate and something being learned? [2]

The Structure and Function of the Brain and Nervous System

You must be able to:

- Describe the divisions of the nervous system (central nervous system and peripheral nervous system)
- Describe the role of the autonomic nervous system in the fight or flight response
- Understand the James-Lange theory of emotion.

The Divisions of the Human Nervous System

- The central nervous system (CNS) comprises the brain and spinal cord.

  - The brain is involved in psychological processes and the maintenance of life.
  - The spinal cord is involved in the transfer of messages to and from the brain to the peripheral nervous system (PNS). It is also involved in reflex actions such as the startle response.

- The PNS transmits messages to the whole body from the brain, and vice versa.
- The PNS has two divisions: the **somatic** system and the autonomic system.

  - The somatic system transmits and receives messages from the senses (e.g. visual information from the eyes and auditory information from the ears).
  - The somatic system also directs muscles to react and move.
  - The somatic nervous system consists of sensory and motor neurons.

  - The autonomic system helps to transmit and receive information from the organs and is divided into the sympathetic (which increases activity) and the parasympathetic (which decreases activity) systems.

The Autonomic Nervous System and The Fight or Flight Response

- The fight or flight response is triggered from the autonomic nervous system (ANS), most notably the sympathetic branch.
- The fight or flight response is designed to help an individual manage physically when under threat. It is also activated in times of stress when the body perceives a threat.
- The fight or flight response helps a person react quicker than normal and ensures that the body is able to tackle the threat by either attacking or running away.

Key Point

The nervous system in humans is divided into the central nervous system (CNS) and the peripheral nervous system (PNS).

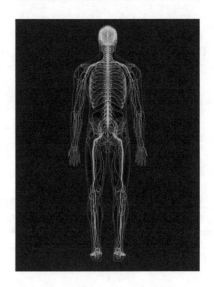

- The fight or flight response occurs in a number of steps, or stages.
  - In the first stage of the fight or flight response, the hypothalamus recognises that there is a threat and sends a message to the adrenal gland.
  - The adrenal medulla then triggers the release of adrenaline to the endocrine system and noradrenaline to the brain.
- These stages lead to a number of bodily changes, including:
  - increased heart rate
  - muscular tension
  - faster breathing rate
  - pupil dilation
  - reduced function of the digestive and immune system.

The James-Lange Theory of Emotion

- The James-Lange theory, proposed by William James and Carl Lange, suggests that emotional experience is the result, not the cause, of perceived bodily changes.
- James illustrated the theory with the following example. We might think that if we meet a bear we become frightened and we run. The James-Lange theory, however, would suggest that we are frightened *because* we run. In a similar way, we feel sad because we cry or afraid because we tremble.
- People require feedback from bodily changes and they label their subjective experience based on this feedback: I am trembling, therefore I must be afraid.
- An alternative explanation (Cannon-Bard theory) argues that the ANS responds in the same way to all emotional stimuli, as explained by the fight or flight response.

Quick Test

1. What are the two systems contained within the human nervous system?
2. The brain and spinal cord are part of which system?
3. Which system controls the fight or flight response?
4. Who developed the James-Lange theory of emotion?

Key Word

somatic

Neuron Structure and Function

You must be able to:

- Describe the functions of the three different types of neuron
- Describe Hebb's theory of learning and growth
- Explain how signals are passed from one neuron to another and how this might be excited or inhibited.

Sensory, Relay and Motor Neurons

- Different types of neuron serve different functions and are specialised to carry out particular roles.

  - Sensory neurons tell the rest of the brain about the external and internal environment by processing information taken from one of the five senses (sight, hearing, touch, smell, taste).
  - The motor neuron carries an electrical signal to a muscle, which will cause the muscle to either contract or relax.
  - Relay neurons carry messages from one part of the central nervous system to another. They connect motor and sensory neurons.

> **Key Point**
>
> Different types of neurons carry out different functions.

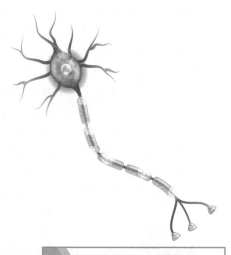

Hebb's Theory of Learning and Neuronal Growth

- Hebb's theory states that when one neuron sends a signal to another neuron, and that second neuron becomes activated, the connection between the two neurons is strengthened.
- The more one neuron activates another neuron, the stronger the connection between them grows.
- Hebb described this using the phrase 'what fires together, wires together'. In other words, with every new experience, the brain rewires its physical structure. This is commonly known as Hebbian learning.
- It is thought that Hebbian learning occurs through a mechanism known as long-term potentiation (LTP).
- LTP results in stronger connections between nerve cells and leads to longer lasting changes in synaptic connections.
- These changes in connections are thought to be responsible for learning and memory.

> **Key Point**
>
> The more often connections are made between neurons, the stronger that connection becomes.

The Process of Synaptic Transmission: Release and Uptake of Neurotransmitters

- The synapse is a specialised gap between neurons through which the electrical impulse from the neuron is transmitted chemically.
- Synaptic transmission refers to the process whereby messages are sent from neuron to neuron.

- During synaptic transmission, the electrical nerve impulse travels down the neuron, prompting the release of brain chemicals called neurotransmitters at the pre-synaptic terminal. These chemicals are then released into the synaptic fluid in the synapse.
- Examples of neurotransmitters are serotonin and dopamine.
- The adjacent neurons must then quickly take up the neurotransmitters from the fluid and convert them into an electrical impulse to travel down the neuron to the next synaptic terminal. The procedure is then repeated.

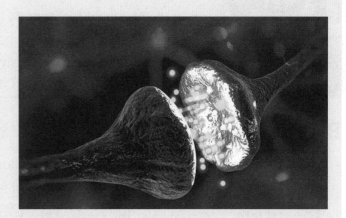

Excitation and Inhibition

- Not all messages prompt activation in the same way because it depends on the action potential of the post-synaptic neuron and the message type received. Only certain neurotransmitters can unlock a message channel in certain receptors in the post-synaptic neuron.
- We can think of this as a lock and key system whereby the right key (neurotransmitter) has to fit into the right lock (receptor) in order to open up the specific ion channel. Ions then flow through the membrane into the neuron along the specific pathways.
- This flooding of ions can cause a potential in the dendrites. This potential can be **excitatory** or **inhibitory**.

Excitatory potentials	Make it more likely for the neuron to fire. If the synapse is more likely to cause a post-synaptic neuron to fire, it is called an excitatory synapse.
Inhibitory potentials	Make it less likely to fire. If the message is likely to be stopped at the post-synaptic neuron, it is called an inhibitory synapse.

Quick Test

1. What are the three types of neuron?
2. How did Hebb describe the action of neuronal growth?
3. What is a synapse?

Key Words

synapse
excitation
inhibition

Localisation of Function in the Brain

You must be able to:

- Describe the main brain structures
- Describe what is meant by localisation of function
- Describe the function of the motor, somatosensory, auditory and language areas of the brain
- Explain Penfield's study of the motor and somatosensory cortex.

Brain Structures

- The brain consists of a number of structures, including the frontal lobe, temporal lobe, parietal lobe, occipital lobe and cerebellum.

Frontal lobe	Situated at the front of the brain and responsible for carrying out higher mental functions such as thinking, decision making and planning.
Temporal lobe	Situated behind the temples and responsible for processing auditory information from the ears (hearing).
Parietal lobe	Located at the back of the brain and responsible for processing sensory information that is associated with taste, temperature and touch.
Occipital lobe	Situated at the lower back of the brain and responsible for processing visual information from the eyes.
Cerebellum	Located in the lower brain and responsible for balance and coordination.

Localisation of Function in the Brain

> Localisation of function refers to the view that particular areas of the brain are responsible for specific functions, such as vision and language.

- **Motor area:** the primary motor cortex is responsible for movement, whereby it sends messages to the muscles via the brain stem and spinal cord.
  - The motor cortex is important for complex movement but not basic functions like coughing or crying.
  - Within the motor cortex there are areas which control specific parts of the body.
- **Somatosensory area:** this is concerned with the sensation of the body and is situated next to the motor cortex.
  - The somatosensory cortex perceives touch. The amount of somatosensory cortex required dictates the amount needed for that area of the body.

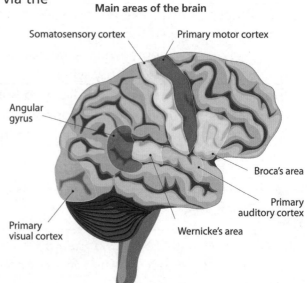

Main areas of the brain

Somatosensory cortex

Primary motor cortex

Angular gyrus

Broca's area

Primary auditory cortex

Wernicke's area

Primary visual cortex

- **The visual area:** this has two visual cortices, one situated in each hemisphere of the brain. The primary visual cortex is the occipital lobe. This is the main visual centre.
  - An area of the visual cortex known as Area V1 is thought to be specifically necessary for visual perception, and people with damage to this area report no vision of any kind (including in dreams).
  - The visual information is transmitted along the pathways, one containing the components of the visual field and the other being involved in the localisation within the visual field.
- **Auditory area:** the human brain has two primary auditory cortices, one in each hemisphere. The auditory cortices in both hemispheres receives information from both ears via two pathways that transmit information about what the sound is and its location.
  - If the primary auditory cortex is damaged, it does not lead to total deafness. However, if the sounds require complex processing (such as music) then this ability is lost.
- **Language area:** most language processing takes place in Broca's and Wernicke's areas. In most people, both areas are situated in the left hemisphere.

Penfield homunculus

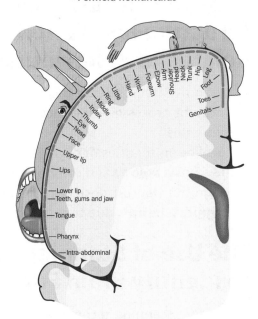

Penfield's Study of the Motor and Somatosensory Cortex

- Penfield, a neurosurgeon, was the first person to map the brain's sensory and motor cortices using a technique known as neural stimulation.
- Often, in order to study the brain, it is necessary to surgically remove parts of the cortex. However, it is also possible to study the brain by using microelectrodes that can stimulate certain areas.
- While employing neural stimulation to epilepsy patients, Penfield discovered that the amount of cortical tissue involved in certain functions differs.
- This means that the more sensitive areas (e.g. the face) require a larger proportion of the cortex than others (such as the trunk), which do not require high levels of sensitivity.
- This is represented in an image known as the Penfield homunculus.

> **Key Point**
>
> The amount of cortical tissue required differs for different functions. The more sensitive the area, the more cortical tissue is required.

> **Key Words**
>
> frontal lobe
> temporal lobe
> parietal lobe
> occipital lobe
> cerebellum
> somatosensory
> localisation
> Penfield homunculus

> **Quick Test**
>
> 1. What is meant by localisation of function?
> 2. What is the temporal lobe area responsible for?
> 3. What is the cerebellum responsible for?

An Introduction to Neuropsychology

You must be able to:

- Describe what is meant by cognitive neuroscience
- Describe the main scanning techniques for studying the brain
- Describe Tulving's 'gold' memory study
- Understand how neurological damage can affect motor abilities and behaviour.

Cognitive Neuroscience: How the Structure and Function of the Brain Relates to Behaviour and Cognition

- Cognitive **neuroscience** focuses on the biological basis of thought processes – specifically, how neurons explain thought processes.
- It relies on theories of cognitive science, and evidence from **neuropsychology** and computer modelling.
- Cognitive neuroscience includes the study of patients with cognitive deficits due to brain damage or strokes.

The Use of Scanning Techniques to Identify Brain Functioning

- Modern scanning techniques rely on matching behavioural actions with physiological activity.
- Because the person is usually conscious while being scanned, they can be directed to produce a particular action, such as performing a memory task.
- A number of scanning techniques are used to identify brain functioning.
  - **fMRI (Functional Magnetic Resonance Imaging):** MRIs record the energy produced by molecules of water after the magnetic field is removed, producing a static picture. fMRIs can show activity as it occurs. This is done by measuring the energy released by haemoglobin (the protein content of blood). When haemoglobin has oxygen, it reacts differently to when it does not have oxygen.
  - **CT or CAT (Computerised Axial Tomography) scan:** CAT scans use an X-ray beam to produce a picture of the physiology of the brain. The picture is not moving like an fMRI but is capable of identifying lesions (damage) and any unusual physiology.
  - **PET (Positron Emission Tomography) scan:** PET scans produce a moving picture of brain activity using radioactive glucose injected into the bloodstream. The scanner picks up the places in the brain where the most glucose is being consumed because these indicate which areas are most active.

Key Point

Cognitive neuroscience is concerned with the biological basis of thought processes.

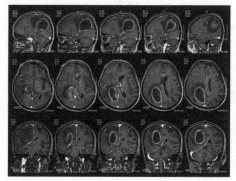

MRI scan

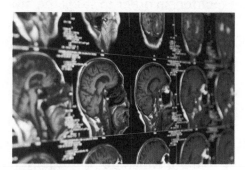

CAT scan

Key Point

Brain scanning techniques help neuroscientists pinpoint particular areas of the brain responsible for specific functions.

Tulving's Gold Memory Study

- Tulving's study (1989) is a good example of how brain scans help scientists understand cognitive processes.
- The study was conducted for two reasons:

  1. To investigate the difference in the processing of episodic memory and semantic memory tasks.
  2. To assess the effectiveness of neuroimaging as a means of investigating mental processes.

- Participants, including Tulving himself, were first injected with a small amount of radioactive gold and then asked to retrieve two types of memory – an episodic memory (that is, a personal experience) and a semantic memory (a general knowledge memory).
- Brain scans revealed that episodic memories resulted in greater activation in the frontal lobes, while semantic memories showed greater activation in the posterior region of the cortex.
- This study indicated that brain scans provide a useful means of identifying cognitive functioning.

Neurological Damage, Motor Abilities and Behaviour

- Damage to the brain can cause a number of deficits in both motor ability and behaviour.
- A stroke occurs when there is not enough oxygen going to the brain. Lack of oxygen can be due to blood vessels becoming blocked or a reduction in blood flow due to the narrowing of blood vessels.
  - The abilities that are affected by a stroke depend on where in the brain the damage has occurred.
  - If the damage occurs in the motor cortex, for example, the stroke victim might not have any movement. This could include reflex actions. Reflex actions can return but recovery varies between patients.

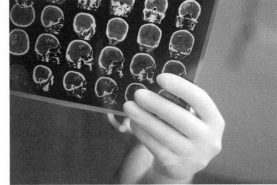

- Damage to the brain due to other factors (e.g. disease or damage caused by an accident) can impact on other brain functions. For instance, damage occurring in the part of the brain responsible for short-term memory can result in the sufferer being unable to form new memories.

Quick Test

1. What is meant by cognitive neuroscience?
2. Name the main types of scanning techniques.
3. What causes a stroke?

Key Words

neuroscience
neuropsychology
fMRI
CT scan
PET scan

Where space is not provided, write your answers on a separate piece of paper.

The Possible Relationship Between Language and Thought

1 How does Piaget's theory of language and thought differ from the Sapir-Whorf hypothesis? [2]

2 How does some evidence challenge Piaget's theory? [3]

3 **a)** Name the **two** types of the Sapir-Whorf hypothesis. [2]

b) How do these **two** types differ? [2]

Differences Between Human and Animal Communication

1 How do animals use non-verbal communication to attract a mate? Give **two** examples. [2]

2 Describe how **two** non-human animals might warn others of their species about danger, such as the presence of a predator. [2]

3 How do honeybees communicate the whereabouts of pollen-rich flowers to the rest of the hive? [4]

4 What are the main differences between human and non-human animal communication? [2]

5 What do human communication systems allow humans to do that is absent in non-human behaviour? [2]

Non-verbal Communication

1 In what ways does verbal communication differ from non-verbal communication? [4]

2 Describe the difference between open and closed postures. [4]

3 a) What is meant by postural echo? [1]

b) What is the purpose of postural echo? [1]

4 How might a person use touch to show empathy? [2]

5 What factors affect personal space? [3]

Explanations of Non-verbal Behaviour

1 According to Darwin, why did humans develop methods of non-verbal communication? [2]

2 Why is Darwin's theory associated with nature rather than nurture? [3]

3 Children who have been blind since birth still display the same facial expressions as sighted children. Why does this provide evidence for Darwin's evolutionary theory of non-verbal communication? [2]

4 What do we mean when we claim that non-verbal behaviour is learned? [2]

5 **a)** In Yuki *et al.*'s 2007 study, how did American and Japanese people differ in terms of their non-verbal communication? [4]

b) Why does Yuki *et al.*'s study support a nurture theory of non-verbal communication? [3]

Where space is not provided, write your answers on a separate piece of paper.

The Structure and Function of the Brain and Nervous System

1 Which **one** of the statements about the human nervous system is correct? Shade **one** box only. [1]

A The autonomic nervous system is responsible for thinking. ◯

B The central nervous system is part of the peripheral nervous system. ◯

C The peripheral nervous system consists only of relay neurons. ◯

D The somatic nervous system consists of sensory and motor neurons. ◯

2 What is the function of the peripheral nervous system? [1]

3 Name the **two** branches of the autonomic nervous system (ANS). [2]

4 Read the text and then answer the question. [6]

> Jake was walking home at night alone when, suddenly, he heard a sound behind him. His heart started to beat fast as he began to run towards the bus stop. From behind him, he heard a voice shout, "Wait for me Jake". As he turned around he saw his friend Will running along the road to catch up with him. Jake stopped and his breathing began to slow down.

Use your knowledge of the central nervous system and the autonomic nervous system to explain Jake's experience.

5 Briefly describe the James-Lange theory of emotion. [4]

Neuron Structure and Function

1 Which **one** of the statements about neurons is correct? Shade **one** box only. [1]

A Motor neurons carry information to the spinal cord. ◯

B Relay neurons carry information from the motor cortex. ◯

C Sensory neurons carry information to the brain. ◯

D Sensory neurons always have longer axons than motor neurons. ◯

2 Briefly explain the function of a motor neuron. [2]

3 What is meant by Hebbian learning? [3]

4 Name **one** neurotransmitter. [1]

5 Describe the lock and key system. [2]

Localisation of Function in the Brain

1 Briefly describe the function of the motor centre of the brain. [2]

2 What does the somatosensory cortex perceive? [1]

3 What is anomia? [1]

4 What is neural stimulation? [1]

An Introduction to Neuropsychology

1 What kinds of people might cognitive neuroscientists study? [2]

2 Describe how modern scanning techniques have increased our understanding of the relationship between brain and behaviour. [4]

3 a) What did Tulving inject into his participants? [1]

b) In Tulving's study, which part of the brain was activated when participants were asked to recall an episodic memory? [1]

4 During a stroke, what causes the blood vessels to become blocked? [1]

5 Following a stroke, different abilities can be affected. What determines the ability affected? [1]

An Introduction to Mental Health

You must be able to:

- Describe the main characteristics of mental health
- Explain cultural variations in beliefs about mental health problems
- Describe how mental health is linked to the increased challenges of modern living
- Describe how society is challenging the stigma related to mental health problems.

Characteristics of Mental Health

- Some behaviour can prevent people from functioning adequately, such as the inability to cope with everyday life.
- If behaviour causes distress leading to an inability to function properly, e.g. an inability to work or to engage in satisfying interpersonal relationships, this can be viewed as a mental health problem.
- Ideal mental health is said to consist of a number of factors:
  - a positive attitude towards oneself
  - personal growth and development (self actualisation)
  - feelings of independence (autonomy)
  - resisting stress
  - an accurate perception of reality
  - being able to cope with life and the changing environment (environmental mastery).
- If these factors are absent, people often suffer from mental health problems.

> **Key Point**
>
> Ideal mental health includes positive engagement with society and coping effectively with challenges.

Cultural Variations in Beliefs about Mental Health Problems

- Social norms are unwritten rules that people are expected to abide by.
  - Social norms include appropriate public behaviour, control of aggression, politeness, and control of culturally and socially offensive language.
- Social norms change between cultures and over time. What might be considered as a mental illness in one culture or point in time might not be the same in other cultures or at a different historical period. For instance, homosexuality was once thought to be a mental illness but today few countries view it as such.
- Some cultures might consider hearing voices as divine, as talking with spirits or conversing with God.
- Some governments have been known to label political opponents as mentally ill and confine them to mental institutions.
- Some behaviours might be thought of as abnormal in some cultures but not in others (e.g. public nudity).

> **Key Point**
>
> Mental health changes over time and within different cultures.

Increased Challenges of Modern Living

- Modern society has led to geographical isolation from family and emotional support networks. This can increase levels of loneliness and the feeling of not knowing who to turn to in times of crisis.
- The increase in people living alone has led to a rise in disorders such as depression and anxiety.
- It has been suggested that the rise in technology and the internet has been responsible for higher levels of mental health problems, although there is little evidence to support this view at present.
- Increased pressure at work and at school has also been blamed on the rise of disorders such as depression and anxiety.

Increased Recognition of the Nature of Mental Health Problems

- In recent years there has been a greater emphasis on the normalising of mental health issues.
- Employers are now encouraged to take into account the wellbeing of their employees and to support them through recovery.
- With the recognition of men's mental health problems and the high level of suicide amongst men, more organisations are beginning to direct their attention towards this group (e.g. The Campaign Against Living Miserably, or CALM).
- A number of charities have been formed over the past few years (e.g. Time To Change) to reduce the stigma attached to mental health problems.
- Many high-profile celebrities and politicians have spoken openly about their mental health problems in an attempt to reduce stigma.

Quick Test
1. What is meant by ideal mental health?
2. How can modern life affect mental health?
3. Name one organisation that is trying to end mental health stigma.

Key Words
self actualisation
recovery
stigma

Effects of Mental Health Problems on Individuals and Society

You must be able to:

- Describe how poor mental health can affect individuals (e.g. damage to relationships)
- Describe how poor mental health can affect wider society, such as crime rates and the economy.

Individual Effects

- Mental health issues can cause problems for people on an individual basis.
- Living with a person with significant mental health problems can put a strain on relationships.
  - For example, living with a person who has a mental illness can lead to the partner experiencing feelings of guilt and shame, and blaming themselves.
- In romantic relationships, social life and physical intimacy might change.
  - For example, the couple might not socialise as often as they used to, or engage in other social activities.
- A survey was conducted by the mental health charity Mind (2013). Sixty three per cent of people with mental health problems who told their partner about their condition said that their partners "weren't fazed" and were "really understanding".
- Mental health issues can:
  - impact day-to-day living, such as personal hygiene and generally looking after yourself
  - lead to loss of interest in socialising and engaging in activities that were once considered enjoyable
  - have a wider impact on physical wellbeing by reducing the function of the immune system and leading to a greater susceptibility to infection.

Social Effects

- Like any illness, sufferers require care and treatment.
- This leads to a greater need for social care, including social workers and mental health professionals.
- If social care is lacking or under stress through shortages in trained staff, this has an impact on the treatment that can be offered to patients.
- More funding for social care would increase patient care but put greater strain on the economy in general, as there would be less money to invest elsewhere.
- Some mental illnesses can lead to sufferers breaking the law, leading to increased crime rates.
    - Drug addiction, for example, can result in people stealing in order to raise money to sustain their addiction.
    - Alcohol addiction can increase acts of aggression in some individuals.
- However, people with mental health issues (especially those with mood disorders) are rarely violent and are much more likely to be a danger to themselves than to members of the public.
- When people are diagnosed with conditions such as depression and anxiety, work absence due to mental health issues increases. This results in a negative impact on businesses and consequently the economy in general.
- While there is less stigma today surrounding mental illness, many people might be concerned about divulging their illness to their employer.

> **Key Point**
>
> Mental health issues can impact negatively on health services and the economy.

> **Key Point**
>
> Mental health problems can affect both individuals and society in negative ways.

> **Quick Test**
>
> 1. How might mental health problems affect a person on an individual level?
> 2. How can mental health problems negatively impact society?
> 3. How might businesses be negatively affected by mental health problems?

> **Key Words**
>
> guilt
> shame
> blame

Characteristics of Clinical Depression

You must be able to:

- Explain the differences between bipolar and unipolar depression, and sadness
- Describe the characteristics of unipolar depression
- Describe how unipolar depression is diagnosed using the ICD criteria.

Clinical Depression

- Depression is one of the mood (or affective) disorders.
- Mood disorders involve a prolonged and major disturbance of mood and emotions.
- Depression and sadness differ in duration (how long the episodes last). Depression lasts for a long time while sadness does not.
- There are two main types of depression: unipolar depression and bipolar depression.
- Both types differ in terms of how the symptoms present themselves and can be distinguished from sadness by their duration and the resulting changes in mood and behaviour.

  - When clinical depression (also known as major depressive disorder) occurs on its own, it is called unipolar depression.
  - If mania occurs with depression, then it is called bipolar disorder or bipolar depression (it is also sometimes referred to as manic depression).
  - Mania can also occur on its own (manic disorder) but is still often referred to as bipolar disorder.

- Mania can be described as a sense of euphoria or elation.

  - People with mania tend to have a great deal of energy and rush around, but rarely get anything done.
  - They lack a sense of purpose in their actions and survive on very little sleep.

- People with bipolar depression alternate between mania and depressive episodes.

> **Key Point**
>
> Depression can be categorised as either bipolar or unipolar.

Classification and Diagnosis of Unipolar Depression

- A person suffering from depression experiences a general slowing down and loss of energy.
- Depression can begin at any time of life but is rarely seen in pre-adolescent children.
- The average age of onset is the late twenties, but the age of onset has decreased over the last fifty years, during which time depression's prevalence has increased (i.e. there are more people being diagnosed with depression and they are getting younger).
- Depression is more prevalent in women than in men, although this could be because men are less likely to seek help.
- The International Classification of Diseases (ICD) identifies three main behaviours that must be present for a diagnosis of unipolar depression:

  – persistent sadness/low mood
  – loss of interest/pleasure
  – fatigue/low energy.

- In addition, the ICD identifies a number of symptoms that often accompany the key behaviours. These include:

  – disturbed sleep
  – poor concentration
  – low self-confidence
  – poor or increased appetite
  – suicidal thoughts or acts
  – agitation
  – guilt/self-blame.

> **Key Point**
>
> The ICD criteria identify a number of symptoms that must be present for a diagnosis of depression to be made.

> **Quick Test**
>
> 1. What is depression?
> 2. What is mania?
> 3. What is bipolar depression?
> 4. What are the three main behaviours associated with unipolar depression?

> **Key Words**
>
> sadness
> duration
> unipolar
> bipolar
> symptoms
> mania

Theories of Depression and Interventions

You must be able to:

- Describe both biological and psychological explanations of depression
- Explain the use of biological therapies in the treatment of depression
- Explain the use of psychological therapies in the treatment of depression.

Biological Explanations of Depression – The Influence of Nature

- Biological explanations of depression indicate that depression is caused by internal factors (the influence of nature rather than nurture), including brain chemicals and genes.
- It has been found that people suffering from clinical depression have lower levels of the neurotransmitter serotonin.
- Most modern anti-depressant medication helps to alleviate symptoms by regulating the levels of serotonin in the brain.
- However, cause and effect is difficult to establish. It could be that depression results in lower levels of serotonin, rather than lower levels leading to depression.
- Depression might also be caused by a mutated gene.
- This gene has been found to reduce levels of serotonin and is much more likely to be found in people suffering from depression.
- One problem with biological explanations of depression is that they assume that the illness has an internal cause. They can overlook external influences such as home life and upbringing.

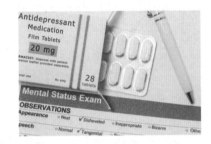

Psychological Explanations of Depression – The Influence of Nurture

- Aaron Beck (1967) believed that depression was the result of a negative outlook.
  - According to this view, depressed people acquire a schema – a blueprint by which they view the world. Depressed people develop a view of the world (schema) that is pessimistic.
- Attributional style is another explanation.
  - This view states that people with depression will often attribute negative events to sources that are internal (their fault), stable (their circumstances won't change, even with effort) and global (their depression is the result of some personal defect or personality characteristic).
- Seligman (1967) believed that depression is the result of learned helplessness.

> ### Key Point
>
> Depression can be explained as both biological and psychological.

– When people continually fail, or bad things happen to them, they begin to believe that this is the way it will always be, no matter what they try to do to change it. They learn to be helpless.

Interventions and Therapies for Depression

- Interventions and therapies for depression are often seen as **reductionist**. They reduce the causes of depression down to, for example, brain chemicals, and improve mental health by treating the symptoms.
- Other interventions are seen as **holistic** – they treat the symptoms but also tackle the causes of depression – e.g. poverty, home life and lack of meaning in life.
- The most common treatment for depression is antidepressant medication.
- There are two main types of antidepressants: tricyclic antidepressants and **SSRI** antidepressants.

  – Tricyclic antidepressants block the transporter mechanism that absorbs both serotonin and another neurotransmitter called noradrenaline.
  – SSRI (selective serotonin re-uptake inhibitors) work in a similar way to tricyclic antidepressants but mainly block serotonin only. The best-known SSRI antidepressant is Prozac (fluoxetine).

- A number of psychotherapies (or talking therapies) are used to help alleviate depression.
- Psychotherapy is a term used for a number of different treatments for mental illness that involve talking with a specially trained therapist.
- One of the most popular types of psychotherapy is cognitive behavioural therapy (**CBT**).
- CBT is based on the premise that the way we think about things impacts on our psychological wellbeing.
  – CBT emphasises the role of **maladaptive** thoughts and beliefs as the main cause of depression. When people think negatively about themselves and their lives they become depressed.
- Wiles (2013) found that people who have not responded fully to antidepressants benefit in the long-term from receiving CBT in addition to their usual treatment.

Key Point

Depression can be treated with medication, or by psychotherapy, such as CBT.

Key Words

serotonin
reductionist
holistic
SSRI
CBT
maladaptive

Quick Test

1. What is a schema?
2. What does SSRI stand for?
3. What is CBT?

Characteristics of Addiction

You must be able to:

* Define addiction
* Explain the difference between addiction and substance abuse
* Describe the criteria for diagnosing addiction.

Addiction

* **Addiction** or dependence refers to a behaviour that leads to dependency.
  - For example, an addiction to alcohol results in a dependency where individuals feel that they are unable to survive without it.
* Addictions also lead to other changes, including changes in behaviour (psychological changes) and in levels of brain chemicals.
* Addiction differs from substance misuse or **abuse** in that the substance is taken to excess but does not necessarily lead to addiction.
  - For example, a person might drink large amounts of alcohol but never feel that they couldn't live without it.

> **Key Point**
>
> Addiction includes a dependence on substances and activities.

Classification and Diagnosis of Addiction

* The International Classification of Diseases (ICD) describes addiction as "A cluster of physiological, behavioural, and cognitive phenomena in which the use of a substance or a group of substances takes on a much higher priority for a given individual than other behaviours that once had greater value".
* A diagnosis of dependence syndrome is made if three or more symptoms have appeared together for at least one month, or have occurred together repeatedly within a twelve-month period.
* These symptoms include, but are not limited to:
  - a strong desire or sense of compulsion to take the substance despite harmful consequences
  - impaired capacity to control substance-taking behaviour
  - pre-occupation with substance use and the giving up of activities once deemed important
  - a physiological **withdrawal** state when the substance is reduced or ceased.
* Many psychologists suggest that addiction need not be centred around a substance, but can also include an experience which becomes addictive.

> **Key Point**
>
> Symptoms of addiction include compulsions, loss of control and pre-occupation.

- This suggestion leads to a broadening of the definition to include behaviours such as shopping and gambling.
- Walters (1999) argues that addiction can be defined as "the persistent and repetitive enactment of a behaviour pattern". This behaviour pattern includes:
  - *progression* (increase in severity)
  - *pre-occupation* with the activity
  - *perceived* loss of control
  - *persistence* despite negative long-term consequences.
- Griffiths argues that addiction can be extended to other activities, including watching TV, playing computer games and using the internet. Such behaviours are *potentially* addictive.
- According to Griffiths, these behaviours share the same core components as addiction:

Salience	The activity becomes the most important one in the person's life.
Mood modification	The activity produces an arousing 'buzz' or 'high'.
Tolerance	Increasing amounts of activity are needed to achieve the same effects.
Withdrawal symptoms	Discontinuation or sudden reduction of the activity produces unpleasant feelings and physical effects.
Conflict	Conflict between the addict and the people around them, such as family and friends, or with other activities and interests.
Relapse	Reverting to earlier patterns of addiction soon after giving up.

Griffiths argues that mobile phone use is potentially addictive

Quick Test

1. What is meant by addiction?
2. What is meant by substance abuse?
3. What are the main symptoms of addiction?

Key Words

addiction
abuse
withdrawal

Theories of Addiction and Interventions

You must be able to:

- Describe biological theories of addiction, including heritability
- Describe Kaij's twin study of alcohol abuse
- Describe psychological theories of addiction
- Explain one biological intervention and one psychological intervention for addiction.

Biological Theories of Addiction

- Biological explanations of addiction concentrate on areas that can be viewed on the nature side of the nature–nurture debate.
- Family and twin studies indicate that genes contribute to the development of addictive behaviour.
- Heritability (the extent to which traits are inherited) estimates range from between 50% and 60% in both men and women.
- Kaij (1960) studied the rates of alcohol abuse in identical and fraternal twins in Sweden.
  - He found that the concordance rate (the presence of the same trait in both twins) for identical twins was 54% and that for fraternal twins it was only 28%.
  - Kaij concluded that there are genetic and hereditary factors involved in alcohol addiction.
  - This means that children with parents who are alcohol dependent have a much greater chance of developing dependence disorders.
- Research indicates a link between the D2 dopamine receptor (DRD2) and severe alcoholism. More specifically, two-thirds of deceased alcoholics had the A1 variant of the DRD2 gene.

Key Point

Addiction can be explained in terms of biology (e.g. genes) and psychology (e.g. peer pressure).

Psychological Theories of Addiction

- Social learning theory (SLT) proposes that learning occurs through observation and communication. It explains addiction in terms of how and why addictive behaviour is caused through social interaction.
- DeBlasio and Benda (1993) found the influence of peers to be a primary factor in the uptake of alcohol and drugs in adolescents.
- Young people who smoke are more likely to associate with other young people who smoke, indicating that they are attempting to conform to the norms of the reference group, or to peers whom they admire.

Interventions and Therapies for Addiction

Aversion Therapy

- **Aversion therapy** works by conditioning the individual into experiencing an unpleasant reaction when engaging in the unwanted activity.

  - When an unpleasant stimuli is paired with the unwanted behaviour, the behaviour becomes associated with the unpleasant feeling.
  - Drugs can be used that, when combined with an addictive substance (e.g. alcohol), result in a feeling of nausea. The individual then associates the activity (drinking alcohol) with feeling sick.
  - People can be taught to use **negative visualisation** or to focus on unpleasant thoughts when their mind wanders towards the undesirable activity.

Self-management Programs

- People often benefit from self-help groups where they can gain support from other people who are struggling with addiction.
- The most well-known of these is the 12-step program used by Alcoholics Anonymous.
  - The 12-step program of personal recovery involves a number of milestones on the journey to breaking the addiction.
  - Steps begin with an acceptance of the addiction. Steps are taken with the help of a sponsor – an experienced member who can offer individual support.
  - The 12-step program has proved useful for other addictions, including drugs and gambling.
- As mentioned on page 117, while some therapies and interventions can be thought of as reductionist (talking about one aspect of addiction and mental health), others are more holistic and can be combined with several treatments for improved outcomes.

 Key Point

Treatment for addiction can involve biological and psychological interventions.

 Key Words

heritability
fraternal
social learning theory
aversion therapy
negative visualisation

 Quick Test

1. What is meant by heritability?
2. Where were the participants from in the Kaij study?
3. Who studied the effect of peer pressure on addiction?

Where space is not provided, write your answers on a separate piece of paper.

The Structure and Function of the Brain and Nervous System

1 **a)** Name the components that make up the central nervous system. [2]

b) Explain the functions of the components you named in a). [2]

2 Describe the peripheral nervous system. [2]

3 What is meant by the fight or flight response? [4]

4 What is the function of the autonomic nervous system? [1]

5 How does the James-Lange theory differ from other explanations of human emotion? [3]

Neuron Structure and Function

1 Describe the purpose of sensory neurons. [2]

2 What did Hebb mean by the phrase "what fires together, wires together"? [2]

3 What is the result of long-term potentiation, or LTP? [2]

4 Describe the process of synaptic transmission. [6]

5 What are neurotransmitters? [1]

6 Explain the difference between excitation and inhibition. [2]

Localisation of Function in the Brain

1 Using the example of memory, explain what is meant by localisation of function. [4]

2 Describe the function of the somatosensory centre of the brain. [3]

3 Describe the function of the visual centre of the brain. [3]

4 **a)** How can neurosurgeons study the brain without having to remove parts of the cortex? [2]

b) What did Penfield discover? [2]

An Introduction to Neuropsychology

1 What do cognitive neuroscientists study? [1]

2 Describe the main difference between MRI and fMRI. [2]

3 How does a CAT scan produce an image of the brain? [1]

4 Describe the procedure of Tulving's gold memory study. [3]

5 What would happen if a person suffered a stroke in their motor cortex? [2]

6 Apart from a stroke, what else might cause damage to the brain? [1]

Where space is not provided, write your answers on a separate piece of paper.

An Introduction to Mental Health

1 What kind of behaviour can prevent people from functioning adequately? [1]

2 Some behaviour can cause distress to the person experiencing it. One example is the inability to work. Name **one** other example. [1]

3 A positive attitude towards yourself and personal growth and development are two factors that encourage ideal mental health. Name **two** other factors. [2]

4 Social norms are unwritten rules that people are expected to abide by. Name **two** social norms. [2]

5 What kinds of mental health problems might loneliness and feelings of isolation lead to? [2]

6 Name **two** organisations that exist to help people cope with mental health problems or reduce stigma. [2]

Effects of Mental Health Problems on Individuals and Society

1 Living with a person with significant mental health problems can put a strain on relationships. Give **one** example of how the problems might do this. [2]

2 Living with a mental health problem can lead to poor physical health. Explain why this might be the case. [2]

3 What can impact on the ability to treat and care for people with mental health problems? [1]

4 Some conditions, such as addiction, can lead to sufferers becoming aggressive and breaking the law. What other criminal activity might they engage in, and why? [2]

5 Why might people be reluctant to tell their employer about their mental health problem? [2]

Characteristics of Clinical Depression

1. What is the difference between sadness and depression? [1]

2. What is clinical depression also known as? [1]

3. What symptom of bipolar depression isn't present in unipolar depression? [1]

4. State **two** symptoms often seen in people who are diagnosed with unipolar depression. [2]

5. At what stage of life does unipolar depression usually develop? [1]

6. Why might depression be more common in women? [2]

Theories of Depression and Interventions

1. What do biological explanations of depression indicate? [2]

2. Which neurotransmitter is most commonly associated with depression? [1]

3. Depression has been linked to a mutated gene. How might this cause depression? [1]

4. a) What is the most common treatment for depression? [1]

   b) What two types of drugs are used to treat depression? [1]

5. Name **one** type of psychotherapy used to treat depression. [1]

Characteristics of Addiction

1 What is meant by addiction? [1]

_____

2 Give **one** example of a substance addiction. [1]

_____

3 How is abuse different from addiction? [1]

_____

4 One symptom of addiction is a strong desire or sense of compulsion to take the substance despite harmful consequences. Name **two** other symptoms. [2]

_____

_____

Theories of Addiction and Interventions

1 Describe **one** study into the heritability of addiction. [4]

2 What is the role played by peers in the development of addictions? [2]

3 Katie has been diagnosed with an addiction to alcohol. When Katie is with her friends they encourage her to drink more. Her father and older sister have also been diagnosed with an addiction to alcohol.

Which of the following statements are true? Shade **two** boxes. [2]

A One treatment that might be offered to Katie is aversion therapy. ◯

B Katie might have a genetic vulnerability to alcohol addiction. ◯

C One biological explanation for Katie's addiction could be peer pressure. ◯

4 How would a psychologist use aversion therapy to cure someone of alcohol addiction? [3]

5 **a)** What is meant by a self-management program? [2]

b) What is the most well-known self-management program? [1]

Psychological Problems

Where space is not provided, write your answers on a separate piece of paper.

An Introduction to Mental Health

1 What behaviours might suggest that a person is not coping well with everyday life? [3]

2 What factors indicate ideal mental health? [6]

3 a) In what ways might culture affect attitudes towards mental illness? [2]

b) Suggest **one** behaviour that was once thought of as abnormal but is no longer considered to be by much of society. [1]

4 How might being geographically closer to family help prevent the onset of mental health problems? [2]

5 How might stigma surrounding mental health problems make some conditions worse? [2]

Effects of Mental Health Problems on Individuals and Society

1 How can living with a partner with a mental illness put strain on the relationship? [3]

2 How might mental illness affect a person's day-to-day life? [2]

3 How does mental illness increase the possibility of poor physical health? [2]

4 An increase in mental health issues can put a strain on a number of social services. What specific services might this include? [2]

5 Why might some mental health conditions lead people to engage in criminal activities? [1]

6 How might mental illness put a strain on employers? [2]

Characteristics of Clinical Depression

1 Depression is a mood disorder. What are the main characteristics of mood disorders? [1]

2 What is bipolar depression also known as? [1]

3 Explain the main difference between unipolar and bipolar depression. [2]

4 What are the main characteristics of mania? [4]

5 a) List the **three** main behaviours that are characteristic of unipolar depression. [3]

b) List **three** additional symptoms that are also often present in depression. [3]

Theories of Depression and Interventions

1 a) What is the relationship between serotonin and depression? [1]

b) How might the relationship in **a)** be criticised? [2]

2 What did Beck believe caused depression? [2]

3 How do SSRI antidepressant drugs work? [2]

4 How does CBT reduce the symptoms of depression? [2]

Characteristics of Addiction

1 Describe the difference between addiction and substance abuse. [2]

2 Explain why addiction can be related to behaviours and habits and not just substances. [2]

3 Describe Walters' behaviour pattern of addiction. [4]

4 What is meant by salience in relation to addiction? [1]

5 What is meant by relapse? [1]

6 You are concerned that your friend, Ella, might be addicted to playing computer games. Briefly describe the symptoms she is displaying that gave rise to your concerns. [3]

Theories of Addiction and Interventions

1 What do Kaij's results tell us about the nature of alcohol abuse? [2]

2 What is the link between the D2 dopamine receptor and addiction? [2]

3 Why are young people who smoke more likely to have friends who also smoke? [2]

4 a) What is aversion therapy? [2]

b) How do self-management programs differ from aversion therapy? [3]

Mixed Questions

Where space is not provided, write your answers on a separate piece of paper.

Cognition and Behaviour

1 State a possible alternative hypothesis for an experiment that aims to study the effect of background noise levels on stress. [4]

2 Explain the role of rehearsal in memory, according to the multi-store model. [2]

3 Besides the eye, name **one** other body area involved in the perception of vision and explain what it does. [2]

4 Briefly explain the interview and survey methods of research. [4]

5 Explain **one** brain development change that occurs before birth and **one** that occurs after birth. [4]

6 Discuss the capacity and duration of the memory stores known as STM and LTM. [4]

7 Complete the following two sentences. [2]

a) A _____ chart is one of the most important ways of displaying data in

psychology. It can be used to show the mean scores of different conditions in an experiment.

b) Correlation is used to analyse primary data gathered from a survey, or secondary data. It

shows the direction and _____ of a relationship between two co-variables.

8 Which theory of perception thinks that illusions are important examples of how complex and difficult perception truly is. Why? [3]

9 Briefly explain **one** of the binocular cues to depth. [3]

_____

_____

_____

10 What **three** terms are used to mean putting information into a memory store, keeping it there, and then taking it out when needed? [3]

_____

_____

_____

11 Complete the sentences by choosing the best words from the selection below. You do not have to use all the words. [4]

areas	set	language	people	motivation	languages

Perception varies between individuals and is affected by a number of factors including

_____, emotion and expectations. Together, these factors are called the

perceptual _____. Another factor that can play a role is culture – the beliefs

and behaviour of a particular group of _____, usually associated with specific

_____.

12 What is this statement describing? A stimulus that causes a person to see something different from what is actually there, or where there are two or more possible interpretations of the same image. [1]

_____

13 Explain how the encoding and storage of human memories is different to recording and saving a video or computer file. [2]

_____

_____

_____

14 Tick (✓) or cross (✗) the statements about factors affecting memory to indicate whether they are true or false. [4]

Statements about factors affecting memory	True (✓) or false (✗)?
Information is better remembered if it is unusual and distinctive.	
Participants in the War of the Ghosts study forgot things because the cultural concepts in the story were unfamiliar.	
It's easier to remember things in a different location from where we first learned them.	
Loftus found that false memories could be generated within an experiment.	

15 In a random sample, every member of the target population must have the same chance of being selected. Explain why this is not the case if a sample is chosen by asking passers-by on a school corridor during the school day. [3]

16 Explain **two** things that could happen to a child's schemas when they see a type of vehicle that they have never seen before. [4]

17 Complete the following **two** sentences. [2]

a) Experimental design means the way that participants are _____ to the conditions of a study.

b) In a repeated measures design, _____ must be used to avoid order effects biasing the results.

18 To what extent could the **two** sides of the nature versus nurture debate *both* be true? Explain your answer. [3]

19 Briefly explain **two** things that Willingham has said about how learning works best. [2]

Social Context and Behaviour

1 Name **two** methods used to treat depression. [2]

2 You are talking with a person you have just met and notice that they begin to mirror your actions. What are they doing and why are they doing it? [2]

3 What is the function of a relay neuron? [1]

4 What **four** factors affect conformity? [4]

5 Someone suffering with alcohol addiction could get help from a self-management program like the 12-step program. What other treatment is available? [1]

6 Why might a person break eye contact while engaged in a conversation? [1]

7 Which response is triggered from the autonomic nervous system? [1]

8 Why might you feel uncomfortable when someone stands very close to you? [2]

9 What **four** factors affect obedience to authority? [4]

10 How would you know if a person was addicted to alcohol? [3]

....

....

....

11 The brain and spinal cord are part of which division of the nervous system? [1]

....

12 What **four** factors affect bystander intervention? [4]

13 The sympathetic and parasympathetic branches are part of which division of the nervous system? [1]

....

14 Describe the posture of a person who is being defensive. [3]

....

....

....

15 How would you know if a person was suffering from depression rather than just sad? [1]

....

16 Name the scanning technique that produces a moving image. [1]

....

Answers

Pages 6–7
1. Short-term memory (STM)
2. Semantic

Pages 8–9
1. Encoding
2. Retrieval

Pages 10–11
1. Attention
2. Semantic encoding

Pages 12–13
1. STM has a limited capacity.
2. **Possible strengths**: provides basic outline which forms the basis of many later models; supported by serial position curve; supported by evidence of separate STM/LTM, e.g. brain damage patients. **Possible weaknesses**: over-simplistic; doesn't account for different types of STM or LTM; view of encoding based on rehearsal is not accurate.
3. Those in the middle.

Pages 14–15
1. The story was from a culture with which they were not familiar.
2. **Any two from:** state, timing, interference, context

Structures of Memory
1. C
2. Limited capacity, limited duration
3. A Procedural B Episodic C Semantic

Processes in Memory
1. An active process
2. C
3. A

The Multi-Store Model of Memory 1 and 2
1. a) The serial position curve
   b) Murdock's serial position curve supports the model, **[1]** the primacy effect is explained by items being rehearsed into LTM, **[1]** the recency effect is explained by a few items remaining within a limited capacity STM. **[1]**
2. Encoding, semantic, words
3. No – often rehearsal alone is not enough.

Factors Affecting Memory
1. Interference, distinctive, easier
2. Different mood, drugs such as caffeine, consumption of alcohol. Also accept a different physical location.
3. B

Pages 18–19
1. Sensation
2. True
3. Colour constancy

Pages 20–21
1. Occlusion
2. Texture gradient
3. Convergence

Pages 22–23
1. The Kanizsa triangle
2. Ambiguity
3. They misinterpret the depth cue of linear perspective.

Pages 24–25
1. The direct/bottom-up theory of perception
2. The constructivist/top-down theory of perception

Pages 26–27
1. It caused participants to perceive food as looking brighter/more vivid.
2. A perceptual set

Structures of Memory
1. Up to approximately 30 seconds
2. A temporary store
3. Unlimited/it does not get full
4. Understanding the meaning (because it uses semantic encoding).
5. **Any two from**: the first letter, a question, an image, or an aspect of the learning context.
6. **A** Hippocampus, LTM **B** Frontal lobe, STM

Processes in Memory
1. B
2. D
3. A–iii, B–i, C–ii
4. Repeating, understand, link, spaced
5. Information is only taken into memory if a person pays attention to it. **[1]** This typically happens when they find things interesting or emotional in some way/if they don't pay attention, things will not enter STM and therefore will not be processed and encoded to LTM. **[1]**
6. The three sections of the exam require recognition, cued recall and free recall respectively. **[3]** The best answers will compare two or more types, noting, for example, that cued recall is easier than free recall. **[1]**
7. It is important for memory, as more exposure increases the chance of encoding. **[1]** However, simply repeating things does not always lead to encoding, particularly if information is hard to understand. **[1]** More important processes are active, such as linking new information to what is already known/ retrieving information from memory in a way that is spaced out over time helps to consolidate it. **[1]** Answers could also refer to the multi-store model of memory, which makes the over-simplistic claims that rehearsal is the only means of encoding items to LTM. **[1]**

The Multi-Store Model of Memory 1 and 2

1. MULTI-STORE MODEL

2. Atkinson & Shiffrin; sensory memory, short-term memory and long-term memory; attention; rehearsal; rehearsal
3. Reading out a list of random words to a group of participants. **[1]** Each participant would have to write down all of the words that they could remember. **[1]** The researcher would count how many times each word was recalled, with the expectation that words at the beginning and end of the list would be recalled more frequently on average. **[1]**
4. The student is able to access the question from the auditory store in sensory memory. **[1]** Now that they are paying attention, they can transfer this question to their short-term memory, where it can be held for a few seconds. **[1]** The student will also need to recall meaningful/factual information from their long-term memory in order to answer the question. **[1]**
5. Sensory memory is a very brief store. **[1]** The visual store was found by Sperling (1960) to have a large capacity but a duration of only 0.5 seconds. **[1]** The acoustic store is thought to last around 2 seconds. **[1]**
6. Curve, first, list, STM
7. A–iii, B–i, C–ii, D–iv

Factors Affecting Memory
1. a) Bartlett
   b) Additions, subtractions, transformations (to familiar), preservation of detached detail
2. A
3. It came from a culture that was unfamiliar to the participants. **[1]** Therefore they lacked schema knowledge to connect it to. **[1]**
4. Culture, timing, interference, context

Perception and Sensation
1. A neuron
2. Due to light constancy. **[1]** When people perceive objects, the brain makes allowances for lighting and therefore objects still appear the same to us. **[1]**
3. Visual cortex (or sensory cortex/occipital lobe of the cerebral cortex)

Visual Cues and Depth Perception
1. Depth perception is essential for survival. **[1] Accept two from the following:** environmental risks to species if they couldn't tell how far away a threat was, or how far

they would fall if they jumped off something; predator species need to perceive how close a prey animal is before attacking; modern human examples such as sport and driving.
2. Cues should be named [**1 for each**] and given a brief but recognisable explanation. [**1 for each**] Answers should focus on monocular cues such as occlusion (one object in front of another shows that it is closer, e.g. plants in front of the water); height in plane (further objects appear higher up, e.g. trees in background); linear perspective. Others are acceptable if accurate and relevant.
3. No (they look blurry and less detailed).

Illusions
1. No. [**1**] There are illusions and distortions that can occur. [**1**]
2. The Kanizsa triangle
3. True, false, false, false

Theories of Perception
1. James Gibson
2. Direct, inferences, affordances
3. a) The constructivist theory.
   b) An inference involves working something out from incomplete information. [**1**] Accept any appropriate example, e.g. seeing half of a bus that is partially obscured by another object such as a building, and working out that it must be a whole bus. [**1**]

Factors Affecting Perception
1. The perceptual set
2. Illusions, hallucinations (distortions to perception also acceptable)
3. Answers should focus on expectations and emotions. If a person is hungry or in a different mood, they can see something differently. [**1**] Seeing the scene with different expectations could also affect how they perceive it. [**1**] Culture and motivation do not tend to change as quickly, but could do so over long time periods. [**1**] Answer should back up one point with Bruner and Minturn/Gilchrist and Nesberg's research. [**1**]

Pages 34–41 **Revise Questions**

Pages 34–35
1. The axon
2. a) brain stem
   b) Cerebral cortex
   c) Cerebellum
3. More complex

Pages 36–37
1. Any appropriate answer, e.g. personality, intelligence, crime, mental health
2. Parenting, culture
3. It is not expressed. (Accept epigenetics.)

Pages 38–39
1. Assimilation, accommodation
2. Centration
3. Pre-operational

Pages 40–41
1. Education/schooling
2. McGarrigle and Donaldson's 'naughty teddy' study (1974)

Pages 42–43
1. No
2. Growth mindset

Pages 44–47 **Review Questions**

Perception and Sensation
1. Receptor cells
2.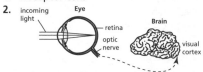
3. Answers must explain that sensation is the process of receiving information from the outside world to the senses, e.g. vision, hearing, [**1**] while perception involves interpreting that information, automatically filtering it and making use of memories and assumptions. [**1**]
4. **Any two from:** colour constancy, light constancy, size constancy, shape constancy.
5. No. [**1**] The perceptual system is very complex. The human brain automatically adjusts for things like lighting conditions and objects moving around – it is possible but difficult to program a computer to do this. [**1**] Also, human sensation relies on very complex networks of receptor cells that help us to build up an image of the world/could mention real-world examples, e.g. self-driving cars, facial recognition software. [**1**]

Visual Cues and Depth Perception
1. Occlusion is a monocular depth cue, [**1**] whereby one object partially covering another allows people to perceive that it must be closer. [**1**]
2. Answers (top to bottom): linear perspective, texture gradient, retinal disparity, height in plane
3. a) Using binocular cues to depth gives more precise depth perception, and for predators this is very important to survival (more important than peripheral vision from side-facing eyes).
   b) It would be less likely to hunt successfully, e.g. misjudging a pounce on the animal or running after it when it was too far away, etc.
4. Monocular, relative, occlusion
5. a) Vanishing point
   b) It makes paintings look more realistic, so that a two-dimensional picture can give a sense of depth and distance.

Illusions
1. Perception
2. It is a 2D shape that tends to be interpreted as a cube [**1**] but there are two possible ways that it could be facing, making it possible for a person to mentally 'flip' the way they perceive the shape. [**1**]
3. Rubin's vase
4. A–ii, B–iii, C–i
5. Depth cues guide us to distance but can be misinterpreted/misleading. [**1**] Various supporting points could be made, e.g. explanation of example(s) of illusions where depth cues are an issue, e.g. Ponzo illusion, Müller-Lyer/

examples from art – artists use depth cues to indicate depth and distance in paintings, such as by drawing clouds at different heights above the horizon (height in plane) and in different levels of detail (texture gradient). [**1 per explained point**]

Theories of Perception
1. James Gibson – direct theory; Richard Gregory – constructivist theory
2. The direct theory (bottom-up processing). [**1**] Animals have simpler thought processes than humans, so if they perceive the world in similar ways to us, then perception can't be based to a large extent on cognitions such as memories, inferences, etc. [**1**]
3. B
4. D
5. Visual cliff, hollow face
6. It is a cue in the environment that allows a person or animal to perceive their surroundings. [**1**] The existence of affordances supports the direct (bottom-up) theory of perception, [**1**] because it suggests that the environment provides enough information for organisms to perceive it without the need for using inferences or schema knowledge (or could give examples of affordances such as depth cues). [**1**]

Factors Affecting Perception
1. Individual differences
2. D
3. B
4. Demonstrates that depth cues can be interpreted in different ways by different cultures. [**1**] This shows one aspect of perceptual set – that culture influences how people perceive the world, due to experiences and expectations. [**1**] However, any conclusions from images like this are limited in that they are only based on pictures. [**1**] They don't show that people from different cultures perceive real-world environments differently. [**1**]
5. Gilchrist and Nesberg (1952) study [**1**] where people were asked to judge the brightness of food colours, such as the red of a tomato, and found it more vivid when they were hungry. [**1**] Bruner and Minturn (1955), [**1**] where people were shown an ambiguous figure that could either be perceived as a letter 'B' or the number '13'. The context (other numbers or other letters) affected their expectations. [**1**] Also accept relevant studies such as the Hudson/Deregowski research on culture.

Pages 48–49 **Practice Questions**

Brain Development
1. **Any two from:** axon, cell body, nucleus, axon terminal, etc.
2. True
3. The ability of the brain to respond to circumstances and modify its neural structure, [**1**] even after childhood/adolescent brain development processes are complete. [**1**]

4. The brain stem is a region of the brain, responsible for autonomic functions, whereas a stem cell is an individual cell that develops early in pregnancy and can later turn into a neuron. (**1 mark for each correct definition, does not need to be fully explained.**)

Nature and Nurture
1. Nature
2. A twin study
3. From top to bottom: true, false, true, true
4. Nurture side puts more emphasis on parenting/upbringing and life experiences rather than genetics when explaining personality, intelligence, mental health, etc. **[1]** Answer should include the role of parents/environment/social background (rather than genetics), e.g. in educational success. **[1]** Study of epigenetics suggests that life experiences can impact on gene expression, so the two are interlinked. **[1]** Could also mention the importance of an enriched rather than deprived environment, or the role of culture in behaviour. **[1]**

Piaget's Theories 1 and 2
1. Schemas
2. Egocentrism/egocentric
3. The child starts to make logical operations, **[1]** is less egocentric **[1]** and no longer shows centration/can conserve volume in the 'tall glass' task. **[1]**
4. Assimilation. **[1]** The boy does not yet have a schema for antelope, so he mentally links it to the closest schema that he has – horse. **[1]**

Learning
1. Verbalisers and visualisers
2. Influencing, styles, visual, coding
3. **Any one from**: praise, success and failure, feedback and messages from teachers and parents
4. Yes **[1]** because learning facts provides essential schema knowledge to which new learning can be connected. **[1]**

Pages 50–59 **Revise Questions**

Pages 50–51
1. Random sampling
2. Bias

Pages 52–53
1. The dependent variable, or DV
2. **Any suitable answer, such as:** If caffeine harms people's ability to fall asleep, then participants in the 500 mg caffeine condition will take longer to fall asleep than those in the 0 mg of caffeine condition.

Pages 54–55
1. Independent groups (or matched pairs)
2. Background noise/distractions

Pages 56–57
1. Order effects, e.g. they may improve due to practice.
2. It breaches the ethical principle of confidentiality.
3. Counterbalancing

Pages 58–59
1. Quantitative data
2. The case study method

Pages 60–61
1. A bar chart
2. A strongly positive correlation

Pages 62–65 **Review Questions**

Brain Development
1. Autonomic functions. **Any one example from**: breathing, heartbeat

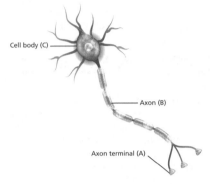

Cell body (C)

Axon (B)

Axon terminal (A)

3. Because without neurons, the brain has not yet developed the structures that are required for sensory processing (thalamus and visual cortex), thinking, memory (cerebral cortex), etc.
4. The thalamus
5. D
6. B
7. Brain, axons, newborn, pruning
8. The child's brain continues to develop through to adolescence and beyond, **[1]** and this occurs mainly through the strengthening of connections and pruning of unnecessary ones. **[1]** It is important to have a stimulating environment that challenges the child and allows for creative play. **[1]** A deprived environment can set back brain development and take years to recover from, or even have permanent effects. **[1]**

Nature and Nurture
1. D
2. B
3. Nature, DNA, expression
4. The nature side
5. Genes do not have a direct effect on development but instead are modified by life experience, a process known as epigenetics. **[1]** If a certain environmental condition is present then the gene will be expressed; if not, then it won't be. **[1]**
6. A–i, B–iii, C–ii
7. Consider whether the girls are identical twins. If they are not, then Maryam may have a higher level of intelligence than her sister, helping to explain her higher grades according to the nature side of the nature versus nurture debate. **[2]** Both seem to have a similar background – they have the same parents, are the same age, and were both encouraged to study hard. **[1]** If the girls are identical twins, then their different personality and achievement can't be explained via genes. **[1]** It could be that Maryam's friends have

encouraged her to work hard and do the same university course (experiences/nurture) or that she was lucky enough to get better teachers. **[1]** Good answers could also discuss possible interactions between genes and the environment, e.g. perhaps the school was more encouraging to extroverted students. **[1]**

Piaget's Theories 1 and 2
1. Assimilation
2. The formal operational stage
3. A–iv, B–i, C–ii, D–iii
4. A
5. C
6. Must describe a suitable study, e.g. the policeman doll study or the naughty teddy study. **[1]** Answer should include researcher name(s) and year. **[1]** Should describe procedure as well as findings/results, e.g. policeman doll: 90 per cent of four year olds succeeded; naughty teddy: majority of children under the age of six were correct. **[2]**
7. Stella is in the pre-operational stage of development. **[1]** In this stage, children can represent one object with another, such as making a brick represent a car. **[1]** However, children are also very egocentric at this stage, so Stella doesn't realise that taking the blue brick away from Fiona would upset her. **[1]**

Learning
1. Learning styles
2. a) In a growth mindset, abilities are seen as open to improvement and mistakes are viewed as useful feedback, **[2]** whereas for someone with a fixed mindset, abilities are not seen as open to change/improvement with effort/practice, and mistakes are viewed as a threat (to self-efficacy). **[2]**
   b) Blackwell et al.'s (2007) study of maths learning in school, or any other appropriate answer
3. **Any two answers from**: no scientific evidence that learning style makes a difference to learning; it makes no sense to try to learn items in a way that doesn't fit the material; it is best to combine the senses where possible, e.g. via dual coding
4. Self-efficacy
5. Growth mindset, **[1]** because Mehul thinks that a skill is not fixed but can be improved. **[1]**
6. Andy appears to have a fixed mindset regarding his English ability. **[1]** He thinks he is a visual learner, but as learning styles theory lacks supporting scientific evidence, he would be best to try other strategies. **[1]** His teacher has told him that he should combine his chart with verbal information, a strategy known as dual coding (or could mention that Andy may be a visualiser – someone who prefers to learn with visual information). **[1]**

Pages 66–69 **Practice Questions**

Sampling
1. Opportunity sampling
2. Systematic sampling
3. Generalising, representative, large

4. The target population
5. Any appropriate answers, e.g.: As with any opportunity sample, the people who are available have particular characteristics. [1] Friends of the researcher might all be of similar ages, or have similar personalities and interests. If they are also students, they might be above average on intelligence and other cognitive abilities. [1]

Variables and Hypotheses
1. Hypothesis (also accept alternative hypothesis/experimental hypothesis/ null hypothesis)
2. Independent, dependent [**half a mark for each correct answer**]
3. Control means manipulating one variable (the IV) while keeping extraneous variables from impacting on the results. [1] This means ensuring that everything other than the IV is exactly equal across all conditions. [1] Could give an example, such as giving all participants the same time/instructions, or discuss the role of lab/field experiments in terms of controlling the research environment. [1]
4. A–ii, B–iii, C–i
5. Alternative hypothesis

Design of Experiments 1 and 2
1. A repeated measures design
2. From top to bottom: true, false, true, false
3. A field experiment
4. Order, counterbalancing, conditions

Non-experimental Methods
1. Interviews and surveys
2. Naturalistic, categories, reliability
3. Qualitative data (accept primary)
4. a) Numerical data
   b) Verbal or other non-numerical data
   c) Data directly obtained by researcher, e.g. interviewing a participant
   d) Indirectly obtained data that was originally used for another purpose
5. Open [1] and closed questions [1]. The open question should allow the participant to answer in any way they want; [1] the closed question should allow only limited answer options, e.g. yes/no. [1]

Correlation and Data Handling
1. Adding up all the numbers and dividing by how many numbers there are.
2. The mean of each condition (such as scores on a test) could be displayed on a separate bar along the x-axis, [1] with the DV shown on the y-axis. [1]
3. Stronger, spread, direction, upward
4. Graph A shows a negative correlation, Graph B a positive correlation (both strong), Graph C zero/no correlation at all (or very weak)

Pages 70–75 Revise Questions

Pages 70-71
1. Conformity is a type of social influence involving a change in belief or behaviour in order to fit in with a group.
2. Asch
3. 75%

Pages 72–73
1. Responding as instructed to a direct order
2. Milgram
3. Adorno

Pages 74–75
1. The way a person acts when they witness an emergency
2. Piliavin (*et al.*)
3. When the presence of a crowd or group leads to the loss of sense of individual identity
4. **Any one from**: use CCTV cameras; restrict access to alcohol; increase policing

Pages 76–81 Review Questions

Sampling
1. A biased sample is one which is not representative of the target population [1] because certain characteristics are more or less likely to occur, such as a higher or lower age range, a distribution of socio-economic or ethnic background that differs from the target population, etc. [1]
2. Every member of the target population must have the same chance of being selected.
3. Representative, random numbers
4. Involves selecting a sample that has the same proportions as the target population; e.g. an equal mix of sexes, or people of different religious backgrounds in the same ratio as the target population. [2] **Strength**: ensures that selected characteristics are representative of the target population. [1] **Weakness**: only ensures representativeness of some characteristics; others are ignored. [1]
5. A
6. B
7. a) sampling, b) the sample, c) generalising, d) bias

Variables and Hypotheses
1. Conditions
2. The dependent variable. [1] Any appropriate example, e.g. the score on a test in a memory experiment. [1]
3. Manipulates, cause-and-effect, IV, DV
4. **Any two from:** the normal distribution is symmetrical; the mean, mode and median are all equal; scores near the mean are very common, and get rarer as they get more extreme
5. Same day revision/short spacing; next day revision/medium spacing; next week revision/long spacing
6. A
7. C
8. This is not a fair test/extraneous variables are not well controlled. [1] Using the school cafeteria (field experiment) will lead to background noise, which might distract students. It could be especially noisy for students who take part at lunch time, leading to bias in the results. [1] Students might do better or worse in the experiment depending on how interested they are in sports stars or planets. These variables should have been kept constant for all participants.

[1] It is a bad idea to test some people in the morning and some at lunchtime, as they may vary on important EVs such as tiredness/hunger. [1]

Design of Experiments 1 and 2
1. (Research) ethics/ethical standards
2. A
3. D
4. Order effects – when a participant does condition 2, everyone has already seen the illusion in condition 1. [1] Could have been avoided by counterbalancing conditions or using an independent groups design. [1]
5. Field experiment: could go to a real lecture and give half of the participants caffeine and none as the control condition (or placebo, e.g. decaffeinated drink). [1] Lab experiment: would have to be conducted in controlled conditions, perhaps by testing students viewing a video of a lecture one at a time in a lab. [1] An appropriate design should be chosen [1] and justified [1] e.g. independent groups design should be used, because watching the same lecture twice would lead to significant order effects.
6. **Repeated measures**: every participant does every condition; order effects. **Independent groups**: participants complete only one condition; participant variables.
7. Random allocation helps to ensure that participant variables are randomly divided among the conditions, [1] and avoids systematic bias. [1]
8. A control condition

Non-experimental Methods
1. Questions with a limited selection of possible answers, such as in a multiple choice question. [1] **Research method:** surveys or interviews [1]
2. a) **Any one from**: experiment, observation, survey, interview
   b) Case study (accept correlation)
3. **Strength**: gathers real-life behaviour as it happens. **Weakness: any one from**: Can risk invasion of privacy; if participants are informed about the observation, this can affect their behaviour
4. **From top to bottom**: false, true, false, false
5. A
6. C
7. The case study method would be used, but this could involve a number of other techniques. [1] Brain scans would be necessary in this case, and probably also personality tests, ability/IQ tests, etc. [1] It would be useful to gain secondary data in the form of scores on tests or descriptions of the patient's behaviour prior to the injury, e.g. any tests that were done while at school. [1]
8. Data from a single observer can be unreliable. [1] Therefore, studies tend to train observers, and get two or more people to observe the same behaviour. This increases the reliability of results. [1] Inter-observer reliability could also be mentioned.

Correlation and Data Handling

1. The difference between the lowest and highest score. [1] Shows how spread out the data are overall, but is not a very sensitive/powerful statistic. [1]
2. C
3. B
4. Visually, a histogram does not have gaps between the bars. [1] The graphs are used for different purposes: a bar chart usually represents the conditions of an experiment; a histogram shows survey responses from groups that vary along a specific variable, e.g. different age groups. [1]
5. A weak correlation means that the two co-variables are not closely linked; this can be either in a positive or a negative direction. [1] A negative correlation means that as one variable increases, the other decreases; this relationship can be either weak or strong. [1]
6. The survey provides primary data while the school grades are secondary data (also acceptable: one of them could be referred to as quantitative data). [2] The two variables would be analysed using a correlation study. Each variable would be shown along one axis of a scatter graph. This would display a pattern, allowing interpretation of the relationship between reading level and school grades. [2] A possible (correlational) hypothesis: the number of books read is positively correlated with/has a strong relationship with school grades. Accept other appropriate answers. [1]
7.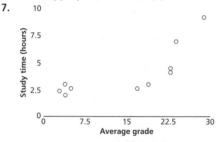

    Accept other appropriate graphs.
8. Mean, dividing, middle, two, common

Pages 82–83 **Practice Questions**

Conformity

1. Anonymity reduces the desire to conform [1] because others are unaware of this non-conformity. [1]
2. Susan is well known for her skill in maths so you're surprised that she gave an incorrect answer. [1] When the second student is asked and also gives the incorrect answer you assume that you are wrong. [1] Rather than look stupid or incompetent you conform to the group norm, [1] even though you know the answer to be incorrect. [1]
3. a) Participants were first asked to look at a 'target' line drawn on a card. [1] They then had to compare it to three lines drawn on another card and say which one was the same length as the target line. [1] Two of the lines on the comparison card were obviously wrong and one was obviously right. [1] Only one of the participants

was genuine – the others were confederates of the experimenter who had been told to give the wrong answer. [1] The genuine participant was usually one of the last to give their judgement [1] so that they could hear the answers given by the confederates. [1]

   b) Researchers have to abide by ethical guidelines [1] that include a duty of care to their participants. Participants shouldn't be put under undue stress. [1]
   c) In a laboratory setting, variables can be controlled.
   d) Participants often conformed to the group's answers [1] even though they were obviously wrong. [1]

Obedience

1. In condition A, the level of obedience was higher because the actor wore a uniform. [1] Wearing a uniform suggests legitimate authority. [1]
2. The university is seen as having a higher status than the venue in town [1] and therefore the experiment is seen as more legitimate and important. [1]
3. Proximity influences levels of obedience – when participants could see their victims, levels of obedience fell.
4. When people are in an agentic state they allow other people to direct their actions. [1] Their actions are attributed to the person giving the instruction and not the responsibility of the person carrying out the instruction. [1]
5. Authoritarian personality
6. They discovered a correlation between obedience and authoritarian personality type.

Prosocial and antisocial behaviour

1. How a person acts when they witness an emergency
2. **Any one from:** similarity to victim (e.g. race, gender), number of people present and low cost of helping
3. Piliavin *et al.* (1969) investigated bystander behaviour on the New York subway. Students acted out a scene where one of them (the 'victim') collapsed on a subway train. [1] The victim was sometimes black and sometimes white, acted drunk, or used a cane, or appeared to be ill. [1] In some versions, one of the team would go and help the victim. [1] Two other members of the team observed the reactions of the other passengers on the train. [1]
4. Zimbardo (1963) replicated Milgram's electric shock study [1] but participants either wore a name badge or had their faces concealed with a hood. [1] Those wearing the hoods gave more shocks than those with name badges, [1] supporting the idea of deindividuation. [1]
5. It means that deindividuation is seen across cultures [1] so it isn't influenced by social or cultural differences. [1]

Pages 84–91 **Revise Questions**

Pages 84–85

1. Piaget's theory (language determines thought) and the Sapir-Whorf

hypothesis (thinking is dependent on language)
2. When a child uses and repeats words before understanding the concepts behind them
3. Goldstein

Pages 86–87

1. Survival
2. Von Frisch
3. Waggle dance

Pages 88–89

1. A type of communication that doesn't rely on spoken or written words
2. Regulating the flow of conversation, signalling attraction and expressing emotion
3. A posture that is revealing and leaves sensitive areas vulnerable
4. A posture that is defensive and protecting

Pages 90–91

1. That it is evolutionary
2. Matsumoto studied sighted and blind judo athletes and found that both groups produced the same facial expressions in certain emotional situations.
3. Yuki *et al.*

Pages 92–93 **Review Questions**

Conformity

1. People are likely to give the obviously wrong answer to a question if the majority also give the same wrong answer, [1] but a number of factors can affect levels of conformity. [1]
2. Lack of unanimity [1] reduces the chances of the participant succumbing to normative conformity (seeking the approval of the group). [1]
3. The more confederates who made the incorrect judgements, [1] the more likely the participant was to conform. [1]
4. **Any one from:** anonymity, task difficulty
5. He made participants believe that all the people in the experiment were volunteers [1] when, in fact, they were confederates of the experimenter and were told to give an incorrect answer. [1]
6. **Any one strength from:** The study was highly controlled and was therefore able to establish a very clear pattern of conformity by most of the participants on one or more of the trials; results have been replicated several times so the study is reliable. [1]
   Any one weakness from: The study can be criticised on ethical grounds because the participants often displayed stress reactions as they struggled to decide what answer they were going to give; the study was carried out in a laboratory setting in order to control variables, so we cannot be sure that the behaviour displayed is typical of that seen in real life. [1]

Obedience

1. Conformity involves changing your behaviour in order to be accepted by the majority, [1] whereas obedience refers to responding as directed to an order being given by an authority figure. [1]

2. To see how far people would go in obeying an instruction from an authority figure, [1] even if it involved harming another person. [1]
3. **Any two from**: proximity; symbols of authority (white coat); agency; culture; status of situation
4. Influence from authoritarian parents
5. **Any one from**: easily manipulated; can be explained in terms of educational level
6. Because the study is correlational – it could be that a tendency towards obedience caused people to be more authoritarian. We cannot establish cause and effect. [1]

Prosocial and Antisocial Behaviour
1. a) This behaviour can be explained using the theory of diffusion of responsibility. [1] The more people who witness an emergency, the less responsible for helping they feel. [1]
   b) If Fatima had been on her own when she saw the man fall, she would have felt more responsible [1] and would have been more likely to help. [1]
2. People who appeared ill [1] or less able to help themselves, such as a person using a walking stick. [1]
3. Anonymity increases feelings of deindividuation [1] and leads to people acting more confidently. [1]
4. a) When people find themselves in crowds they begin to lose their sense of individuality (this is called deindividuation). [1] When we are a member of a crowd we also feel more anonymous [1] and are more likely to do things that go against our personal beliefs, [1] such as becoming involved in acts of aggression. [1]
   b) **One from**: install CCTV cameras; remove or restrict access to alcohol
   c) **Any one from**: using CCTV cameras at football matches decreases the feeling of anonymity; individuals know they might get caught on camera and punished for their actions.

The Possible Relationship Between Language and Thought
1. a) Piaget thought that development takes place in a number of stages and that language development is the result of cognitive (or thought) development. [1] According to Piaget, a child must first be able to use ideas and concepts before being able to use language. [1] However, a child might use and repeat words before understanding the concepts behind these words. Piaget called this egocentric speech. [1]
   b) To convey ideas and information
2. The weak version of the Sapir-Whorf hypothesis suggests that language influences thought.

Differences Between Human and Animal Communication
1. Animals only communicate to pass messages about survival, reproduction,

territory and obtaining food (such as a rabbit thumping to warn of predators for survival). [1] Humans communicate information about many aspects of their lives, such as how they are feeling, by smiling when they are happy or frowning when they are uncertain. [1]
2. The waggle dance of the honeybee
3. **Any two from**: song in birds; leaving marking on trees (e.g. wild boar); scenting territory using urine (e.g. dogs)
4. Distance is based on the duration of the dance.
5. Symbols are sounds, gestures, material objects or written words [1] that have a specific meaning to a group of people. [1]
6. The discussion of possible future outcomes [1] based on present situations and expected outcomes. [1]

Non-verbal Communication
1. Verbal: **any two from**: Rebecca passing a note; Abi laughing out loud; teacher telling off
   Non-verbal: **any two from**: Rebecca smiling; Abi waving; Abi frowning
2. Looking away can signal to the speaker that the listener isn't interested.
3. Because the listener wishes to speak
4. Hands held up to the chin [1] or the head is lowered to protect the throat; [1] arms and legs are crossed. [1]
5. a) An imaginary area that people view as their own territory.
   b) People react in a number of ways, including feeling uncomfortable and adjusting their own position in order to regain territory.

Explanations of Non-verbal Behaviour
1. Non-verbal communication is an evolutionary mechanism – it is evolved and adaptive. [1] All mammals (both human and non-human) show emotions through facial expression. [1] This behaviour is universal and, therefore, evolutionary. [1] Types of non-verbal behaviour persist in humans because they have been acquired for their value throughout evolutionary history. [1]
2. Lack of ecological validity because Yuki used computer-generated faces to test participants and not real faces. [1] Demand characteristics – participants were aware that they were taking part in a study so may not have given true responses. [1] Findings cannot be generalised because the study only looked at one element of emotion (happy/sad) and not any other emotions. [1] Yuki used students in the study – other groups might have reacted differently. [1]
3. If something is innate then we are born with it. [1] If something is learned we are not born with it but learn it through our experiences and observations. [1]

Pages 96–97
1. Central nervous system and peripheral nervous system
2. Central nervous system

3. Autonomic nervous system
4. William James and Carl Lange

Pages 98–99
1. Sensory, motor, relay
2. 'What fires together, wires together'
3. A specialised gap between neurons through which the electrical impulse from the neuron is transmitted chemically.

Pages 100–101
1. It is the view that particular parts of the brain are responsible for specific functions.
2. Hearing
3. Balance and coordination

Pages 102–103
1. It is concerned with the biological basis of thought processes.
2. fMRI, CAT, PET
3. Insufficient oxygen going to the brain

The Possible Relationship Between Language and Thought
1. Piaget's theory states that language determines thought [1] and the Sapir-Whorf hypothesis suggests that thinking is dependent on language. [1]
2. Some children have severe learning difficulties but normal language development, [1] suggesting that language development isn't dependent on cognitive development. [1] Some studies have found that language development can accelerate cognitive development. [1]
3. a) Strong and weak version
   b) The strong version says that language determines thought and the weak version says that language influences thought.

Differences Between Human and Animal Communication
1. Peacocks attract a mate using their plumage. Male birds of paradise engage in a complex dance to attract females.
2. Magpies chatter; rabbits thump their paws on the ground
3. They engage in the waggle dance. [1] The direction the bee moves in relation to the hive indicates direction. [1] If the bee moves vertically, the direction to the source is directly towards the sun. [1] The duration of the waggle dance signifies the distance to the source from the hive. [1]
4. Humans have an open vocal system and a larger bank of symbols to use in communication.
5. To discuss the past, plan for the future and discuss future events.

Non-verbal Communication
1. Verbal communication relies on the use of words; [1] non-verbal communication doesn't rely on spoken or written words. [1] Non-verbal communication can include body posture or gestures. [1] It can also include certain aspects of language such as tone of voice. [1]

2. Open postures involve leaving the body vulnerable, [1] including having the chin raised, arms placed to the side (not folded) and legs uncrossed. [1] A closed posture ensures that vulnerable areas are protected by folding arms and crossing legs. [1] A closed posture is thought to be a defensive posture. [1]
3. a) The mirroring or the adoption of the same posture as the person doing the talking.
   b) Encourages mutual positive feelings
4. **Any appropriate answer, such as:** tapping somebody lightly on the shoulder; gently stroking their hand; hugging them; holding their hand
5. Cultural norms, gender, status

Explanations of Non-verbal Behaviour
1. Non-verbal communication is an evolutionary mechanism, [1] allowing species to adapt and evolve. [1]
2. It assumed that non-verbal behaviour is innate, [1] i.e. it is something we are born with rather than a behaviour we learn from the environment. [1] It is therefore nature rather than nurture. [1]
3. In order to learn facial expressions from others, it is necessary to see other people use those expressions. [1] A child who has been blind since birth is unable to learn from what they cannot see, so the expressions they make must have been present at birth. [1]
4. Learned behaviour arises through observing others. [1] Learning theories would argue that non-verbal behaviour is a learned response to watching other people display such behaviour. [1]
5. a) Americans responded to visual cues associated with the mouth [1] and Japanese people responded to eyes. [1] For example, while an American would identify a happy person from their upturned mouth, [1] a Japanese person would focus on creases around the eyes. [1]
   b) Yuki found that American and Japanese people focus on different areas of the face to identify emotional states. [1] If non-verbal behaviour was evolutionary, all cultures should identify emotions in the same way, [1] but because Yuki found a difference, non-verbal behaviour must be learned. [1]

The Structure and Function of the Brain and Nervous System
1. D
2. The PNS transmits messages to the whole body from the brain, and vice versa.
3. Sympathetic and parasympathetic
4. The CNS is in control when Jake is aware of the sound behind him and he decides to run. [1] The CNS later recognises Will's voice and that there is no real danger. [1] The fight or flight response is activated. [1] The ANS can be seen in the increased heart rate and ability to run. [1] When the threat recedes, the ANS switches back to the parasympathetic action [1] and breathing rate slows. [1]

5. The theory suggests that emotional experience is the result, not the cause, of perceived bodily changes. [1] For example, we might think that if we meet a bear we become frightened and we run. [1] James-Lange theory, however, would suggest that we are frightened *because* we run. [1] In a similar way, we feel sad because we cry or afraid because we tremble. [1]

Neuron Structure and Function
1. C
2. It carries an electrical signal to a muscle, [1] which will cause the muscle to either contract or relax. [1]
3. It is the theory that states when one neuron sends a signal to another neuron, and that second neuron becomes activated, the connection between the two neurons is strengthened. [1] The more one neuron activates another neuron, the stronger the connection between them grows. [1] With every new experience, the brain rewires its physical structure. [1]
4. **Any one from:** serotonin or dopamine
5. During synaptic transmission, [1] the right key (neurotransmitter) has to fit into the right lock (receptor) to open up the specific ion channel. [1]

Localisation of Function in the Brain
1. The primary motor cortex is responsible for movement [1] by sending messages to the muscles via the brain stem and spinal cord. [1]
2. Touch
3. When a person struggles to find the word that they need
4. The technique of using microelectrodes to stimulate parts of the brain

An Introduction to Neuropsychology
1. People with cognitive deficits [1] due to brain damage or strokes. [1]
2. Techniques such as fMRI rely on matching behavioural actions with physiological activity. [1] Because the person being scanned is usually conscious, [1] they can be directed to produce a particular action [1] such as performing a memory task while being scanned. [1]
3. a) Radioactive gold
   b) Frontal lobes
4. Lack of oxygen
5. The area in which the damage occurred

Pages 110–111
1. Positive engagement with society and coping effectively with challenges.
2. Geographical isolation from family and emotional support networks, which in turn increases levels of loneliness and the feeling of not knowing who to turn to in times of crisis; technology and internet usage; increased pressure at work and school
3. Any appropriate organisation, e.g. Time To Change

Pages 112–113
1. Living with a person with significant mental health problems can put a strain on relationships.
2. If social care is lacking, or under stress through shortages in trained staff, this has an impact on the treatment that can be offered to patients; can lead to higher crime rates; effect on economy through time off work
3. Increased staff absence

Pages 114–115
1. One of the mood (or affective) disorders – mood disorders involve a prolonged and major disturbance of mood and emotions
2. A sense of euphoria or elation
3. Depression with mania
4. Persistent sadness/low mood, loss of interest/pleasure, fatigue/low energy

Pages 116–117
1. A blueprint by which depressed people view the world
2. Selective serotonin re-uptake inhibitors
3. Cognitive behavioural therapy – a type of psychotherapy that helps people to think in more constructive ways

Pages 118–119
1. Addiction or dependence refers to a behaviour that leads to dependency.
2. When a substance is taken to excess but does not necessarily lead to addiction.
3. A strong desire or sense of compulsion to take the substance despite harmful consequences, impaired capacity to control substance-taking behaviour, pre-occupation with substance use and the giving up of activities once deemed important, a physiological withdrawal state when the substance is reduced or ceased.

Pages 120–121
1. The extent to which traits are inherited
2. Sweden
3. DeBlasio and Benda

The Structure and Function of the Brain and Nervous System
1. a) Brain and spinal cord
   b) The brain is involved in psychological processes and the maintenance of life [1]; the spinal cord is involved in the transfer of messages to and from the brain to the peripheral nervous system (PNS). [1]
2. The PNS transmits messages to the whole body from the brain, and vice versa. [1] The PNS has two divisions: the somatic system and the autonomic system. [1]
3. The fight or flight response is designed to help when we feel that we are under threat. [1] It helps a person react quicker than normal. [1] It is triggered from the autonomic nervous system, specifically the sympathetic branch, and gets the body ready to fight or run away from the threat. [1] It leads to a number of bodily changes, e.g. increased heart rate, faster breathing, pupil dilation, etc. [1]

4. Helps to transmit and receive information from the organs
5. It proposes that the way in which we experience an emotional event is triggered by our bodily response [1] rather than the other way around. [1] For example, we get anxious because our heart is beating very fast (or any other appropriate example). [1]

Neuron Structure and Function
1. They tell the rest of the brain about the external and internal environment [1] by processing information taken from one of the five senses (sight, hearing, touch, smell, taste). [1]
2. With every new experience, the brain rewires its physical structure [1]; the more often the activity occurs, the stronger the connection becomes. [1]
3. Stronger connections between nerve cells [1] and longer lasting changes in synaptic connections. [1]
4. The electrical nerve impulse travels down the neuron, [1] prompting the release of neurotransmitters at the pre-synaptic terminal. [1] The neurotransmitters are released into the synaptic fluid in the synapse. [1] The adjacent neurons must then take up the neurotransmitters from the fluid [1] and convert them into an electrical impulse to travel down the neuron to the next synaptic terminal. [1] The procedure is then repeated. [1]
5. Chemicals within the brain that transmit signals
6. Excitatory potentials make it more likely for the neuron to fire; [1] inhibitory potentials make it less likely to fire. [1]

Localisation of Function in the Brain
1. Refers to the view that particular parts of the brain are responsible for specific functions, [1] such as vision and language. [1] In the case of memory, a person could suffer memory impairment through infection or trauma and retain long-term memories but be unable to create new memories [1] due to damage to the part of the brain responsible for short-term memory. [1]
2. Concerned with the sensation of the body; [1] the somatosensory cortex perceives touch; [1] the amount of somatosensory cortex required dictates the amount of somatosensory cortex needed for that area of the body. [1]
3. The visual centre of the brain is concerned with visual perception. [1] More specifically, an area of the visual cortex known as Area V1 is thought to be specifically necessary for visual perception; [1] people with damage to this area report no vision of any kind (including in dreams). [1]
4. a) Neural stimulation; [1] microelectrodes are used to stimulate parts of the brain to test their function [1]
   b) The amount of cortical tissue required differs for different functions; [1] the more sensitive the area, the more cortical tissue is required. [1]

An Introduction to Neuropsychology
1. How the function of neurons affects thought and behaviour
2. Traditional MRI scans produce static images; [1] fMRIs can produce moving images captured in real time [1]
3. Uses an X-ray beam to produce a picture of the physiology of the brain.
4. Participants were injected with a small amount of radioactive gold [1] and then asked to retrieve two types of memory: an episodic memory (that is, a personal experience) [1] and a semantic memory (a general knowledge memory). [1]
5. They would lose at least some movement, such as reflex actions and the inability to walk or to lift their arms. [1] This movement can return over time but is sometimes permanently lost. [1]
6. Any appropriate answer, such as accidents; certain types of infection

Pages 125–127 Practice Questions

An Introduction to Mental Health
1. The general inability to cope with everyday life
2. The inability to engage in satisfying interpersonal relationships
3. **Any two from**: feelings of independence (autonomy); resisting stress; an accurate perception of reality; being able to cope with life and the changing environment (environmental mastery)
4. **Any two from**: appropriate public behaviour; control of aggression; politeness; control of culturally and socially offensive language
5. Anxiety; depression
6. Any appropriate answers, such as The Campaign Against Living Miserably (CALM) and Time To Change

Effects of Mental Health Problems on Individuals and Society
1. The partner may experience feelings of guilt and shame [1] and even blame themselves. [1]
2. Chronic mental health problems can lead to a weakened immune system [1] and make people more susceptible to infection. [1]
3. The number of trained mental health professionals and social workers
4. Theft [1] to obtain money to feed their addiction [1]
5. Stigma; [1] the employee might believe that people will treat them differently if they divulge their illness. [1]

Characteristics of Clinical Depression
1. Depression has a longer duration (it lasts longer).
2. Major depressive disorder.
3. Mania
4. **Any two from**: persistent lowering of mood, decrease in activity/energy, change in sleep pattern, reduced self-esteem or self-confidence, ideas of guilt or worthlessness, loss of pleasurable feelings, agitation, loss or increase in appetite, loss of concentration, suicidal thoughts or acts

5. It usually develops after adolescence/in adulthood.
6. Men are less likely to seek help [1] so are never diagnosed. [1]

Theories of Depression and Interventions
1. Depression is caused by internal factors (nature rather than nurture), [1] including brain chemicals and genes. [1]
2. Serotonin
3. The gene has been found to reduce levels of serotonin.
4. a) Antidepressant medication
   b) Tricyclics and SSRIs
5. Cognitive behavioural therapy (CBT)

Characteristics of Addiction
1. A behaviour that leads to dependency
2. Any appropriate answer, e.g. alcoholism, drug addiction
3. Abuse doesn't include dependency.
4. **Any two from**: impaired capacity to control substance-taking behaviour; pre-occupation with substance use and the giving up of activities once deemed important; a physiological withdrawal state when the substance is reduced or ceased

Theories of Addiction and Interventions
1. Kaij (1960) [1] studied the rates of alcohol abuse in identical and fraternal twins. [1] He found that the concordance rate for identical twins was 54% and that for fraternal twins it was only 28%. [1] He concluded that there are genetic and hereditary factors involved in alcohol addiction. [1]
2. DeBlasio and Benda found the influence of peers to be a primary factor in the uptake of alcohol and drugs in adolescents. [1] Young people who smoke are more likely to associate with other young people who also smoke. [1]
3. A and B
4. They could use a drug that reacts with alcohol [1] and makes the person feel nauseous. [1] The addict would learn to associate alcohol with the feeling of being sick. [1]
5. a) A group of people with the same or similar problem who come together for support and help in overcoming their addiction.
   b) The 12-step program

Pages 128–129 Review Questions

An Introduction to Mental Health
1. Feeling bad about yourself (including the way you look); [1] showing signs of stress or the inability to cope; [1] feelings of having no control over life [1]
2. A positive attitude towards yourself, [1] personal growth and development (self-actualisation), [1] feelings of independence (autonomy), [1] resisting stress, [1] an accurate perception of reality, [1] and being able to cope with life and the changing environment (environmental mastery). [1]
3. a) Different cultures have different norms and values, [1] so something that might appear ordinary or normal in one culture can be seen as abnormal in another. [1]
   b) Homosexuality

4. More support networks to fall back on in times of need. [1] Families can support people in a number of ways, including psychological support, comfort, understanding and feelings of belonging. [1]

5. Mental illness can lead some people to feel alienated because of the negative feelings towards it. People might equate mental illness to psychological weakness and associate it with violence and extreme unusual behaviour. [1] This leads to an awkwardness around sufferers and they could feel isolated because of it, making the condition worse. [1]

Effects of Mental Health Problems on Individuals and Society

1. It can lead to the partner experiencing feelings of guilt and shame. [1] They might even blame themselves for their partner's illness. [1] Behaviour can change, resulting in the relationship being less intimate. [1]

2. It can lead to some people neglecting themselves, such as their personal hygiene. [1] They might become less interested in activities they once found enjoyable and socialise less often. [1]

3. Certain conditions, such as chronic anxiety and depression, can put a strain on the immune system, [1] making people more susceptible to infections. [1]

4. Health services [1] and social services [1]

5. To obtain money to buy the addictive substances they crave

6. Some conditions, such as stress-related problems and depression, can lead to people having to take long periods off work. [1] This can lead to understaffing in some workplaces. [1]

Characteristics of Clinical Depression

1. A prolonged and major disturbance of mood and emotions.

2. Manic depression or bipolar disorder

3. Bipolar depression is characterised by periods of mania followed by periods of low mood. [1] Unipolar depression doesn't include manic episodes. [1]

4. A sense of euphoria or elation. [1] People with mania have a great deal of energy [1] and can survive on very little sleep. [1] Despite this, however, they have difficulty focusing and rarely get very much done. [1]

5. a) Persistent sadness, loss of interest and pleasure in activities, fatigue and low energy
   b) **Any three from**: disturbed sleep, poor concentration, low self-confidence, poor or increased appetite, suicidal thoughts or acts, agitation, guilt/self-blame

Theories of Depression and Interventions

1. a) People with depression often display low levels of the neurotransmitter serotonin.
   b) The assumption is that low levels of serotonin are responsible for depression. [1] However, there is a problem with cause and effect in that depression might lead to lower

levels of serotonin rather than be caused by it. [1]

2. Negative self-schemas [1] which lead people to think pessimistically [1]

3. They help to regulate the levels of serotonin in the brain. [1] They block the transporter mechanism that absorbs the serotonin. [1]

4. It helps people to think differently about how they perceive events – encourages more positive and adaptive ways of thinking. [1] Maladaptive thoughts can be challenged and held up to scrutiny where they are found to be false. [1]

Characteristics of Addiction

1. Addiction refers to a behaviour that leads to dependency; [1] abuse refers to taking the substance in excess but doesn't necessarily lead to dependency. [1]

2. Certain behaviours and habits can cause people to become dependent on them (such as playing computer games). [1] These behaviours share the same core components as addiction. [1]

3. Progression (increase in severity); [1] preoccupation with the activity; [1] perceived loss of control; [1] persistence despite negative long-term consequences [1]

4. The addictive activity becomes the most important aspect of the addict's life.

5. The reverting to the patterns of addiction that existed prior to recovery.

6. Ella will have become gradually more consumed by playing games and will find it difficult to think about anything else. [1] Activities she once found interesting and exciting (such as playing sports or socialising with friends) will have become far less important. [1] She might be spending large amounts of time on her own playing games. [1]

Theories of Addiction and Interventions

1. There is a genetic component to alcohol abuse [1] because identical twins had higher concordance rates (54%) than fraternal (non-identical) twins (28%). [1]

2. Research found that deceased alcoholics were more likely to possess the A1 variant of the DRD2 gene, [1] suggesting that the cause of alcoholism might be genetic. [1]

3. Addiction is learned through observation. [1] This would suggest that people are more likely to engage in potentially addictive behaviour if they witness the behaviour being carried out by others, especially peers. [1]

4. a) A technique that pairs the addictive behaviour with an unpleasant experience or sensation. [1] For example, drugs can be taken that cause nausea when a cigarette is smoked. [1]
   b) Self-management programs rely on group support and a series of steps on the path to recovery, [1] while aversion therapy attempts to apply the principles of conditioning. [1] Aversion therapy obtains faster results than self-management programs. [1]

Pages 130–134 **Mixed Questions**

Cognition and Behaviour

1. Any appropriate example, such as 'If noise has an effect on stress, then people who complete a task in a noisy environment will score higher on a measure of their stress level than people who complete the task in a quiet environment.' [4]

2. It has two main roles: it maintains information in STM [1] and encodes it into LTM. [1]

3. The brain/visual cortex; [1] this builds up an image of the world by combining information from a network of receptor cells and integrating it with memories/assumptions. [1]

4. Both are non-experimental methods which involve asking questions to participants. [1] Interview is done face-to-face; surveys via paper or on screen. [1] Both could use two types of question, but interviews tend to feature open questions and surveys closed questions. [1] Interviews allow follow-up to questions, whereas an advantage of surveys is that they are private, so could prompt a higher level of honesty in responses. [1]

5. Before – **any two from**: beginning of brain formation in week 3; development of stem cells; true neurons forming from day 42; brain areas largely complete by midway through pregnancy; many connections forming (axons/fibres linking cells). After – **any two from**: pruning of axonal connections; rapid learning and strengthening connections; structural changes until mid-20s; (neuro)plasticity throughout life.

6. Limitations of STM, i.e. approximately seven items in terms of capacity (**two seconds of rehearsal time is also acceptable**), [1] and a duration of up to 30 seconds before items decay. [1] In LTM, both capacity and duration should be described as unlimited. [2]

7. a) bar b) strength

8. The top-down/constructivist theory. [1] Illusions show that the world is sometimes ambiguous, and therefore people can't perceive it just from information that reaches the senses. [1] Therefore, according to constructivist theory, it is necessary to make inferences and use knowledge about the world stored in memory in order to build up a mental picture of the world. [1]

9. Retinal disparity: [1] differences between the images from the two eyes gives a cue to distance, [1] as the difference is larger when the object is close. [1] **Or** convergence/eye convergence: [1] a cue from the muscles that move our eyes, [1] as the eyes have to rotate slightly for closer objects. [1]

10. Encoding, storage, retrieval

11. Motivation, set, people, areas

12. An illusion

13. It is an active process, [1], which can be distorted by things such as prior knowledge/expectations. [1]

14. **From top to bottom**: true, true, false, true

15. Asking passers-by is an opportunity sample, not a random sample. [1] There are various ways that such a sample could be biased – accept any appropriate answer. For instance: some people might not be in school; some are more likely to be in the corridor while others are in class/in the school library, etc. People who take a particular school subject are more likely to be on a particular corridor (e.g. a science corridor). People who are missing class for various reasons are more likely to be in the corridor. Certain pupils are more likely to have a free period, e.g. older pupils with a lighter timetable. [2]

16. They could link it to an existing schema (e.g. "it's a type of train") [1] or create a new schema for this new category of vehicle [1], i.e. they could assimilate [1] or accommodate [1] the stimulus.

17. a) allocated
    b) counterbalancing

18. The two sides may be correct on different occasions. Some psychological attributes might be largely genetic, while others are linked to upbringing and culture. [1] Genetic aspects could also have an effect on later life experiences, meaning that the two interact. [1] Genes and the environment interact biologically (epigenetics) meaning that aspects of the 'nurture' side such as upbringing could affect things usually associated with the nature side, i.e. based on gene expression. [1]

19. **Any two answers from**: facts are necessary in order to connect new ideas; we shouldn't just teach skills; it's best to avoid teaching the theory of learning styles because there is no scientific evidence for it; it's important to combine different sensory inputs – dual coding; a style of learning needs to be appropriate to the material.

Social Context and Behaviour

1. Antidepressant medication; [1] cognitive behavioural therapy (CBT) [1]
2. Postural echoing; [1] to increase positive feelings between you [1]
3. They carry messages from one part of the central nervous system to another.
4. Presence of an ally, [1] size of majority, [1] anonymity, [1] task difficulty [1]
5. Aversion therapy
6. The listener wants to speak.
7. Fight or flight
8. They have invaded your personal space. [1] Personal space is an imaginary area around us that we think of as our territory. [1]
9. Proximity, [1] symbols of authority, [1] status of the situation, [1] agency [1]
10. They would feel unable to survive without it; [1] drinking would take priority over all other behaviours; [1] there would be specific behavioural changes. [1]
11. The central nervous system
12. Number of people present; pluralistic ignorance; similarity of victim to helper; cost of helping
13. The autonomic nervous system
14. They will be protecting vital parts of their body such as the chest and genital region. [1] Arms will most likely be folded across the chest [1] and if they are seated, legs will be crossed. [1]
15. The symptoms would last longer.
16. fMRI

Glossary

abuse – the use of a substance (often a drug) in amounts that are harmful to the user

accommodation – the process of changing a schema or developing a new one when faced with information that cannot be assimilated into a person's current schemas

acoustic encoding – encoding information to memory based on its sound

active process – a cognitive process that requires effort and attention, for example problem-solving or rehearsal in working memory

adaptive – a behaviour that evolves in order to increase the chances of reproductive success

addiction – a condition that results when a person ingests a substance or engages in activity that over time becomes compulsive and interferes with ordinary life responsibilities

Adorno – German philosopher and sociologist who developed the theory of the authoritarian personality

affordances – information from the environment that aids perception, for example depth cues

agentic – a state in which a person behaves as if an agent of another, assuming no responsibility for their actions or the consequences

(random) allocation – a basic principle of experimental design which states that the choice of condition or order of conditions that a participant completes must be random to avoid bias

alternative hypothesis – a scientific prediction of the effect that the IV will have on the DV, with a rationale based on past research

ambiguity – more than one possible interpretation; the basis of several illusions

the Ames Room – a specially constructed room that appears ordinary when viewed from the front but is actually distorted, causing an illusion of size

assimilation – the process of fitting new information into an existing schema

attention – the cognitive function of focusing on a stimulus; people have a limited amount of attention which must be divided among active tasks

authoritarian – the favouring or enforcing of strict obedience to authority at the expense of personal freedom

autonomic – involuntary or automatic; referring to the autonomic nervous system

autonomous – having the freedom to act independently

aversion therapy – creates in the individual a strong aversive (i.e. dislike) response to the source of the addiction

axon – part of a neuron; the nerve fibre which carries signals to other neurons

bar chart – a graph displaying statistical results based on the height of two or more bars; commonly used to compare conditions of an experiment

Bartlett – memory researcher, Sir Frederic Bartlett, was the first professor of psychology in the United Kingdom

bias – ways in which data or judgements are distorted or skewed

binocular – a visual cue to depth/distance which depends on comparing the differences between what is sensed by the two eyes

bipolar – a disorder where people alternate between periods of depression and mania

blame – feeling responsible for a fault or a wrong; people who are close to individuals with mental health problems will often believe that they are somehow at fault for the illness

bottom-up processing – a type of perceptual processing based on the information received via sensation, considered to be primary by the direct theory

brain stem – part of the brain; responsible for autonomic functions such as breathing and heartbeat

bystander intervention – a psychological phenomenon in which someone is less likely to intervene in an emergency situation when others are present than when they are alone

capacity – in cognitive psychology, the amount of information that can be held in a memory store at one time

case study – an in-depth study of one individual or a small group

categories of behaviour – types of behaviour that might be recorded during observational research, generally phrased broadly so that many possible actions could fall within a single category

cause-and-effect relationship – relationship between two variables where a change in one variable directly causes a change in the other, i.e. there is causation

CBT – cognitive behavioural therapy; a type of psychotherapy that attempts to correct faulty thought patterns

cell body – part of a neuron; the central part of the cell containing the nucleus

centration – the tendency of children in Piaget's pre-operational stage to focus on one element of a problem and ignore others

cerebellum – part of the brain; responsible for precise physical movement and coordination

cerebral cortex – part of the brain; responsible for cognition, including thinking, perception and most memory processes

closed posture – a defensive posture involving the protection of vulnerable parts of the body

closed questions – questions that give participants a pre-determined choice of possible answers

colour constancy – the perceptual constancy where the brain makes allowances for the variable appearance of colours under different conditions

concrete operational stage – a developmental stage from Piaget's theory; children aged 8 and above can make logical operations and are able to conserve volume and other properties

conditions – parts of an experiment which are compared, each relating to a different value of the IV

confederate – a person hired by the researcher to act as a participant when they are, in fact, part of the experiment

confidentiality – ethical principle regarding the treatment of data and participant details; information must be held securely and personal information should not be released

conformity – the process of giving in to real or imagined pressure from a group

conservation – awareness that the appearance of an object or set of objects can transform without its properties fundamentally changing; Piaget believed that this emerges in the concrete operational stage of development.

constructivist theory – a psychological theory which states that a person's schemas can influence and distort what they remember and perceive

context – a factor that affects memory; it's easier to remember things in the same context as where they were first learned

control – keeping extraneous variables constant and minimised during experimentation, allowing the researcher to test for cause and effect between the experimental variables

control condition – a condition of an experiment which is conducted to form a baseline for comparison

convergence – a binocular cue to depth based on muscular movements; the eyes rotate inwards to a greater extent when viewing an object that is closer

correlation – a statistical analysis technique that aims to show how two variables are linked

correlation strength – how closely connected two co-variables are in a correlational study, in either a positive or negative direction

counterbalancing – varying the order of experimental conditions to balance out any possible order effects

co-variables – the variables studied in a correlation study

CT scan – a type of scanning technique that uses an X-ray beam to produce a picture of the physiology of the brain

cue – a piece of information which helps a memory to be retrieved

cued recall – retrieval from memory where the individual has a prompt or reminder of some kind

culture – the beliefs and behaviour of a particular group of people, usually associated with specific areas or countries; a factor that affects both memory and perception

debriefing – information given to participants at the end of a study

deception – an ethical flaw in research whereby a researcher will withhold details or give false information to participants

deindividuation – the tendency of people in a large, arousing, anonymous group to lose inhibitions, sense of responsibility and self-consciousness

dependent variable (DV) – the variable that is measured in an experiment, resulting in the data that a researcher analyses

deprivation – time spent in an environment which limits or harms a child's ability to develop healthily; a lack of suitable stimulation can harm intellectual development

depth cues – affordances in the environment that allow a person or animal to perceive depth or distance

depth perception – the perceptual process of interpreting how close or far away objects are

diffusion of responsibility – the tendency for an individual to feel less responsible in the presence of others because responsibility is distributed among all the people present

direct theory – a psychological theory which states that perception is based on sensation rather than on expectations and inferences

displacement – in cognitive psychology, forgetting from STM where items are pushed out because of its limited capacity

distortion – an aspect of a memory which differs from what was originally experienced

dual coding – the finding that combining both verbal and visual information during learning improves the rate at which people later remember information

duration – the length of time a memory store can retain information before it is forgotten

Dweck – Carol Dweck, a cognitive psychologist with an interest in education, and the originator of the theory of growth and fixed mindsets

effort after meaning – a term used by Bartlett to describe people's motivation to reconstruct and distort information in memory in order to make sense of it

egocentrism – inability to think about the feelings of others or to view situations from their perspective, or the tendency to avoid doing so

emotion – feelings such as happiness, worry and fear; bodily feelings such as hunger are sometimes included

encoding – taking new information into memory; an input process

epigenetics – the study of how the environment impacts on whether genes are – or are not – expressed

episodic memory – long-term memory for life events

ethical guidelines – code of conduct set out by a professional organisation such as the British Psychological Society, aiming to ensure that research meets ethical standards

ethical standards – set of principles which must be followed by researchers to ensure that research is ethically sound and does not harm participants

evolution – the process by which different kinds of living organism are believed to have developed from earlier forms during the history of the earth

excitation – a positive change in voltage that occurs when a neurotransmitter binds to an excitatory receptor site

expectations – a factor in the perceptual set; people's perceptions are influenced by what they expect, which is in turn influenced by past experience

extraneous variable (EV) – any variable other than the IV which could potentially affect the DV

false memory – events that appear in memory but didn't actually happen

fiction – the basis of some illusions, fictions are where something is perceived despite not being (fully) available to the senses

field experiment – any experiment which is conducted in a participant's natural environment

fixed mindset – a set of attitudes based around the idea that ability levels are fixed, and that how well someone does at a task is largely due to factors outside of their control

fMRI – a scanning technique that measures the energy released by haemoglobin; an fMRI scan produces a moving picture

formal operational stage – a developmental stage from Piaget's theory; children aged 11 and above can solve abstract problems

fraternal – non-identical twins

free recall – retrieval from memory where the stimulus is not present and there is no cue

frontal lobe – one of the four main lobes of the cerebral cortex; this area is essential for STM/working memory processes

gene expression – where a gene causes the body to produce a protein, potentially impacting on brain structure and behaviour

generalise – to conclude that the findings from a research study also hold true for the wider population

genes – sequences of DNA held within every cell in the body

genetics – the study of genes and their effects on the characteristics of living organisms

Gestalt approach – a psychological perspective which states that people have a tendency to perceive objects as wholes rather than many parts, and therefore to mentally connect objects that appear to belong together

gestures – movements of part of the body, especially a hand or the head, to express an idea or meaning

Gibson – J.J. Gibson, the main figure behind the direct theory of perception

Gregory – Richard Gregory, the main figure behind the constructivist theory of perception

growth mindset – a set of attitudes based around the idea that ability levels can be changed, and therefore how well someone does at a task is largely due to effort and learned skill

guilt – a feeling of responsibility or remorse for an offence, crime, wrongdoing, etc., whether real or imagined

hallucinations – perception in the absence of any relevant sensation

harm – ethical principle which states that research participants must be treated with respect and should come to no physical or psychological harm, including stress

height in plane – a monocular cue to depth; objects that are more distant appear closer to the horizon line

heritability – an estimation of how much variation in a phenotypic trait in a population is due to genetic variation among individuals in that population

hippocampus – an area of the brain essential to encoding new long-term memories

histogram – a graph displaying statistical results based on the height of a series of bars; commonly used to represent a continuous set of groups among a target population

holistic – the treatment of the whole person, taking into account mental and social factors rather than just the symptoms of a disease

hollow face illusion – an image of the back of a mask which tends to be perceived as a face, supporting the constructivist theory of perception

illusion – a stimulus which causes a person to see something different from what is actually there, or where there are two or more possible interpretations of the same image

independent groups – an experimental design where each participant takes part in only one experimental condition

independent variable (IV) – the variable that is manipulated in an experiment

individual differences – ways in which people differ from each other, for example culture

inferences – assumptions and problem solving which is done to convert sensations into a coherent perception of the world; the need for inferences implies that the information received by the senses is insufficient for perception to take place

informed consent – ethical principle which states that research participants must give their consent in full knowledge of what they are consenting to

inhibition – a negative change in voltage that occurs when a neurotransmitter binds to an inhibitory receptor

innate – something (such as an ability) that is present at birth

input process – a cognitive process such as encoding where information is entered for the first time

interference – a type of forgetting where information is forgotten because it gets confused with other information

internalise – when a belief or value is integrated with a person's identity

inter-observer reliability – the extent to which different observers record the same data from the same observation

interview – a research method which involves asking people questions about their behaviour or thoughts face-to-face

invasion of privacy – an ethical flaw in research whereby a researcher breaches a participant's right to privacy in terms of their actions or data

the Kanizsa triangle – a fiction illusion where corners of a triangle are shown, and people tend to perceive a whole triangle

laboratory experiment – an experiment in a lab, i.e. any controlled environment that allows the effects of distractions to be minimised

leading question – a question that prompts inaccurate recall of memories

learning styles – a controversial educational theory which suggests that people learn best if a task suits their preferred modality: auditory, visual or kinaesthetic

light constancy – the perceptual constancy where objects are perceived as the same regardless of lighting conditions

linear perspective – a monocular cue to depth; parallel lines tend to appear closer together as they become more distant

localisation – the idea that different parts of the brain are responsible for specific behaviours, or that certain functions are localised to certain areas in the brain

Loftus – memory researcher Elizabeth Loftus is an expert in the formation of distorted or false memories

logical operation – a symbolic task involving making a deduction or calculation

long-term memory (LTM) – a permanent memory store which encodes information on the basis of meaning

maladaptive – not adjusting adequately or appropriately to the environment or situation

mania – a behaviour marked by great excitement, euphoria and overactivity

matched pairs – an experimental design where each participant takes part in only one experimental condition and is matched by characteristics such as age or gender with participants in the other conditions, rather than randomly allocated

mean – a statistic which shows the arithmetic average of a set of data

median – a statistic which shows the midpoint of a set of data by finding the centre-most score

mode – a statistic which shows the midpoint of a set of data by finding the most common score

monocular – cues to depth that are apparent using only one eye

Motion parallax – the way that the visual scene world changes when a person or animal moves; closer objects appear to move more, and more distant ones move less

motivation – a desire to do, perceive or remember something; a factor in the perceptual set

Müller-Lyer illusion – an illusion of length which appears like a pair of arrowheads around a line

multi-store model – a theory of memory which states that the main stores of memory are separate, but connected together via attention and rehearsal

natural experiment – research method with the overall structure of an experiment but which lacks experimenter control over the independent variable and the allocation of participants to conditions.

naturalistic observation – observing a participant in an everyday context such as their workplace

nature – one side of the nature–nurture debate which states that genes are much more important than the environment, and that they largely determine what kind of personality and skills someone will develop

naughty teddy study – a task which was used to test for the conservation of number in children

the Necker cube – an ambiguous figure of a cube

negative correlation – a correlational relationship between two variables, where increases in one variable are associated with decreases in the other

negative visualisation – a technique that involves imagining the worst possible outcome of a situation or an unpleasant result of a specific behaviour

neurons – the cells of the nervous system, which communicate via electrochemical signals and whose functioning underlies all sensory and brain processes

neuropsychology – a branch of psychology that involves the study of the brain and nervous system, and how these relate to behaviour

neuroscience – the scientific study of the nervous system; a multidisciplinary science, drawing from fields including anatomy, molecular biology, mathematics, medicine, pharmacology, physiology, physics and psychology

neurotransmitters – chemicals released by neurons, stimulating responses in other neurons

normal distribution – a distribution of data where the middle values are common while more extreme ones are progressively rarer, resulting in a bell-shaped curve

normative conformity – a type of conformity that arises due to the desire to be accepted by the group

null hypothesis – a baseline scientific prediction which assumes that the IV will not have an effect on the DV

nurture – one side of the nature–nurture debate which states that upbringing and life experiences are more important than genes, and that what happens to a person during their life will largely determine what kind of personality and skills they will develop

observation – research method which involves studying behaviour as it happens and recording data in the form of notes or videos

occipital lobe – one of the main lobes of the brain, located at the bottom, back part of the cortex. The occipital lobe is responsible for processing visual information from the eyes.

occlusion – a monocular cue to depth; objects that partially cover other objects tend to be perceived as closer

open posture – a form of non-verbal communication where the body is left vulnerable (such as arms unfolded and legs apart). It implies that the person adopting the posture is listening and receptive to the other person

open questions – questions that allow the participant to answer in any way they want

open vocal system – the vocal system found in humans that allows them to combine known symbols with new symbols in order to create new meanings

opportunity sampling – selecting research participants on the basis of convenient availability

order effects – any way in which the order of conditions completed by participants in a repeated measures experimental design could affect results

output process – a memory process such as retrieval where information is retrieved or used

paralinguistics – the study of vocal (and sometimes non-vocal) signals beyond the basic verbal message or speech

parietal lobe – one of the four main lobes of the brain; responsible for processing sensory information

Penfield homunculus – a physical representation of the human body, located within the brain, describing the proportion of cortex required by each area of the body

perception – the process where the brain interprets the information that reaches the senses and builds up a coherent mental representation of the world that allows us to function

perceptual constancy – way in which the perceptual system makes allowances for changes in the environment, adjusting the information that reaches the senses

perceptual set – a group of assumptions and emotions that affect perception, biasing how people perceive the world

PET scan – a scanning technique that produces a moving picture of brain activity using radioactive glucose injected into the bloodstream

Piaget – researcher Jean Piaget was a Swiss developmental psychologist responsible for a stage theory of cognitive development

plasticity – the ability of brain cells and structures to adapt their function to respond to new environmental conditions throughout life

pluralistic ignorance – in social psychology, a situation in which a majority of group members privately reject a norm, but incorrectly assume that most others accept it, and therefore go along with it

policeman doll study – a variation on the three mountains problem which suggested that young children are less egocentric than previously thought

Ponzo illusion – an illusion based on misinterpreted depth cues, where images closer to a vanishing point look larger

positive correlation – a correlational relationship between two variables, where both increase and decrease together

postural echo – the mirroring of body postures between two or more participants

posture – a position of the body; in body language, posture can be open or closed (defensive)

pre-operational stage – a developmental stage from Piaget's theory; children aged 7 or below learn to use one object to represent another, but are egocentric and exhibit centration

primacy effect – part of the serial position effect, where words at the start of a list are better remembered than those in the middle

primary data – new data obtained directly from the participant(s)

procedural memory – long-term memory for skills

qualitative data – data in the form of spoken/written words or in another non-numerical form

quantitative data – data in the form of numbers

questionnaire – a research method which involves asking people questions about their behaviour or thoughts on paper or via a computer

random allocation – selecting participants to take part in experimental and/or control conditions using a random process in order to avoid bias

random numbers – a set of numbers in a random order; used to carry out random sampling

random sample – ensuring that every member of the target population has the same chance of being selected

range – statistic which shows the distribution of a set of data via the difference between the lowest and highest score

recency effect – part of the serial position effect, where words at the end of a list are better remembered than those in the middle

receptor cells – sensory cells such as rods and cones which respond to external cues such as light and sound

recognition – retrieval from memory where the information or stimulus is repeated and the person compares it to what is in their memory

reconstructive memory – the process of using schema knowledge to fill gaps when retrieving a memory

recovery – in addiction, the diminishing of the physical and psychological need for the addicted-to substance

reductionist – analysing and describing a complex phenomenon in its most simple form

rehearsal – the process of maintaining information in STM by repeating it again and again, potentially playing a role in encoding new information to LTM

relative size – a monocular cue to depth; smaller objects of the same type tend to be perceived as more distant

repeated measures – an experimental design where participants all take part in every condition of the experiment

representative – a sample which has the same characteristics as the target population as a whole

research methods – a group of techniques used to gather and analyse data in psychology

retinal disparity – a binocular cue to depth; the difference between the visual images to the eyes reduces as objects become more distant

retrieval – in memory, accessing stored information and bringing it back to mind when needed

right to withdraw – ethical principle in research ensuring that participants can stop their participation at any time

Rubin's vase – an illusion which can be interpreted as either two faces looking towards each other, or as a vase

sadness – an emotion associated with feelings of loss, despair or sorrow

sample – a group of people that take part in an experiment or other research study, selected from among the target population

scatter graph – a graph that shows relationships in correlation studies via a pattern of points

schema – a memory structure based on a concept that people derive from life experience and which is influenced by their culture; forms the basis of long-term memories and also of children developing understanding of the world, as studied by Piaget

secondary data – data which has been generated before for a different purpose, and is obtained and analysed by a researcher

self actualisation – the realisation of one's talents and potentialities

self-efficacy – a person's sense of whether they are good or bad at a task

semantic memory – long-term memory for facts and meanings

semantic encoding – encoding information to memory based on its meaning

sensation – the process which occurs when receptor cells in the senses process external cues such as light and sound

sensorimotor stage – a developmental stage from Piaget's theory; children up to the age of 2 focus on interacting with physical objects, and develop object constancy

sensory cortex – part of the cerebral cortex; the area responsible for processing sensory information and therefore essential for perception

sensory memory – a very brief memory store, allowing sensations such as sounds and images to be retained for up to two seconds without being processed

serial position curve – a U-shaped graph showing recall of a series/list, which tends to show better recall at the beginning and the end (the primacy and recency effects)

serotonin – a neurotransmitter associated with depression

shame – a painful feeling of humiliation or distress

shape constancy – the perceptual constancy where the brain makes allowances for changes in an object's apparent shape as it is viewed from different angles

short-term memory (STM) – a temporary memory store with limited capacity, which encodes information on the basis of sound; also known as working memory

size constancy – the perceptual constancy where the brain allows for changes in an object's apparent shape as it is viewed from different distances

social learning theory – proposes that learning is a cognitive process that takes place in a social context and can occur purely through observation or direct instruction

social loafing – the phenomenon whereby a person exerts less effort to achieve a goal when they work in a group than when they work alone

somatic – relating to body; distinct from the mind

somatosensory – part of the sensory system concerned with the conscious perception of touch, pressure, pain, temperature, position, movement and vibration, which arise from the muscles, joints, skin and fascia

SSRI – selective serotonin re-uptake inhibitors; a class of antidepressant drugs that increase the level of serotonin

standardised instructions – the presentation of standard information to all participants in a research study or experimental condition, in order to minimise random error or bias

state – a factor that affects memory; it's easier for people to remember things when they are in the same physical state as when it was first learned; includes their mood, arousal level and the consumption of drugs

statistics – mathematical operations used to interpret and make sense of data, and summarise it in a simplified form

stem cell – a type of bodily cell which plays a key role in the early development of the brain and other organs; can transform into different types of cell

stigma – a mark of disgrace associated with a particular circumstance, quality or person; with regards to mental illness, stigma occurs when people look negatively on those with psychological problems

storage – the process of maintaining information in memory over time, avoiding forgetting or distortions

store – an area of memory such as short-term memory, long-term memory and the sensory stores

stratified sampling – selecting research participants in a way which maintains the same proportions as the population, in categories that the researcher considers to be important

symbols – sounds, gestures, material objects or written words that have a specific meaning to a group of people

symptoms – physical or psychological features indicating the presence of a disease

synapse – the junction between the axon of one neuron and the cell body or dendrite of a neighbouring neuron

systematic sampling – selecting research participants according to a regular pattern

target population – the group of people who the researcher is interested in studying

temporal lobe – one of the main lobes of the brain responsible for processing auditory information

texture gradient – a monocular cue to depth; the texture of objects can be seen in less detail as they become more distant

thalamus – part of the brain; responsible for basic sensory processing and relaying signals to the cortex

theory of cognitive development – an explanation or model of how cognitive abilities such as thought and language develop through life, and especially during childhood

three mountains problem – an experimental task involving model mountains, used to test egocentrism

timing – a factor that can affect memory, with delays either harming or improving later memory performance

top-down processing – a type of perceptual processing involving inferences and prior knowledge, considered to be primary by the constructivist theory

twin studies – research studies which compare the psychology of identical and non-identical twins within the same families, or after adoption

unipolar – a type of depression that occurs in the absence of mania

upbringing – the way a child is looked after by their parents or guardians

vanishing point – the point towards which lines appear to converge as they become more distant

variable – any characteristic, attribute or environmental condition that can have different values

verbaliser – a person with a preference for learning via words

visual cliff – an experiment involving a sheet of glass which is safe to walk on but looks like a cliff edge; it was used to support the idea that perception is innate

visual encoding – encoding information to memory based on its appearanc

visualiser – a person with a preference for learning via images

Willingham – Daniel Willingham, a cognitive psychologist with an interest in education, and a critic of learning styles

withdrawal – the unpleasant physical reaction that accompanies the process of ceasing to take an addictive drug

References

Adorno, T. W., Frenkel-Brunswik, E., Levinson, D. J. and Nevitt, S. R. (1950) *The Authoritarian Personality.* Oxford: Harpers.

Argyle, M. (1972) *Non-verbal communication in human social interaction.* In Hinde, R.A. (ed.) *Non-verbal communication.* Boston: Houghton Mifflin.

Asch, S. E. (1951) *Effects of group pressure upon the modification and distortion of judgement.* In Guetzkow, H (ed.) *Groups, leadership and men.* Pittsburgh, PA. Carnegie Press.

Atkinson, R.C. and Shiffrin, R.M. (1968) *Human memory: A proposed system and its control processes.* In K.W. Spence and J.T. Spence (Eds.) *The Psychology of Learning and Motivation*: Vol. 2. London: Academic Press.

Bartlett, F.C. (1932) *Remembering: A Study in Experimental and Social Psychology.* Cambridge: Cambridge University Press.

Beck, A. T. (1967) *Depression: Clinical, experimental and theoretical aspects.* Philadelphia: University of Pennsylvania Press.

Blackwell, L.S., Trzesniewski, K.H. and Dweck, C.S. (2007) 'Implicit theories of intelligence predict achievement across an adolescent transition: A longitudinal study and an intervention', *Child Development,* 78 (1), 246–263.

Bruner, J. S. and Minturn, A. L. (1955) 'Perceptual identification and perceptual organization', *The Journal of General Psychology,* 53 (1), 21–28.

Carmichael, L., Hogan, H.P. and Walker, A.A. (1932) 'An experimental study of the effect of language on the reproduction of visually perceived form', *Journal of Experimental Psychology*, 15 (1) 73–86.

DiBlasio, F.A. and Benda, B.B. (1993) 'Adolescent sexual intercourse: Family and peer influences', *School Social Work Journal,* 18 (1), 17–31.

Elms, A. C. and Milgram, S. (1966) 'Personality characteristics associated with obedience and defiance toward authoritative command', *Journal of Experimental Research in Personality*, 1 (4) 282–289.

Gilchrist, J. C. and Nesberg, L. S. (1952) 'Need and perceptual change in need-related objects', *Journal of Experimental Psychology*, 44 (6), 369–376.

Gregory, R. (1974) *Concepts and Mechanisms of Perception*, London: Duckworth.

Griffiths, M. (1999) 'Internet addiction: Fact or Fiction?' *The Psychologist*, 12 (5) 246–250.

Hall, E.T. and Hall, M.R. (2001) *Part 1: Key concepts: Underlying structures of culture.* In Hall, E.T. and Hall, M.R. *Understanding cultural differences: Germans, French and Americans.* London: Nicholas Brealey Publishing Company.

Heshka, S. and Nelson, Y. (1972) 'Interpersonal speaking distance as a function of age, sex and relationship', *Sociometry*, 35 (4) 491–498.

Hollinghurst, S., Jerrom, B., Kessler, D. and Kuyken, W. (2013) 'Cognitive behavioural therapy as an adjunct to pharmacotherapy for primary care based patients with treatment resistant depression: results of the CoBalT randomised controlled trial', *The Lancet*, 381 (9864) 375–384.

Hudson, W. (1960) 'Pictorial depth perception in sub-cultural groups in Africa', *Journal of Social Psychology*, 52 (2) 183–208.

Hughes, M. (1975) *Egocentrism in preschool children.* Unpublished doctoral dissertation. Edinburgh University.

International Classification of Diseases, *The ICD-10 Classification of Mental and Behavioural Disorders: Clinical descriptions and diagnostic guidelines*, available at www.who.int/substance_abuse/terminology/ICD10ClinicalDiagnosis.pdf (accessed January 24, 2017).

Kaij, L. (1960) *Alcoholism in twins: Studies on the etiology and sequels of abuse of alcohol.* Almqvist & Wiksell.

Kraemer, D. J., Rosenberg, L. M. and Thompson-Schill, S. L. (2009) 'The neural correlates of visual and verbal cognitive styles', *The Journal of Neuroscience,* 29 (12) 3792–3798.

Loftus, E.F. & Palmer, J.C. (1974) 'Reconstruction of automobile destruction: an example of the interaction between language and memory', *Journal of Verbal Learning and Verbal Behaviour,* 13, 585–589.

Matsumoto, D. and Willingham, R. (2009) 'Spontaneous facial expressions of emotion of congenitally blind individuals', *Journal of Personality and Social Psychology*, 96 (1) 1–10.

McGarrigle, J. and Donaldson, M. (1974) 'Conservation accidents', *Cognition*, 3, 341–350.

Milgram, S. (1963) 'Behavioural study of obedience', *The Journal of Abnormal and Social Psychology*, 67 (4) 371-378

Mind (2013) *Mental health and romantic relationships research released today,* available at www.mind.org.uk/news-campaigns/news/mental-health-and-romantic-relationships-research-released-today/#.WlhoHOSmnzR (accessed January 25, 2017).

Murdock Jr, B. B. (1962) 'The serial position effect of free recall', *Journal of Experimental Psychology,* 64 (5) 482.

Piliavan, I. M., Rodin, J. and Piliavin, J. A. (1969) 'Good Samaritanism: An underground phenomenon?' *Journal of Personality and Social Psychology*, 13 (4) 289–299.

Rubin, Z. (1970) 'Measurement of romantic love', *Journal of Personality and Social Psychology*, 16 (2) 265–273.

Scoville, W.B. and Milner, B. (1957) 'Loss of recent memory after bilateral hippocampal lesions', *Journal of Neurology, Neurosurgery and Psychiatry,* 20, 11–21.

Seligman, M.E. and Maier S.F. (1967) 'Failure to escape traumatic shock', *Journal of Experimental Psychology*, 74 (1) 1.

Sperling, G. (1960) 'The information available in brief visual presentations', *Psychological Monographs,* 74 (11) 1–29.

Tulving, E. (1989) 'Remembering and knowing the past', *American Scientist*, 77 (4) 361–367.

Walters, G.D. (1999) *The addiction concept: Working hypothesis or self-fulfilling prophesy?* Boston: Allyn & Bacon.

Wiles, N., Thomas, L., Abel, A., Ridgway, N., Turner, N., Campbell, J., Garland, A., Hollinghurst, S., Jerrom, B., Kessler, D., Kuyken, W., Morrison, J., Turner, K., Williams, C., Peters, T. and Lewis, G. (2013) 'Cognitive behavioural therapy as an adjunct to pharmacotherapy for primary care based patients with treatment resistant depression: results of the CoBalT randomised controlled trial', *Lancet*, 381 (9864) 375–84.

Yuki, M., Maddux, W.W. and Masuda, T. (2007) Are the windows of the soul the same in East and West? Cultural differences in using the eyes and mouth as cues to recognize emotions in Japan and the United States, *Journal of Experimental Social Psychology*, 43 (2) 303–311.

Zimbardo, P.G. (1969) *The cognitive control of motivation.* Glenview, Il: Scott, Foresman and Co.

Index

Collins

AQA GCSE Revision
Psychology

Psychology

AQA GCSE

Workbook

Jonathan Firth, Marc Smith

Contents

Cognition and Behaviour

Social Context and Behaviour

Exam Papers

Revision Tips

Rethink Revision

Have you ever taken part in a quiz and thought '*I know this*!', but, despite frantically racking your brain, you just couldn't come up with the answer?

It's very frustrating when this happens, but in a fun situation it doesn't really matter. However, in your GCSE exams, it will be essential that you can recall the relevant information quickly when you need to.

Most students think that revision is about making sure you **know** stuff. Of course, this is important, but it is also about becoming confident that you can **retain** that *stuff* over time and **recall** it quickly when needed.

Revision That Really Works

Experts have discovered that there are two techniques that help with all of these things and consistently produce better results in exams compared to other revision techniques.

Applying these techniques to your GCSE revision will ensure you get better results in your exams and will have all the relevant knowledge at your fingertips when you start studying for further qualifications, like AS and A Levels, or begin work.

It really isn't rocket science either – you simply need to:

- **test yourself** on each topic as many times as possible
- **leave a gap** between the test sessions.

It is most effective if you leave a good period of time between the test sessions, e.g. between a week and a month. The idea is that just as you start to forget the information, you force yourself to recall it again, keeping it fresh in your mind.

Three Essential Revision Tips

1. **Use Your Time Wisely**
   - Allow yourself plenty of time.
   - Try to start revising six months before your exams – it's more effective and less stressful.
   - Your revision time is precious so use it wisely – using the techniques described on this page will ensure you revise effectively and efficiently and get the best results.
   - Don't waste time re-reading the same information over and over again – it's time-consuming and not effective!

2. **Make a Plan**
   - Identify all the topics you need to revise (this All-in-One Revision & Practice book will help you).
   - Plan at least five sessions for each topic.
   - One hour should be ample time to test yourself on the key ideas for a topic.
   - Spread out the practice sessions for each topic – the optimum time to leave between each session is about one month but, if this isn't possible, just make the gaps as big as realistically possible.

3. **Test Yourself**
   - Methods for testing yourself include: quizzes, practice questions, flashcards, past papers, explaining a topic to someone else, etc.
   - This All-in-One Revision and Practice book provides seven practice opportunities per topic.
   - Don't worry if you get an answer wrong – provided you check what the correct answer is, you are more likely to get the same or similar questions right in future!

Visit our website to download your free flashcards, for more information about the benefits of these revision techniques, and for further guidance on how to plan ahead and make them work for you.

www.collins.co.uk/collinsGCSErevision

Memory

Where space is not provided, write your answers on a separate piece of paper.

Structures of Memory

1 What is meant by a memory cue? [2]

2 Which of the following statements is true of long-term memory? Shade **one** box only. [1]

A It is subject to forgetting through interference. ⬜

B It is based in the frontal lobe of the brain. ⬜

C Its memories all disappear over time. ⬜

D It only includes memory for skills. ⬜

3 Explain what effects brain damage can have on memory. [4]

4 Tick (✓) or cross (✗) the statements about memories to indicate whether they are true or false. [4]

Statements about memories	True (✓) or false (✗)?
Memories are always forgotten eventually	
It is hard to remember old memories out of context	
Memories can be triggered by a cue	
LTM and STM are processed in the same area of the brain	

5 Name the brain areas that are essential for the healthy functioning of:

a) STM .... [1]

b) LTM .... [1]

6 Name and briefly describe **three** types of LTM. [3]

7 Give examples of how STM and LTM are used in the real world. [2]

Memory as an Active Process

1 Which of the following examples is the most accurate metaphor for memory?
Shade **one** box only. [1]

A Putting things in a box ⬜   B Recording a video ⬜

C Saving a computer file ⬜   D Solving a problem ⬜

Memory

2 Which of the following can help information to be accurately encoded to LTM?
Tick all that apply.   [6]

A Spacing ☐

B Attention ☐

C Understanding ☐

D Repetition ☐

E Assumptions ☐

F Forgetting ☐

3 Name and briefly explain the **three** main types of retrieval from memory.   [6]

4 Write down whether each of the following examples relate to the memory
processes of encoding, storage or retrieval.   [4]

Example	Encoding, storage or retrieval?
A Reading a news story	
B Telling somebody a joke that you heard last week	
C A person keeping the names of a few food items in mind as they walk to the shops	
D Seeing a place and realising that you have been there before	

5 Complete the sentences by choosing the best words from the selection below.
You do not have to use all the words.   [4]

active	recognition	computer	brain	distorted	effort

Unlike the input and output processes of a _____, the human memory
does not just passively encode and retrieve information when required to do so. Its "working
memory" is used for _____ processing of information in everyday tasks,
such as solving a maths problem. Retrieval of long-term memories does not happen automatically
but involves mental _____, and this process can cause the information
to be _____, as can the process of encoding.

The Multi-Store Model of Memory 1 and 2

1 Which of the following is **not** one of the stores of the multi-store model? Shade **one** box only.   [1]

A Sensory memory ○

C Semantic memory ○

B Long-term memory ○

D Short-term memory ○

2 What term is used to describe superior recall of the first few items from a list?
Shade **one** box only.   [1]

A The primacy effect ○

C The nature–nurture debate ○

B The serial position curve ○

D Episodic memory ○

Memory

3 What type of forgetting happens to items which are held in short-term
memory when new information comes in? [1]

4 **a)** Describe the features of sensory memory. [1]

b) Give an example of how sensory memory is used in everyday life. [3]

5 Discuss the memory processes shown in the following example. [5]

> Fatima is studying for her French exam and has to learn lots of vocabulary. She does this
> by reading each word from her notebook, and then closing the book and testing herself.
> She finds that she always remembers the first few words in the list and the last few, but
> tends to make mistakes in the middle. After a while, Fatima gets tired and starts to lose
> concentration. She is still reading the vocabulary, but not paying as much attention. Now
> she notices that she is making a lot of mistakes, and decides to take a break.

6 Evaluate the multi-store model of memory, using research evidence. [8]

Factors Affecting Memory

1 Name **one** thing that can cause people to form a false memory. [1]

2 Complete the sentences by choosing the best words from the selection below.
You do not have to use all the words. [3]

culture	Bartlett	personality	Loftus	encoded	stories

_____ was the first professor of psychology in the United Kingdom. He was interested

in how long-term memories can be forgotten and distorted, and how this process is affected

by _____. His research used realistic stimuli, such as _____ and pictures.

3 People can use their existing schema knowledge to fill gaps when they are retrieving a memory.

a) What term did Bartlett use for this process? [1]

b) What theory did he develop that is based on this idea? [1]

4 Read the text. Then explain what might have happened to Liam's memory of his holiday. [4]

> Liam, aged 10, went on holiday with his parents last summer. When he returned to
> school, he tried to write a description of what he did on holiday, but found some details
> hard to recall. Later that day he discussed the holiday with his sister, and found that she
> remembered the events quite differently from what Liam had written in class.

5 Consider the factors that affect memory, including the research of Bartlett and Loftus. Describe
four ways in which language is linked to the way people think and remember. [8]

Perception

Where space is not provided, write your answers on a separate piece of paper.

Perception and Sensation

1 Define sensation. [1]

2 Which of the following is **not** a form of visual constancy? Shade **one** box only. [1]

   A Object constancy ◯   **B** Colour constancy ◯

   C Shape constancy ◯   **D** Size constancy ◯

3 Read the text below. Then explain how visual constancies helped Stan to locate his car. [3]

> Stan is leaving a friend's house late at night and can't remember where he parked his new red car. The street is dimly lit with streetlights that give off a yellowish light. He looks around for a minute and then spots his car at the far end of the street.

4 Explain the following diagram. [2]

Lens   Retina   Visual cortex   Optic nerve   Light from object

5 Describe how perception operates in everyday life, using **one** example such as a game of sport. [6]

Visual Cues and Depth Perception

1 Name the **two** main types of depth cues. [2]

2 Explain why depth perception could be important to an animal which has to jump from branch to branch in a tree. [2]

3 Which of the following is **not** a monocular cue to depth? Shade **one** box only. [1]

   A Texture gradient ◯   **B** Disparity ◯

   C Linear perspective ◯   **D** Occlusion ◯

Perception

4 Which of the following examples shows linear perspective? [1]

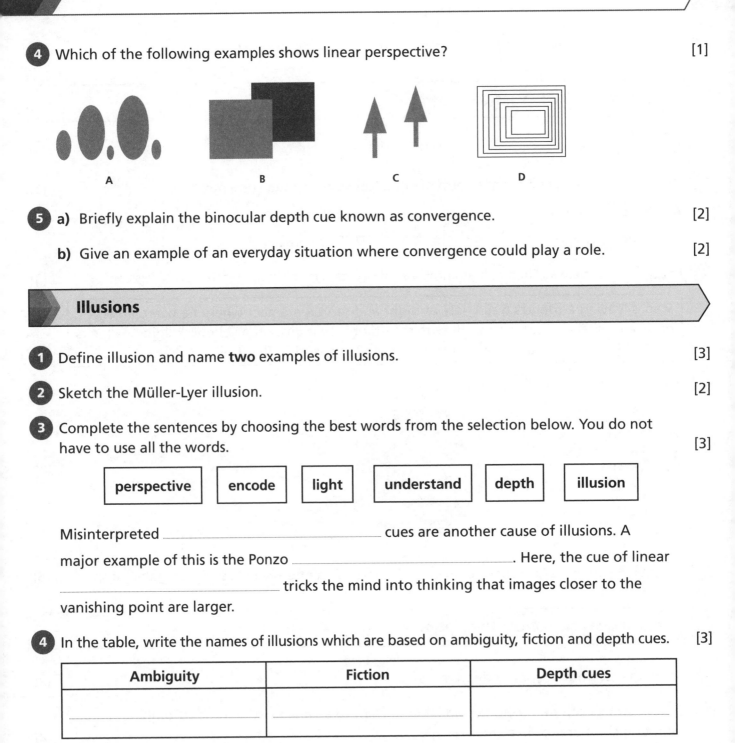

| A | B | C | D |

5 a) Briefly explain the binocular depth cue known as convergence. [2]

b) Give an example of an everyday situation where convergence could play a role. [2]

Illusions

1 Define illusion and name **two** examples of illusions. [3]

2 Sketch the Müller-Lyer illusion. [2]

3 Complete the sentences by choosing the best words from the selection below. You do not have to use all the words. [3]

| perspective | encode | light | understand | depth | illusion |

Misinterpreted _____ cues are another cause of illusions. A

major example of this is the Ponzo _____. Here, the cue of linear

_____ tricks the mind into thinking that images closer to the

vanishing point are larger.

4 In the table, write the names of illusions which are based on ambiguity, fiction and depth cues. [3]

Ambiguity	Fiction	Depth cues

5 The Gestalt approach to psychology can be used to explain certain illusions.

a) What is the main principle of this approach? [1]

b) Name an illusion that it helps to explain. [1]

Perception

6 Which illusion is shown in the following example? [1]

7 The Müller-Lyer illusion is sometimes linked to the way people perceive corners. We are used to seeing the shorter-looking line as the shape of a corner which is close, and the longer-looking line as the shape of a corner further away.

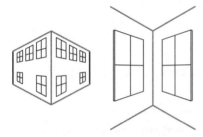

According to this point of view, explain how the Müller-Lyer illusion can be linked to depth cues in perception. [4]

Theories of Perception

1 Define perception. [2]

2 Which type of perceptual processing is the basis of the direct theory of perception? [1]

3 In the table below, note which theory (direct or constructivist) is supported by the various pieces of evidence. [4]

Evidence	Theory
San hunter-gatherer people failing to see the Müller-Lyer illusion	
Human and animal babies in the visual cliff experiment	
The hollow face illusion	
Motion parallax	

Perception

4 Explain the role of expectations and inferences in perception, according to the constructivist theory. [4]

5 Evaluate the direct theory of perception. Consider the arguments and evidence for and against this theory, and try to make at least **five** points. [5]

Factors Affecting Perception

1 Which of the following is **not** a factor that forms part of the perceptual set? Shade **one** box only. [1]

A Expectations ○

B Motivation ○

C Sensation ○

D Emotion ○

2 Identify **two** feelings that can affect perception. [2]

3 Complete the sentences by choosing the best words from the selection below. You do not have to use all the words. [3]

expectations	religion	biased	perception	attention	accurate

A person's perceptual set means a group of assumptions and emotions that affect
_____. Having a perceptual set means that people are _____
in how they perceive the world. Perceptual set includes several factors, in particular motivation, emotion, and a person's _____. Culture can also be considered a factor in a person's perceptual set.

4 Read the text and then answer the questions.

> Thom is visiting a school in another country. While he is there, he looks at a comic book that the local students enjoy and find funny. Thom finds the pictures confusing and doesn't entirely understand what is happening in the comic strips.

a) Define culture. [2]

b) Culture can affect how a person perceives the world. Explain how this might have affected Thom's experience. [6]

Development

Where space is not provided, write your answers on a separate piece of paper.

Brain Development

1 What do developmental psychologists study? [1]

2 What term is used to mean the fibre of a neuron (brain cell), which allows a signal to travel to another area of the brain? Shade **one** box only. [1]

A An axon terminal ⭕ **B** A nucleus ⭕

C A cell body ⭕ **D** An axon ⭕

3 Label **four** areas of the brain on the diagram. For each one, state **one** of its main functions. [8]

4 Explain the role of a stem cell in brain development. [3]

5 Explain how a child's brain develops after birth. [5]

Nature and Nurture

1 Complete the sentences by choosing the best words from the selection below. You do not have to use all the words. [3]

birth	experiences	genes	mindsets	upbringing	teachers

The nurture side of the debate suggests that although genes are important, what truly makes human beings unique is their life _____. It states that one of a person's most important set of experiences is their _____, including the way their parents or guardians looked after them. Parenting seems to play a key role in a child's educational success – some researchers have found that what parents do makes a bigger difference to a child's education than what their _____ do.

Development

2 In the following boxes, briefly explain how the two sides of the nature–nurture debate explain differences in intelligence and personality. [4]

	Nature	Nurture
Intelligence		
Personality		

3 Sometimes the nature–nurture debate is seen as too simplistic. Explain why this is, and describe **one** way in which genetics and the environment might interact. [4]

4 Which of the following are true of twin studies? Tick all that apply. [6]

A Most children share either genes or an environment with their parents, but not both. ☐

B Some twin studies compare the psychology of identical and non-identical twins. ☐

C Cases of identical twins who have been adopted and raised by different families are rare. ☐

D Twin studies are the only useful way of studying the nature–nurture debate. ☐

E Researchers use twin studies to investigate the separate effect of genetics and upbringing. ☐

F A limitation of studies of adopted twins is that the adoptive families are often quite alike. ☐

5 Using your knowledge of psychology, evaluate the evidence for the nature side of the nature–nurture debate. [6]

Piaget's Theories 1 and 2

1 Piaget described a series of stages, the first of which was the sensorimotor stage.

a) What age are children when they reach the end of this stage? [1]

b) Name an ability that a young child develops by the end of this stage. [1]

2 Explain an error of thinking that is made by children in the pre-operational stage of development. Refer to research evidence. [4]

Development

3 What is the name of the developmental stage where children become able to conserve number, realising that a line of counters contains the same number even when spread out? Shade **one** box only. [1]

A Sensorimotor ○   B Pre-operational ○

C Concrete operational ○   D Formal operational ○

4 Read the text below. Explain Hannah's error, referring to the concepts of assimilation and accommodation. [5]

> Hannah has always lived in a village where all of the houses are detached. When she is four years old, her family move to a flat in the city. At first, Hannah assumes that blocks of flats are houses, each containing only a single family. She calls them 'tall houses'. Soon she learns that this is not the case, however.

5 Discuss ways in which Piaget's ideas could be applied to education in primary schools. [8]

6 Piaget's stage theory of development has been criticised. Use your knowledge of psychology to evaluate Piaget's theory. Refer to the work of McGarrigle and Donaldson (1974) and Hughes (1975). [5]

Education

1 What term means a person's belief about how good or bad they are at something? [1]

2 One type of mindset described by Dweck is the fixed mindset.

  a) Explain this mindset. [1]

  b) Name and explain an alternative mindset. [2]

  c) Give an example of what someone with a fixed mindset might say **or** do. [1]

3 Complete the sentences by choosing the best words from the selection below. You do not have to use all the words. [4]

harder	maths	growth	fixed	mixture	slowly	sample

In support of mindset theory, Blackwell and colleagues studied .... attainment in school students. They found that students with a growth mindset continually improved their grades, whereas those with a .... mindset stayed at the same level. However, the theory has been accused of being over-simplistic, with students sometimes given the message that success is just about working ...., and failure is due to having the wrong attitude. There are a lack of reliable ways of measuring which mindset people have, and, in addition, some people appear to have a .... of the two mindsets, or to show different mindsets on different occasions.

4 Which mindset is indicated in the following statements? [6]

a) "I'm not bad at chess – I just haven't got the hang of it yet." ....

b) "I could try a harder project, but I'd rather just stick to something that I know I'll do well at." ....

c) "Maggie is amazing at sport. She's just naturally sporty." ....

d) "Andy can't draw at all. He's hopeless. He shouldn't waste time trying!"

....

e) "People say that I'm good at maths, but what they don't see is that it took me a lot of time to learn the skills. I love trying out new maths problems". ....

f) "Václav is amazing with people. He's a natural leader." ....

5 Using your knowledge of psychology, explain and evaluate the learning styles theory. [8]

6 Briefly explain:

a) visualisers and verbalisers [4]

b) dual coding. [2]

Research

Where space is not provided, write your answers on a separate piece of paper.

Sampling

1 Complete the following sentence: [1]

In a true random sample, every member of the target population has an .... chance of being selected.

2 Look at the example below. Which sampling method is being used? [1]

> Two researchers decide to select participants for a lab experiment in a school setting. They place adverts on a main school noticeboard, announcing that the testing will be taking place every lunchtime, and that anyone over the age of 16 is welcome to participate. They also offer a free cup of tea and a biscuit for anyone who takes part.

3 Identify the key characteristics of a stratified sample, and give an advantage of this type of sample. [2]

4 Complete the sentences by choosing the best words from the selection below. You do not have to use all the words. [3]

representative	conveniently	small	biased	random	opportunity

The most commonly used sampling method is .... sampling. This means selecting a group of research participants on the basis of who is easily available – e.g. a lecturer selecting their own students. The samples obtained using this method are often ...., because the people who are easily available may not be representative of the target population. Typically, the researcher approaches members of the target population that are .... available without taking any other characteristics into account.

5 Explain **one** way that a researcher might select a random sample. [2]

6 In a random sample, every member of the target population must have the same chance of being selected. Explain why this is not the case if a sample is chosen by asking passers-by on a school corridor during the school day. [3]

Variables and Hypotheses

1 Complete the following sentences:

a) The variable that a research manipulates is called the .... variable. [1]

b) The variable that is measured is called the .... variable. [1]

Research

2 What is the term given to a variable that a researcher tries to minimise and keep constant? Shade **one** box only. [1]

A Independent variable ◯   B Dependent variable ◯

C Extraneous variable ◯   D Controlled variable ◯

3 What is the term given to a group of participants whose main function is to act as a baseline for comparison with an experimental group? Shade **one** box only. [1]

A Control group ◯   B Dependent group ◯

C Null group ◯   D Controlled group ◯

4 Read the scenario and answer the questions that follow.

> A sports psychologist wants to study the effect of spaced practice on football players' ability to score penalties. Kath, the researcher, thinks that a given amount of penalty shooting practice will be more successful if it is spaced out over several practice sessions.
>
> Kath obtains a sample of players from a local sports club and allocates them to two experimental groups. One group does an hour of penalties practice on a single afternoon; the other group does three separate 20-minute sessions of penalties practice spread across a week.

a) What was the independent variable in this study? [1]

b) What was the dependent variable? How would the researcher measure it? [2]

c) State a possible alternative hypothesis for the study. [2]

d) Do you think that this study should have used a control group? Explain your answer. [2]

5 What term means the different parts of an experiment which link to different values of an independent variable? [1]

6 Give an example of a normally distributed variable, and state **one** characteristic of such a variable. [2]

Design of Experiments 1 and 2

1 Which ethical standard in research means that people are not forced to continue with a research study, even if they have initially consented to take part? [1]

2 Explain what steps need to be taken at the beginning of a research study, such as an experiment, to ensure that it is ethically sound. [3]

Research

3 Which of the following is a way of avoiding bias when dividing a sample of participants among experimental conditions? Shade **one** box only. [1]

A Stratified sampling ⭕   B Random allocation ⭕

C Counterbalancing ⭕   D Informed consent ⭕

4 Complete the following sentences.

a) A research study which takes place in a participant's natural surroundings is known as a

_____ experiment. [1]

b) The primary ethical concern that applies to all research is that participants must not be

_____ in any way, either physically or psychologically. [1]

c) In an experiment that uses a repeated measures design, counterbalancing must be used

to avoid _____ effects. [1]

5 Read the text below. Explain the main choices of experimental designs that Sam could use, and discuss the strengths and weaknesses of these designs for the experiment that she is going to conduct. [9]

Sam is a psychology student at university. She is conducting a research study into the effect of music on memory for facts, and intends to give participants in her research a list of capital cities to memorise. In one condition of the experiment, the participants will do the task while listening to pop music, and in the second condition they will study the items in silence.

Sam is trying to decide whether to use separate groups of participants for the two conditions, and whether she should consider matching the participants in some way.

Non-experimental Methods

1 What term means data in the form of numbers? [1]

2 Explain the difference between primary and secondary data. [2]

3 Name **one** non-experimental research method which involves asking questions about people's thoughts and behaviour. [1]

4 Which of the following is a non-experimental research method usually conducted on a single participant? Shade **one** box only. [1]

A Case study ⭕   B Laboratory experiment ⭕

C Questionnaire ⭕   D Observation ⭕

Research

5 Give a strength and a weakness of the case study method. [2]

6 Briefly explain how an observation study is conducted. Explain some of the problems with this method of research, and how they might be overcome. [8]

Correlation and Data Handling

1 What term is used for the statistic which involves finding the most common score from a set of data? [1]

2 What type of correlation is shown in this graph? [1]

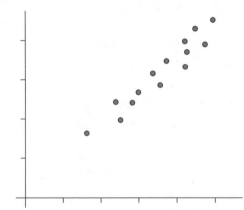

3 Can a strong correlation allow a researcher to conclude that one co-variable has an effect on the other? Explain why or why not. [2]

4 Here are some class scores on a language test. Calculate the mean, median and range. [3]

| 12 14 18 18 19 24 27 29 31 |

5 The following data show two groups' scores on a memory test out of a maximum of 20. The participants in condition 2 used a visualisation technique to help them memorise the information.

Condition 1: 8, 10, 11, 11, 11, 12, 13, 15
Condition 2: 4, 7, 9, 12, 15, 18, 19, 20

   a) For each condition, what was the mean score? [2]

   b) Convert the mean scores to percentages. [2]

   c) Condition 2 has a higher mean and a higher range. What does this suggest? [2]

   d) Sketch a suitable graph to show the mean scores. [2]

Social Influence

Where space is not provided, write your answers on a separate piece of paper.

Conformity

1 Would people always give the wrong answer to a question if the majority also gave the wrong answer? [1]

2 What is meant by the term 'normative conformity'? [2]

3 Which of the following is **not** a situational factor affecting conformity? Shade **one** box only. [1]

A Anonymity ⃝

B Task difficulty ⃝

C Gender ⃝

D The size of the majority ⃝

4 a) In the study conducted by Asch, what percentage of participants gave the wrong answer at least once? Shade **one** box only. [1]

A 85% ⃝

B 75% ⃝

C 65% ⃝

D 55% ⃝

b) Why can't we be sure that the behaviour displayed in the Asch study is typical of real life? [2]

c) Why might you claim that the Asch study was unethical? [2]

5 a) In the Asch study, what happened when participants were allowed to give their answers in private? [1]

b) What happened when the task became more difficult or the answer more ambiguous? [1]

Social Influence

Obedience

1 Which of the following statements is false? Shade **one** box only. [1]

A People are more likely to inflict harm on someone when given an instruction by an authority figure if they can't see the person they are harming. ◯

B People are more likely to inflict harm on someone if a person wearing a white lab coat gives the instruction. ◯

C People are more likely to inflict harm on someone if the person giving the instruction is dressed casually. ◯

D People are more likely to inflict harm on someone if the instruction is given in a prestigious location, such as a university. ◯

2 **a)** Describe a person in an 'agentic state'. [2]

b) What is the alternative to an agentic state? [1]

3 What is meant by 'dispositional factors'? [1]

4 According to Adorno, what kind of personality can lead to higher levels of obedience? [1]

5 What type of parents are more likely to raise children with authoritarian personalities? [1]

6 Elms and Milgram (1966) found a strong correlation between levels of obedience and authoritarian personality type. Does this mean that an authoritarian personality causes higher levels of obedience? Give reasons for your answer. [3]

7 Why might the F-scale be unreliable? [1]

Social Influence

Prosocial and Antisocial Behaviour

1. People are more likely to help in an emergency if there are fewer people present because they feel more responsible.

   a) What term do psychologists use for this behaviour? [1]

   b) When are people less likely to help? [2]

   c) How might 'expertise' make someone more likely to help? [2]

2. In what kind of situation might someone display pluralistic ignorance? [1]

3. Piliavin *et al*. (1969) investigated bystander behaviour in the Subway Samaritan study.

   a) In the study, who were people most likely to help? [1]

   b) Who were people least likely to help? [1]

4. Aggression can be reduced in public places by installing CCTV cameras. How does installing the cameras help? [2]

5. When people are in a crowd they often act more aggressively, due to a loss of personal identity. What is this behaviour called? [1]

6. In what situation might deindividuation lead to prosocial behaviour? [1]

Language, Thought and Communication

Where space is not provided, write your answers on a separate piece of paper.

The Possible Relationship Between Language and Thought

1 a) Who claimed that language determines thought?   [1]

  b) What did he believe about human development?   [1]

2 Complete the sentences below.   [2]

The strong version of the Sapir-Whorf hypothesis states that language _____

thought. The weak version states that language _____ thought.

3 a) Impaired cognitive development is often associated with impaired language development.
     How does this support Piaget's theory?   [2]

_____

_____

  b) Some children have learning difficulties but normal language development. Why does
      this not support Piaget's theory?   [2]

_____

_____

4 According to the Sapir-Whorf hypothesis, what do differences in language determine?   [1]

_____

5 Why might some Native American tribes have difficulty distinguishing between different colours?   [2]

_____

_____

6 How do studies into Native American tribes support the Sapir-Whorf hypothesis?   [1]

_____

Language, Thought and Communication

Differences Between Human and Animal Communication

1 How might non-human animals (such as birds) communicate their superiority over other animals of their own species? [2]

2 Name **two** territorial behaviours. [2]

3 What signals do magpies and rabbits use to communicate a threat from a predator? [2]

Magpie: ....

Rabbit: ....

4 a) Who first translated the movements of the waggle dance? [1]

....

b) Describe the **six** stages of the waggle dance. [6]

....

....

....

....

....

....

....

5 What are symbols in relation to human communication? [4]

....

....

....

....

6 a) What does human communication use that animal communication does not? [3]

b) With reference to **a)**, what does this allow humans to do that animals cannot? [2]

Language, Thought and Communication

Non-verbal Communication

1 Verbal communication is a type of communication that uses words. List **three** ways these words can be communicated. [3]

2 What is the main difference between verbal and non-verbal communication? [1]

3 a) You are having a conversation with a friend and notice that they often break eye contact. Suggest one reason why they might do this. [1]

   b) What information does eye contact provide for the speaker? [1]

   c) How has eye contact been linked with emotional intimacy? [1]

4 In the table below, describe what each term means. [6]

Term	Description
Open posture	
Closed posture	

5 Describe postural echo. [1]

6 What factors affect personal space? [3]

Language, Thought and Communication

Explanations of Non-verbal Behaviour

1 What is the difference between nature explanations of non-verbal behaviour and nurture explanations of non-verbal behaviour? [2]

2 According to Darwin, why does non-verbal behaviour develop? [1]

3 What is meant by the phrase "non-verbal behaviour is universal"? [2]

4 What can studying children who are blind from birth tell us about facial expressions? [2]

5 Name **two** non-verbal behaviours that could be learned by observing people within a specific culture. [2]

6 **a)** The results of Yuki *et al.*'s 2007 study indicated that non-verbal behaviour is innate. Is this statement true or false? [1]

b) Name **two** weaknesses of Yuki's study. [2]

Brain and Neuropsychology

Where space is not provided, write your answers on a separate piece of paper.

The Structure and Function of the Brain and Nervous System

1 The spinal cord is part of the nervous system. What is the function of the spinal cord? [1]

2 The peripheral nervous system has **two** divisions. **One** division is the somatic system. What is the other? [1]

3 The somatic system consists of which **two** types of neuron? [2]

4 **a)** Which part of the nervous system is most associated with the triggering of the fight or flight response? [1]

b) The fight or flight response helps a person react more quickly than normal so that the body is able to tackle a threat. In what **two** ways might the body react? [2]

c) Name the bodily changes that occur during the fight or flight response. [6]

5 According to the James-Lange theory, why would a person feel sad? [1]

Neuron Structure and Function

1 In the table below, note which type of neuron is being described: relay, sensory or motor. [3]

Function	Type of neuron
A This type of neuron tells the rest of the brain about the external and internal environment by processing information taken from one of the other five senses.	
B This type of neuron carries messages from one part of the central nervous system to another. They connect motor and sensory neurons.	
C This type of neuron carries an electrical signal to a muscle, which will cause the muscle to either contract or relax.	

Brain and Neuropsychology

2 a) Name the mechanism by which Hebbian learning occurs. [1]

   b) What does this mechanism result in? [2]

3 What is meant by 'synaptic transmission'? [1]

4 Dopamine is **one** type of neurotransmitter. Name **one** other. [1]

Localisation of Function in the Brain

1 What is the frontal lobe responsible for? Give **three** examples. [4]

2 Name **two** types of sensory information processed by the parietal lobe. [2]

3 Which brain structure is responsible for processing visual information? [1]

4 In the table below, write down which area of the brain is being described: somatosensory, motor or auditory. [3]

Definition	Area of brain
A Responsible for movement; sends messages to the muscles via the brain stem and spinal cord.	
B Concerned with the sensation of the body.	
C Receives information from both ears via two pathways that transmit information about what the sound is and its location.	

5 a) What did Penfield discover? [1]

   b) How did Penfield represent these findings? [1]

Brain and Neuropsychology

Brain and Neuropsychology

1. *The study of how the structure and function of the brain relates to behaviour and cognition.* What is this statement describing? [1]

2. a) Why is it useful for a person to be conscious while being scanned? [2]

   b) Name **three** scanning techniques. [3]

3. Why were Tulving's participants asked to retrieve **two** different types of memory? [1]

4. a) Damage to the brain can result in deficits in behaviour. What else can be affected? [1]

   b) What might non-behavioural deficits result in? [2]

Psychological Problems

Where space is not provided, write your answers on a separate piece of paper.

An Introduction to Mental Health

1 Mental health problems can be defined as the inability to function properly. What type of activities might be affected? [2]

2 Name **three** factors that represent ideal mental health. [3]

3 Name **two** examples of social norms. [2]

4 a) Suggest **one** reason for increased loneliness in modern society. [1]

    b) Name another factor that might affect mental health. [1]

5 Why have mental health charities and support groups targeted men? [1]

Effects of Mental Health Problems on Individuals and Society

1 How can mental health problems:

    a) lead to a change in social life for couples? Give a specific example. [2]

    b) affect day-to-day living? [1]

    c) affect physical wellbeing? [2]

2 Name **one** profession that might be placed under greater strain due to the rise in mental health problems. [1]

3 Some mental health conditions can lead to people breaking the law. Give **one** example. [1]

4 What impact can poor mental health have on businesses? [1]

Psychological Problems

Characteristics of Clinical Depression

1 Define unipolar depression. [1]

2 What distinguishes depression from sadness? [1]

3 Describe a person with mania. [5]

4 Why might it appear that depression is more prevalent in women? [1]

5 a) Name **two** main behaviours that must be present for a diagnosis of unipolar depression. [2]

   b) Name **three** associated behaviours of depression. [3]

Theories of Depression and Interventions

1 Biological explanations of depression indicate that it is caused by internal factors, including brain chemicals and genes.

   a) Using your knowledge of these factors, explain how serotonin and a mutated gene have been associated with depression.

      i) Serotonin [1]

      ii) Mutated gene [2]

   b) Explain **one** weakness of biological explanations of depression. [2]

2 How do schemas affect depression? [2]

3 Attribution theory suggests that people with depression attribute the causes of events to **three** specific explanations. **Two** of these are global and internal. What is the **third**? [1]

4 How do tricyclic antidepressants differ from SSRIs? [2]

5 What is the difference between drug therapy and psychotherapy (e.g. CBT)? [2]

6 What did Wiles (2013) find was the best treatment for people who had not responded well to antidepressants? [1]

Psychological Problems

Characteristics of Addiction

1 Substance abuse is when a person takes a substance to excess. How does this differ from substance addiction? [2]

2 **a)** A diagnosis of addiction is made if three or more particular symptoms have appeared together for how long? [1]

b) Name the **three** symptoms associated with addiction. [3]

3 Name **one** non-substance addiction. [1]

4 According to Walters, the behavioural pattern of addiction includes progression and perceived loss of control. Name **two** other factors. [2]

5 What is meant by the term relapse? [1]

Theories of Addiction and Interventions

1 What types of study have been used to investigate the heritability of addictive behaviours? [2]

2 **a)** What did Kaij study? [2]

b) What fraction of deceased alcoholics were found to have the A1 variant of the DRD2 gene? [1]

3 Why might associating with people who smoke increase the chances of someone smoking? [1]

4 **a)** Describe how aversion therapy could help someone to give up smoking. [4]

b) Apart from taking a drug, name one technique that could be used in aversion therapy. [1]

5 What is the first step of the 12-step program of personal recovery? [1]

Collins

GCSE Psychology
Paper 1: Cognition and Behaviour

Time allowed: 1 hour 45 minutes

The maximum mark for this paper is 100

Materials

For this paper you may have:

- a calculator.

Instructions

- Use black ink or black ball-point pen.
- Answer **all** questions. You must answer the questions in the spaces provided.
- Do all rough work in this book.

Information

- The marks for questions are shown in brackets.
- Questions should be answered in continuous prose. You will be assessed on your ability to:
  - use good English
  - organise information clearly
  - use specialist vocabulary where appropriate.

Name: _____

Section A
Memory

Answer **all** questions in the spaces provided.

---

0 1 Which **one** of these is the type of long-term memory involved in remembering the events of a family holiday? Shade **one** box only. **[1 mark]**

A Semantic memory ◯

B Procedural memory ◯

C Sensory memory ◯

D Episodic memory ◯

0 2 Which **one** of these is the first stage of the multi-store model of memory? Shade **one** box only. **[1 mark]**

A Sensory memory ◯

B Visual cortex ◯

C Encoding ◯

D Sampling ◯

0 3 Which **one** of these is **not** one of the ways in which information was distorted in Bartlett's War of the Ghosts study? Shade **one** box only. **[1 mark]**

A Addition ◯

B Subtraction ◯

C Preservation of detached detail ◯

D Hallucinations ◯

Practice Exam Paper 1

Read the item and then answer the questions that follow.

> Amina is listening to her French teacher. She listens to a new phrase, followed by her teacher's explanation of what it means. However, when Amina tries to write down the phrase, she realises that she has already forgotten it.
>
> She asks the teacher to repeat the phrase, and even though she still doesn't entirely understand it, she is able to write it down in her notes.

0 4 · 1 Explain the duration and encoding of short-term memory (STM). Refer to Amina's French lesson in your answer. **[4 marks]**

_____

_____

_____

_____

_____

0 4 · 2 The capacity of STM may be a normally distributed variable. Explain what this means. **[3 marks]**

_____

_____

_____

_____

_____

Figure 1 shows a model of how memory stores connect.

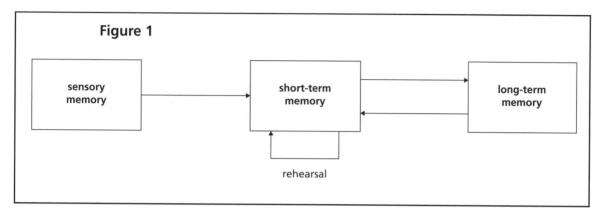

Figure 1

0 5 . 1 Identify the researchers who are known for their work on this model. **[1 mark]**

....

....

0 5 . 2 According to this model, how does information move from one memory store to another? **[6 marks]**

....

....

....

....

....

....

....

....

0 5 · 3 Explain the strengths and weaknesses of this model of memory. You may refer to supporting research evidence. **[8 marks]**

Section B
Perception

Answer **all** questions in the spaces provided.

---

0 6 What is the difference between sensation and perception?   **[2 marks]**

....

....

0 7 Which illusion is usually shown as a double-ended arrow? Shade **one** box only. **[1 mark]**

A Müller-Lyer   ◯

B Ames Room   ◯

C Ponzo   ◯

D Rubin's vase   ◯

0 8 Which **one** of these is a binocular depth cue? Shade **one** box only.   **[1 mark]**

A Occlusion   ◯

B Relative size   ◯

C Retinal disparity   ◯

D Kanizsa triangle   ◯

Figure 2 is used as a road sign in the USA. It shows the state of Idaho, but some people think that it also looks like a face.

Figure 2

IDAHO

3

| 0 | 9 | Explain what is meant by an ambiguous figure, giving at least one further example. [3 marks]

....

....

....

....

Look at **Figure 3**.

Figure 3

| 1 | 0 | Identify and explain two monocular depth cues that would help to perceive the distance of objects in the scene.

[6 marks]

Depth cue 1: ....

....

....

Depth cue 2: ....

....

....

Read the item and then answer the questions that follow.

Duncan is 14. He is waiting for his parents to get home and make an evening meal. He thinks he hears the doorbell but when he goes to check, he finds that there is nobody there. He is feeling hungry and considers eating some crisps, even though he doesn't usually like them.

Practice Exam Paper 1

1 1 . 1 Explain why perception is sometimes inaccurate, referring to Duncan. **[4 marks]**

....

....

....

....

....

1 1 . 2 Describe and evaluate a research study that showed the role of the perceptual set.
[8 marks]

....

....

....

....

....

....

....

....

....

....

Section C
Development

Answer **all** questions in the spaces provided.

---

1 2 · 1 Which of the following means the way that gene expression is influenced by the environment? Shade **one** box only. **[1 mark]**

A Nurture ◯

B Epigenetics ◯

C Mindset ◯

D Egocentrism ◯

1 2 · 2 Which of the following researchers devised the theory of growth and fixed mindsets? Shade **one** box only. **[1 mark]**

A Bruner ◯

B Gibson ◯

C Willingham ◯

D Dweck ◯

Look at **Figure 4** and answer the questions that follow.

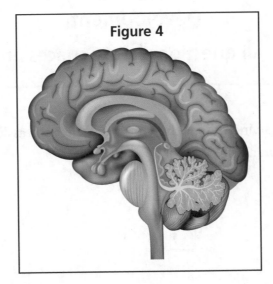

Figure 4

| 1 | 3 | · | 1 | Identify **two** areas of the human brain and state their function. Label the areas on the image. **[4 marks]**

Area 1: ....

Area 2: ....

| 1 | 3 | · | 2 | Explain the development of the human brain **before** birth. **[3 marks]**

....

....

....

....

| 1 | 3 | · | 3 | Explain the development of the human brain **after** birth. **[3 marks]**

....

....

....

1 4 Explain the criticisms of the 'learning styles' theory in education. **[3 marks]**

Figure 5 shows the three mountains experiment.

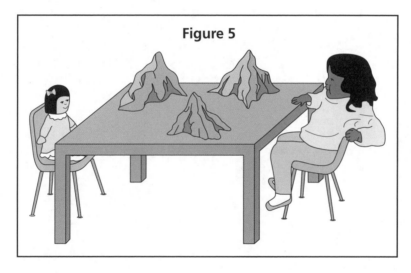

Figure 5

1 5 · **1** Explain how the three mountains experiment was conducted. **[4 marks]**

1 5 . 2 Discuss what the three mountains experiment shows about a child's development. You could mention other research studies. **[6 marks]**

Section D
Research Methods

Answer **all** questions in the spaces provided.

Read the item and then answer the questions that follow.

A researcher conducts a case study into a 25-year-old participant, a man who has suffered brain damage in an accident. The man is given an fMRI brain scan to assess his injury. He is then interviewed by the researcher, and is given a verbal test and an IQ test. His school records are accessed, including IQ tests sat during his teenage years. The participant's diaries are also studied in order to compare his use of language before and after his accident.

1 6 · 1 Identify **two** types of data which were used by the researcher in this study. For each, describe what type of data it is. **[4 marks]**

Example 1:

Example 2:

1 6 · 2 Explain **one** ethical issue that the researcher must take into account when carrying out this case study. **[2 marks]**

Read the item and then answer the questions that follow.

> A team of researchers is studying the effect of two revision strategies (the use of visual images and the use of examples) on students' memory for facts.
>
> In a lab experiment, they randomly allocate each of their student volunteers to one of three conditions:
>
> – a visual images condition
>
> – an examples condition
>
> – a control condition.
>
> Ten short factual paragraphs are given to every participant in all three conditions. Participants in the 'visual images' condition are given an accompanying picture that matches the passage. Participants in the 'examples' condition are given a relevant real-world example at the end of the paragraph. Participants in the control condition are not given any additional information.

1 7 · 1 Which experimental design is used in the experiment above?　　　　**[1 mark]**

....

1 7 · 2 Explain the use of the following aspects of research methods.　　　　**[4 marks]**

Random allocation: ....

....

A control condition: ....

....

1 7 · 3 Explain why researchers need to maintain experimental control. Identify **one** example of this from the item. **[3 marks]**

1 7 · 4 Name a graph which could be used to display the results from this experiment, and sketch how it might look. **[3 marks]**

Read the item and then answer the questions that follow.

A researcher is studying the relationship between stress and the effectiveness of exam revision. He contacts a local maths teacher, and the teacher agrees to let her A-Level class take part in the study. The students who give consent to take part are asked to fill in a stress questionnaire. The researcher then gives them a realistic maths revision task, and one week later he tests their skill at answering maths problems, giving each student a percentage score. In total, 19 students take part.

Figure 6

1 8 . 1 Identify the **two** co-variables in this study.   [2 marks]

....

....

1 8 · 2 The researcher finds a negative correlation between how highly stressed a pupil is and how well they score on the maths task. Sketch what this may look like below.

[2 marks]

1 8 · 3 Which of the following sampling methods did the researcher use?
Shade **one** box only.

[1 mark]

A Random sampling ◯

B Opportunity sampling ◯

C Systematic sampling ◯

D Stratified sampling ◯

1 8 · 4 Identify **one** way in which the researcher could have improved the sample of participants selected for the study. **[1 mark]**

....

1 8 · 5 On the basis of this study alone, why can't the researcher conclude that stress causes revision to be less effective? **[2 marks]**

....

....

....

Collins

GCSE Psychology
Paper 2: Social Context and Behaviour

Time allowed: 1 hour 45 minutes

The maximum mark for this paper is 100

Materials

For this paper you may have:

- a calculator.

Instructions

- Use black ink or black ball-point pen.
- Answer all questions. You must answer the questions in the spaces provided.
- Do all rough work in this book.

Information

- The marks for questions are shown in brackets.
- Questions should be answered in continuous prose. You will be assessed on your ability to:
  - use good English
  - organise information clearly
  - use specialist vocabulary where appropriate.

Name:

Practice Exam Paper 2

Section A
Social Influence

Answer **all** questions in the spaces provided.

---

0 1 Grace is shopping with two of her friends when they decide to have lunch. Both of Grace's friends choose salads. When Grace sees this, she also chooses a salad.

Which one of the following best describes Grace's behaviour? Shade **one** box only. **[1 mark]**

A Bystander intervention ◯

B Conformity ◯

C Deindividuation ◯

D Obedience ◯

Read the item and then answer the questions that follow.

David is talking to Raj and tells him that the previous day he saw a lady collapse in the street.

"How awful," responds Raj. "Did you help her?"

---

0 2 · 1 Outline what is meant by bystander behaviour. **[1 mark]**

....

0 2 · 2 Identify **three** factors that could influence bystander behaviour in this type of situation. **[3 marks]**

....

....

....

0 3 · 1 In Asch's study into conformity, what percentage of participants conformed at least once? **[1 mark]**

....

0 3 · 2 How would you conduct a study into conformity?
In your answer, explain how you would select the participants for the study and **one** feature of the task that participants would be required to do. **[3 marks]**

....

....

....

....

....

Practice Exam Paper 2

Read the item and then answer the questions that follow.

In a research study into obedience, an actor told people to pick up litter in a local park. In Condition A, the actor wore a uniform and in Condition B the actor wore casual clothes. The actor told 50 people to pick up litter in each condition and the results for each were recorded.

Table 1: The number of people who picked up or refused to pick up litter

	Condition A	Condition B
Picked up litter	32	20
Did not pick up litter	18	30

0 4 · 1 In Condition B, 40% of people picked up litter. Calculate the percentage of people who picked up litter in Condition A. **[1 mark]**

0 4 · 2 Use your knowledge of psychology to explain why the level of obedience was different between Condition A and Condition B. **[2 marks]**

0 4 · 3 Explain **two** ways in which this obedience study can be evaluated. **[4 marks]**

0 5 Describe and evaluate **one** way in which deindividuation has been investigated.

You must include the method used, results obtained and conclusion drawn. **[9 marks]**

Section B
Language, Thought and Communication
Answer **all** questions in the spaces provided.

Read the item and then answer the question that follows.

> Katie and Ria are playing hockey. Katie has possession of the ball when Ria raises her hand to indicate that she is free and shouts "Pass!" to Katie. Katie passes the ball to Ria, who then hits it into the back of the goal. Katie shouts "Yes!", while Ria jumps up and down with excitement.

0 6 From the extract above, identify **two** examples of verbal behaviour and **two** examples of non-verbal behaviour.
[4 marks]

Verbal behaviour	Non-verbal behaviour

0 7 Outline **one** difference in animal and human communication. Include an example.
[3 marks]

0 8 Briefly describe Piaget's theory that language depends on thought. **[3 marks]**

....

....

....

....

....

....

0 9 Evaluate Yuki *et al*'s (2007) study of emoticons. **[6 marks]**

....

....

....

....

....

....

....

....

....

Practice Exam Paper 2

Read the item and then answer the questions that follow.

> Researchers observed the behaviour of 20 three-month-old babies. Of these 20 babies, 10 had been blind since birth and 10 were sighted. The researchers observed the number of times each baby smiled over a one-hour period. They recorded the results in the table below.
>
> | | Blind babies | Sighted babies |
> |---|---|---|
> | Number of smiles | 33 | 40 |

1 0 · 1 What does innate mean? **[1 mark]**

1 0 · 2 Explain how the results in the table support the suggestion that non-verbal behaviour is innate. **[6 marks]**

1 0 . 3 Which **one** of the following best describes the target population of this study?
Shade **one** box only.

[1 mark]

A Smiling babies ◯

B Babies ◯

C Blind and sighted babies ◯

D Babies who were three months old ◯

1 0 . 4 What was the research method used in this study?

[1 mark]

....

Practice Exam Paper 2

Section C
Brain and Neuropsychology

Answer **all** questions in the spaces provided.

---

1 1 Which **one** of these statements about the nervous system is correct? Shade **one** box only. **[1 mark]**

A The autonomic nervous system is responsible for thinking. ○

B The central nervous system is part of the peripheral nervous system. ○

C The peripheral nervous system consists only of relay neurons. ○

D The somatic nervous system consists of sensory and motor neurons. ○

1 2 Briefly describe the function of relay neurons. **[2 marks]**

....

....

1 3 Explain the processes involved in the fight or flight response. You must include the role of the hypothalamus, the release of adrenaline and bodily changes. **[6 marks]**

....

....

....

....

....

....

1 4 · 1 For each of the definitions in the table below, shade **one** box to identify the correct structure of the brain. **[3 marks]**

Definition	Occipital	Parietal	Temporal
A Responsible for processing auditory information from the ears (hearing)	○	○	○
B Responsible for processing sensory information that is associated with taste, temperature and touch.	○	○	○
C Responsible for processing visual information from the eyes	○	○	○

1 4 · 2 For each of the definitions in the table below, shade **one** box to identify the correct area of the brain. **[2 marks]**

Definition	Motor	Somatosensory	Auditory
A The area of the brain concerned with the perception of touch and temperature	○	○	○
B The area of the brain concerned with the processing of sound	○	○	○

1 4 · 3 What is meant by localisation of function? **[2 marks]**

Practice Exam Paper 2

1 5 Explain how modern scanning techniques have increased our understanding of the relationship between brain and behaviour. **[6 marks]**

....

....

....

....

....

....

....

....

....

....

1 6 Which **one** of these statements about neurons is correct? Shade **one** box only. **[1 mark]**

A Motor neurons carry information to the spinal cord. ⃝

B Relay neurons carry information from motor neurons. ⃝

C Sensory neurons always have longer axons than motor neurons. ⃝

D Sensory neurons carry information to the brain. ⃝

1 7 Briefly describe the function of a motor neuron. **[2 marks]**

....

....

Section D
Psychological Problems

Answer **all** questions in the spaces provided.

___

| 1 | 8 | Name **two** symptoms often associated with people who are diagnosed with unipolar depression. **[2 marks]**

___

___

| 1 | 9 | Bipolar depression differs from unipolar depression in that it includes episodes of mania. Explain what is meant by mania and describe how a person with bipolar depression might behave. **[3 marks]**

___

___

___

Read the item and then answer the question that follows.

> Lucy has been diagnosed with an addiction to alcohol. Her father and older brother have also been given the same diagnosis. Lucy has tried to cut down on her drinking but when she is with her friends they encourage her to drink more.

| 2 | 0 | Which **one** of these statements is false? Shade **one** box only. **[1 mark]**

    A An intervention that could help Lucy is aversion therapy. ◯

    B Lucy might have a genetic vulnerability to addiction. ◯

    C One biological explanation for Lucy's addiction could be peer pressure. ◯

Read the item and then answer the questions that follow.

Researchers were interested in finding out about the effectiveness of cognitive behavioural therapy (CBT) for unipolar depression, and whether its effectiveness could be improved if combined with medication.

They recruited participants by putting up posters at doctors' surgeries asking for volunteers who had received either medication only, or a combination of medication and CBT. Ten participants were chosen from each group.

Participants completed a questionnaire asking them to rate the effectiveness of the treatment they had received. A response of 0 indicated that the treatment was of no use at all, and a response of 10 indicated that it was highly successful. Results are shown in the table.

Participant	Medication	Participant	Medication and CBT
1	3	11	10
2	6	12	5
3	5	13	7
4	4	14	8
5	6	15	8
6	8	16	9
7	9	17	6
8	4	18	8
9	7	19	10
10	8	20	9

2 1 . 1 Calculate the mean rating for the effectiveness of both groups.　　　**[4 marks]**

....

....

2 1 . 2 Suggest **one** strength and **one** weakness of using the mean.　　　**[2 marks]**

....

....

2 1 · 3 Identify the sampling method used in the study. **[1 mark]**

_____

2 1 · 4 Explain **one** strength and **one** weakness of this sampling method for the study described. **[4 marks]**

_____

_____

_____

_____

2 1 · 5 Suggest a different sampling method the researchers could have used to obtain a more representative sample. Include **one** weakness. **[2 marks]**

_____

_____

_____

_____

2 1 · 6 What do the results of this study suggest about the effectiveness of using CBT and medication to treat unipolar depression? **[2 marks]**

....

....

....

....

2 2 Describe **one** study into the heritability of addiction. **[4 marks]**

....

....

....

....

....

....

Notes

Notes

Notes

Notes

Answers

Structures of Memory

1. Something which helps a memory to be retrieved from LTM, [1] such as the first letter of a word or name. [1]
2. A
3. Ability to encode new long-term memories can be badly harmed. [1] Short-term/working memory potentially damaged by frontal lobe injury. [1] Long-term memory is harmed by damage to the hippocampus or to the cerebral cortex as a whole. [1] Could further explain specifics of one or more case study, e.g. in the case of HM, one type of LTM (procedural) was intact, and it was therefore only semantic/episodic long-term memories that could not be encoded. [1]
4. **From top to bottom**: false, true, true, false
5. a) frontal lobe of the cerebral cortex
   b) the hippocampus
6. **Episodic**: memory for life events; [1] **semantic**: memory for word meanings and facts; [1] **procedural**: memory for skills [1]
7. Must be actual uses of the memory stores that accurately reflect their features. STM: very brief (half a minute, or a little more if maintenance rehearsal is used) and limited in capacity; LTM: permanent and unlimited. Any appropriate examples, such as: STM – holding a phone number for a few seconds; [1] LTM – remembering the names of characters from a TV show. [1] Remembering something for hours or overnight, such as exam cramming, is **not** an example of STM.

Memory as an Active Process

1. D
2. A, B, C, D should be ticked.
3. **Recognition**: seeing an item and matching it to what is in memory; [2] **cued recall**: being supplied with a cue such as the first letter of a word, and then retrieving the item; [2] **free recall**: retrieval without a cue or anything else to help the process – more difficult [2]
4. A: encoding; B: retrieval; C: storage; D: retrieval
5. Computer, active, effort, distorted

The Multi-Store Model of Memory 1 and 2

1. C
2. A
3. Displacement
4. a) A very brief store with a large capacity

b) Any appropriate example, such as: a person is not paying attention to a speaker but a small amount of information enters and remains in their sensory store for up to two seconds, allowing them to direct their attention to it afterwards, e.g. when a student's name is called in the classroom. [2] Answer should correctly indicate sensory store rather than STM/LTM by showing that information fades without attention/is only taken into memory if a person pays attention to it **or** by referring to specific sensory stores. [1]

5. Memory processes: primacy and recency, in her accuracy with the start and end of the word list, and the role of attention. [3] Without paying attention, items will not be successfully transferred from her sensory memory to her short-term memory. [1] Important to take breaks and to use self-testing and spacing to good effect. [1].

6. Answer should identify and explain at least two strengths and two weaknesses. [2 marks for each, if fully explained] Strengths: any two from: clarity of the model; supporting evidence from the serial position curve; limited STM and forgetting via displacement; biological evidence showing separate STM and LTM. **Weaknesses: any two from**: doesn't account for visual encoding in either STM or LTM; concept of rehearsal is over-simplistic as it is not clearly tied to LTM encoding; the model doesn't show the different types of LTM.

Factors Affecting Memory

1. **Any one from**: leading question after an event; false information; assumptions based on a schema
2. Bartlett, culture, stories
3. a) Effort after meaning (also accept redintegration)
   b) Theory of reconstructive memory
4. Answer should include factors and refer to schemas/reconstructive memory/false memories. For example: it is harder to recall events in a different physical context (in class versus on holiday), and Liam may have been in a different mood in school, making it harder. [1] The story task would cause Liam to use reconstructive memory, filling any gaps with schema knowledge about what typically happens on a holiday, [1] leading to Liam and his sister having different memories of the events. [1] It is also possible that one or the other of them has generated a false memory, or that

leading questions have distorted their memories. [1]
5. Any appropriate answers such as the following [2 points for each factor]:
   - Loftus's research into leading questions – wording of a question can affect later memory and even cause a false memory.
   - The War of Ghosts research showed that people's cultural schemas affect how they remember and recount a story, with different wording used/distortions based on how well they understand it.
   - Memory is an active process and can involve reconstruction. Words can act as cues to trigger memories, but people tend to fill the gaps based on assumptions/schemas.
   - Memory is linked to various factors such as state and context. When people hear words, names or phrases out of context, they will be harder to remember.
   - STM encodes acoustically and LTM uses semantic encoding, so people can recall precise wording in the short term but in the long term they tend to remember gist/meaning.

Perception and Sensation

1. The initial processing of external cues such as light and sound by specialist receptor cells in the body.
2. A
3. Colour constancies: despite the colour of the car, little or no red light would be reaching the retina due to the lighting conditions, but the brain makes allowances for this. [1] Shape constancy: he is seeing the car from an angle (and perhaps partly obscured by other cars) as he looks up the street but he is still able to perceive it normally. [1] Size constancy: the brain uses its stored knowledge of car size, so even though the car is far away he can still perceive it accurately – it doesn't look smaller than usual. [1]
4. During sensation, a visual image of the world hits the retina upside down, [1] but the brain is able to make allowances for this and therefore people perceive the world the right way up. [1]
5. Answers will vary depending on the example. One possibility: the need to accurately judge depth and distance when catching a ball, or jumping over a hurdle, or when cycling, vaulting, etc. [1 for description of context]. Could distinguish between sensation and perception, or describe the biological process involved in transmitting information to the brain

via receptor cells. **[1]** The role of one or more visual constancies could be considered, such as recognising the colour of a sport team's strip under artificial lighting such as a floodlit football match; the important role of assumptions and expectations could also be mentioned. **[1 per concept accurately linked to the example]**

Visual Cues and Depth Perception

1. Monocular depth cues; binocular depth cues
2. Depth perception is essential for survival. **[1]** Without the ability to judge depth and distance the animal would be unable to jump safely and could hurt itself, or fall and die. **[1]**
3. B
4. D
5. a) A cue where the muscles that move the eyes have to rotate inwards slightly, **[1]** more so when objects are closer. **[1]**
   b) Any appropriate example, e.g. judging the distance of a ball which is thrown towards you, picking up an object, swatting a fly, etc. **[1]** with a description of how eyes will have to converge more as an object gets closer. **[1]**

Illusions

1. A stimulus that causes a person to see something different from what is actually there, or where there are two or more possible interpretations of the same image, or a much-studied group of stimuli which are either ambiguous or cause people to perceive things that are not actually there. **[1] Any two appropriate examples**, e.g. Ponzo, Müller-Lyer, Necker cube, Rubin's vase, Ames Room, Kanizsa triangle, etc. **[2]**
2. Answer should look like this:

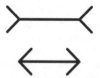

3. depth, illusion, perspective
4. **Ambiguity**: Necker cube (or Leeper's lady); **Fiction**: Kanizsa triangle; **Depth cues**: Ponzo
5. a) Objects tend to be perceived as groups/wholes.
   b) The Kanizsa triangle
6. The Ames Room
7. The illusion can be seen as a misinterpreted depth cue. **[1]** The outward-pointing arrow is perceived as a corner which is closer to the viewer, and the mind automatically adjusts. **[1]** Similarly, the inward-pointing arrow is seen as a corner that is more distant. **[1]** Cultural evidence – people in the San hunter-gatherer society didn't perceive the illusion in

the same way as Western participants (Gregory research). **[1]**

Theories of Perception

1. Theories of Any appropriate answer, e.g. the brain building up a picture of the world using information from the senses **[1]** and interpreting them/combining them with information from memory. **[1]**
2. Bottom-up processing
3. **From top to bottom**: constructivist, direct, constructivist, direct
4. The constructivist theory states that perception is based to a large degree on expectations and experience rather than simply on sensation. **[1]** How people see the world is in part based on what they expect to see. **[1]** Inferences means working out what sensations mean based on past experience **[1]** – it is a form of problem solving which this theory believes to be necessary in order to perceive what the world is like. **[1]**
5. Answers should refer to the work of Gibson, bottom-up processing or the idea that perception is largely based on interpreting sensation as it occurs, including the concept of a single correct interpretation of sensations coming from the environment. **[1]** Evidence supporting the theory could include the idea of motion parallax (or optic flow), environmental affordances such as cues to depth, that all animals may be able to perceive the world in similar ways to humans, and research evidence such as the visual cliff. **[1 mark per point]** Arguments could also be made against the theory and/or for the opposing view, i.e. Gregory's constructivist theory, e.g. based on the role of experience and evidence from the perception of illusions such as the hollow face. **[up to 2 marks]**

Factors Affecting Perception

1. C
2. Any appropriate examples, e.g. hunger, fear
3. Perception, biased, expectations
4. a) The beliefs and behaviour of a particular group of people; **[1]** usually associated with specific areas or countries. **[1]**
   b) Thom and his hosts come from two different countries and therefore have different cultures. **[1]** This can cause them to see things like pictures differently. **[1]** Supporting research, e.g. Hudson (1962), shows how perception of depth cues in pictures depends on culture. **[1]** Role of schemas and expectations in the perceptual set, and how schemas are shaped by culture. **[1]** Culture linked to the role of expectations and experience – the constructivist theory of perception **[1]**; back this up with

relevant evidence into expectations, e.g. the hollow face illusion, Bruner and Minturn's study. **[1]**

Brain Development

1. How the mind and brain change across the lifespan, particularly during childhood, **or** the changes that cause an individual's personality and abilities to develop, and the factors that can harm this process.
2. D
3. **One mark for each correct label and one mark for each correct function** (a single word or phrase is sufficient). **Any four from A: brain stem**: autonomic functions such as breathing and heartbeat; **B: thalamus**: some sensory processing/relaying signals to the cerebral cortex; **C: cerebellum**: precise physical movement/coordinates actions; **D: cerebral cortex**: cognition/thinking/perception/memory processes; visual cortex (at the back of the cerebral cortex): visual processing.
4. In the very early stages of brain development, there are no true neurons; instead the brain is composed of stem cells. **[1]** These are cells that can develop/transform into any bodily cell. **[1]** By day 42 of a pregnancy, true neurons have begun to form from stem cells. Stem cells therefore only play a role in brain development during early pregnancy. **[1]**
5. Brain development continues right through to adolescence and beyond. **[1]** Complexity of neural connections is initially high/a newborn baby has a much more complex level of interconnections in their brain than those of an adult, with more axons **[1]** but pruning of connections allows the brain to attune to the environmental context. **[1]** Deprivation can harm development after birth, while a stimulating environment is helpful (could mention case of adopted orphans). **[1]** Plasticity could be mentioned – the brain is still able to change and develop when we are older due to the ability of neural connections to change **or** could also refer to the nature–nurture debate. **[1]**

Nature and Nurture

1. Experiences, upbringing, teachers
2. **Intelligence/nature side**: certain people are born with superior 'smart genes'. **[1] Intelligence/nurture side**: upbringing and education are important, with good teaching and supportive parenting leading to educational success. **[1] Personality/nature side**: personality is innate, with traits based on genes. **[1] Personality/**

nurture side: personality is based on life experiences, with a child's personality traits developing according to parenting/what happens to them during childhood. [1]

3. Each side is too extreme in its basic form, and both may be correct on different occasions (some psychological attributes might be largely genetic and others based on upbringing/culture). [1] Interaction should refer to epigenetics, i.e. the process where gene expression is modified by life experience. [1] If a certain environmental condition is present then the gene will be expressed, if not then it won't be. [1] Genetic influences on skills and personality could have an effect on later life experiences, and these could in turn affect development. [1]

4. B, C, E, F should be ticked.

5. Essential idea that personality and abilities are due to genetics rather than developmental environment should be made clear. [1] Could refer to the difficulty of drawing conclusions from twin studies – the very small samples/rare cases involving identical twins raised apart and the fact that sometimes their environment is still quite similar. [2] Could note that even identical twins do not share all psychological characteristics - they have their own personality traits, and the correspondence between their intelligence, mental health, etc. is not 100%, showing that the environment must play a role too. [2] It's also not simple to link a psychological factor such as a mental illness or someone's personality to a single gene, as abilities generally link to a mixture of genes, and can change over time. [1]

Piaget's Theories 1 and 2

1. a) 2 years old
   b) Object constancy (becomes aware that objects still exist even when they are out of sight)

2. **Failure to conserve**: [1] pre-operational children lack the ability to mentally reverse an operation and tend to focus on a particular aspect of a problem (e.g. height of water in a glass) while ignoring other aspects. [1] Examples include failure to conserve volume, number, etc. [1] This was shown in Piaget's famous conservation of liquid task (two glasses of different heights). [1] **Egocentrism also an acceptable answer:** [1] the tendency to think about things only from their own point of view. [1] Could give real-world examples and/or refer to the three mountains problem, showing how children in this stage make errors when asked what another person can see. [2]

3. C

4. Assimilation adds new information to an existing schema. [1]

Accommodation creates a new schema to allow for new information which can't be assimilated. [1] Hannah has a schema for house, in which one family lives in a single building. [1] She has not experienced flats, and therefore does not have a schema for them. When she moves to the city, at first she assimilates the blocks of flats into her house schema as 'tall houses'. [1] Soon she learns that a block of flats is not just a tall house, and she accommodates this information by creating a 'flat' schema. [1]

5. Could refer to the different needs of children in different stages. Very young children, in the sensorimotor stage, mainly need lots of objects to interact with. Children in the pre-operational stage roughly correspond to pre-school and early primary – these children are keen to experiment with objects in order to find out more about physical properties, and these years of education provide a lot of active play with water tables, sand tables, etc. They are also egocentric, so their ability to play social games is very limited. By the concrete operational stage, aged 8+, children already understand physical properties so they no longer play as much with physical objects, but can instead do logical work such as basic maths. This stage corresponds to primary/elementary school in many countries. Finally, at the formal operational stage, the children are able to cope with advanced logical processes and abstract concepts, and can learn things like algebra. This stage corresponds to secondary/high school in many countries. **[2 marks per stage – for full marks, an accurate factual point should be made about each of the four stages, and this should be linked to an educational application]**

6. Piaget's stage theory has been influential and is used in both childcare and education. [1] The three mountains problem and demonstrations of ability to/failure to conserve provide useful evidence for the theory. [1] However, McGarrigle and Donaldson's (1974) naughty teddy study shows that in the right circumstances young children can conserve number, so the stage theory may be flawed. [1] The work of Hughes (1975) suggests that children under the age of six are not as egocentric as previously thought. **[1, plus 1 mark for a description of either study's methodology]**

Education

1. Self-efficacy

2. a) People see intelligence and abilities as fixed and not open to improvement through practice and effort.

b) Growth mindset, [1] where abilities are seen as being changeable and dependent on effort, experience and learning. [1]

c) Any appropriate example, such as: "I am just naturally bad at art, I guess I was born that way." Any appropriate actions, e.g. giving up when they think they are failing; not trying to improve or take a class; sticking to easy tasks that they know they will succeed at rather than trying something challenging.

3. Maths, fixed, harder, mixture

4. a) growth b) fixed c) fixed d) fixed e) growth f) fixed

5. Three theorised 'learning styles' (visual, kinaesthetic and auditory) should be explained (could use examples). [3] Should note that this theory is widely used in education. [1] Evaluation should focus on the lack of evidence that using these learning styles has any impact on how well people learn. [1] In particular, material or instruction methods that use their supposed/preferred learning style don't seem to provide any advantage. [1] Could mention Willingham's criticisms, e.g. the idea that the type of instruction should be suited to the material rather than to the learner and that it is best to use dual coding/multiple sensory inputs, or other relevant evidence. [2]

6. a) Visualisers prefer to take information in visually; [1] and verbalisers prefer to take information in through words. [1] Kraemer et al. (2009) found increased brain activity linked to people's preferred way of learning (verbal or visual), [1] but neither group learned better when they used their preferred style, **or** different ways of learning may be just a matter of personal preference. [1]

b) Dual coding is taking in new information both verbally and visually. [1] It's important to combine different modalities, as this increases later memory for the material. [1]

Pages 167–170 **Research**

Sampling

1. Equal

2. Volunteer sampling/self-selecting sampling

3. Categories such as sex, age or education level are kept within set parameters – the researcher ensures that the sample has the same levels of these as the target population as a whole, for example a 50–50 split of males and females. [1] **Advantage**: this ensures representativeness of these characteristics, making it easier to generalise research findings to the target population. [1]

4. Opportunity, biased, conveniently
5. To select a random sample, a researcher will use a numbered list of everyone in the target population. [1] They will use a computer program to select random numbers from this list; [1] **also acceptable**: names from the population could be put in a hat and the required number of names pulled out. [1]
6. Asking passers-by is an opportunity sample, not a random sample. [1] Any appropriate explanations of bias, such as: some people might not be in school, some are more likely to be in the corridor while others are in class/in the school library, etc. People who take a particular school subject are more likely to be on a particular corridor (e.g. a science corridor). People who are missing class for various reasons are more likely to be in the corridor. Certain students are more likely to have a free period, e.g. older pupils with a lighter timetable. [2]

Variables and Hypotheses

1. a) independent
   b) dependent
2. C
3. A
4. a) Spaced (versus non-spaced) practice
   b) Skill at taking a penalty. [1] Any appropriate answer re how to measure: for example, by asking each player to take 10 penalties the following week (against the same goalkeeper) and calculating an average success rate. [1]
   c) Any appropriate answer, e.g.: If spacing is a more effective way to practise penalties, [1] then the spaced practice group will score more penalties on average than the non-spaced group. [1]
   d) A control group who didn't do any shooting practice would provide a useful baseline. [1] We can't know from the study whether either group benefited from the practice – they could both have done worse than they would have without the practice! [1]
5. Conditions
6. Any reasonable answer, e.g. IQ, score on reaction time tests, STM capacity, etc. [1] Any appropriate characteristic, e.g. mean/median/mode are all equal; bell-shaped curve of frequencies; symmetrical distribution. [1]

Design of Experiments 1 and 2

1. Right to withdraw
2. Participants need to give informed consent, which usually involves signing a consent form that gives them information about the nature of the study. [1] They then need to be briefed, so that they understand what

is going to happen and how long it will take. [1] Steps must be taken to ensure that their data will be stored securely and anonymously. [1]
3. B
4. a) field b) harmed c) order
5. Sam could consider using repeated measures, a design where every participant does every condition. [1] This would avoid participant variables, but would lead to order effects as participants get better at the task. [1] She could use counterbalancing to minimise this problem. [1] Independent groups is another option, a design where participants complete only one condition; [1] participant variables can cause a major problem with this design, [1] but can be minimised by using a large sample (possibly impractical for a student). [1] Matched participants is a good compromise in this experiment; [1] matching participants by their memory ability and using two separate groups. [1] This would minimise the role of participant variables while allowing Sam to use two separate groups of participants and therefore use the same materials for both conditions. Given that people have different tastes in music, she could also consider matching by music preferences. [1]

Non-experimental Methods

1. Quantitative data
2. **Primary data**: where the researcher obtains and uses new data directly from the participant(s). [1] **Secondary data**: generated before for a different purpose, and the researcher obtains it and analyses it. [1]
3. Interview **or** survey
4. A
5. **Strength – any one from**: gains great depth and volume of data; useful for unusual cases, e.g. brain damage or psychological disorders; longitudinal, so allows researcher to see changes over time. **Weakness – any one from**: can be difficult to generalise from a single participant to the rest of the population; close relationship with participant can lead to researcher bias, or other relevant points.
6. Observation involves studying behaviour as it happens and recording data in the form of notes or videos. [1] Includes naturalistic observation – observing a participant in an everyday context. [1] Researcher may set out categories of behaviour in advance, with a checklist or observation schedule used to record how often each one occurs. [1] Problems: a single observer can be unreliable; this problem can be overcome by training observers and also by using more than one. [1] Inter-observer reliability means the

extent to which different observers record the same data from the same observation; the results from different observers can be compared to see how similar they are. [1] Ethical issues should be considered: invasion of privacy is where people are observed in a way that violates their rights, such as being watched in private without their consent. [1] This must be avoided, though researchers should be aware that disclosing the observation will impact on the behaviour of participants. [1] One way to minimise this problem is to ensure that participants being observed get used to the observer's presence. [1]

Correlation and Data Handling

1. The mode
2. A strong(ly) positive correlation
3. No. Correlation does not mean causation. [1] Two variables may show a strong relationship, but this isn't enough information for the researcher to know which variable is having an effect on the other, or if some outside/third variable is causing the relationship to occur. [1]
4. mean = 21.33; median = 19; range = 19 (31–12)
5. a) 11.4 [1] and 13.0 [1]
   b) 56.9% [1] and 65% [1] (If the mean was rounded before calculating this, the calculation will be inaccurate.)
   c) Although the visualisation technique was helpful overall, [1] it increased the variability in the scores, meaning that it helped some people but not others. [1]
   d)

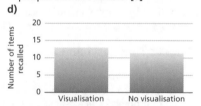

Pages 171–173 **Social Influence**

Conformity

1. No
2. Seeking the approval of the group [1] or the 'desire to be liked' [1]
3. C
4. a) B
   b) It was conducted in a laboratory [1] and is therefore an artificial situation. [1]
   c) Asch used deception [1] by making participants believe that all the other participants were genuine when they were actually confederates of the researcher. [1]
5. a) They were less likely to conform.
   b) People were more likely to adopt the views of the group.

Obedience

1. C
2. a) They allow other people to direct their actions [1] and attribute their actions to the person giving the instruction, rather than themselves. [1]
   b) Autonomous state
3. Things about the individual that might lead to them being more or less obedient (e.g. personality)
4. Authoritarian
5. Those who enforce high levels of discipline.
6. No. [1] A correlation does not imply causation. [1] There could be other factors that lead to higher levels of obedience. [1]
7. It is easily manipulated/people can second guess the questions to avoid being categorised as authoritarian.

Prosocial and Antisocial Behaviour

1. a) Diffusion of responsibility
   b) If helping is going to be time-consuming [1] or could put the helper in danger [1]
   c) If the helper is medically trained (e.g. nurse or doctor) [1] or other skills that can be used to help [1]
2. When they don't see the situation as an emergency
3. a) **One from**: people who were ill; people who carried a cane
   b) People who were drunk
4. Cameras reduce the anonymity of the crowd [1] and make them less likely to act aggressively. [1]
5. Deindividuation
6. Any reasonable answer, e.g. religious gatherings

Pages 174–177 **Language, Thought and Communication**

The Possible Relationship Between Language and Thought

1. a) Piaget
   b) It takes place in a number of stages.
2. Determines; influences
3. a) It suggests that language develops as a result of cognitive development [1] because if a child has problems with cognitive development, this affects their language. [1]
   b) It suggests that language can develop even though cognitive development is impaired. [1] Piaget believed that language could only develop if cognitive development is unimpaired. [1]
4. The types of thoughts people are able to have
5. They have fewer names for colours. [1] For example, the Zuni tribe only uses one word for the yellow-orange region of the spectrum. [1]
6. They have found that the words we use for colours can influence the ability to perceive colours that are not part of our vocabulary.

Differences Between Human and Animal Communication

1. Plumage [1], e.g. peacocks [1] (or any other reasonable example)
2. **Any two from**: song (birds), marking trees (e.g. wild boar), scenting with urine (dogs)
3. **Magpie**: chattering; **rabbit**: paw thumping
4. a) Von Frisch
   b) A bee finds a food source while exploring. [1] It returns to the hive to communicate its location. [1] Using the sun's position as a guide, it waggles its body in the direction of the food source. [1] The food's distance is communicated by adding extra shuffles. [1] The more plentiful the food source, the longer the duration of the dance. [1] After receiving the directions, the rest of the colony fly off to harvest the food. [1]
5. Sounds, [1] gestures, [1] material objects [1] or written words [1] that have a specific meaning to a group of people.
6. a) Past, [1] present [1] and future tense [1]
   b) Discuss/plan possible future outcomes [1] and discuss past events [1]

Non-verbal Communication

1. Speaking, [1] writing, [1] sign language [1]
2. Verbal communication uses words, while non-verbal communication doesn't rely on spoken or written words.
3. a) **Any one from**: they might want to speak; they might not be interested; they are listening but need to filter out distracting information
   b) It can indicate whether the listener approves of what the speaker is saying.
   c) Couples who score highly on measures of love also spend longer in mutual eye contact.
4. **Open posture**: revealing and leaves sensitive areas vulnerable; [1] the head is usually slightly back and the chin slightly raised; [1] arms by the side and the legs uncrossed [1]. **Closed posture**: defensive and protecting; [1] hands are held up to the chin or the head is lowered to protect the throat; [1] arms and legs are crossed [1]
5. The mirroring or adoption of the same posture as the person doing the talking
6. Cultural norms, [1] gender, [1] status [1]

Explanations of Non-verbal Behaviour

1. **Nature**: non-verbal behaviour is innate. [1] **Nurture**: non-verbal behaviour is learned. [1]
2. It conveys an evolutionary advantage.
3. Non-verbal behaviour is seen in all mammals, [1] both human and non-human. [1]
4. Blind children display the same facial expressions as sighted children. [1] This indicates that facial expressions are innate. [1]
5. Any two appropriate examples, such as: shaking hands, kissing on cheek, bowing
6. a) False
   b) **Any two from**: lacks ecological validity, sample bias, findings cannot be generalised

Pages 178–180 **Brain and Neuropsychology**

The Structure and Function of the Brain and Nervous System

1. It transfers messages to and from the brain to the peripheral nervous system.
2. Autonomic system
3. Sensory [1] and motor [1]
4. a) Sympathetic system
   b) Attack the threat; [1] run away from the threat [1]
   c) Increased heart rate; [1] muscular tension; [1] faster breathing rate; [1] pupil dilation; [1] reduced function of the digestive system; [1] reduced function of the immune system [1]
5. Because they cry (emotional experience is the result, not the cause, of perceived bodily changes)

Neuron Structure and Function

1. A = sensory; [1] B = relay; [1] C = motor [1]
2. a) Long-term potentiation (LTP)
   b) Stronger connections between nerve cells [1]; longer lasting changes in synaptic connections [1]
3. The process where messages are sent from neuron to neuron.
4. Serotonin (or another appropriate answer)

Localisation of Function in the Brain

1. It carries out higher order/mental functions. [1] Examples: thinking, [1] decision making [1] and planning [1]
2. **Any two from**: taste, temperature, touch
3. Occipital lobe
4. A = motor; [1] B = somatosensory; [1] C = auditory [1]
5. a) The amount of cortical tissue in certain brain functions differs.
   b) In an image known as the Penfield homunculus

Brain and Neuropsychology

1. Cognitive neuroscience
2. a) So that they can be asked to produce a particular action, [1] such as performing a memory task [1]
   b) fMRI, [1] CT (or CAT), [1] PET [1]
3. In order to identify the parts of the brain involved in the different kinds of memory.
4. a) Motor ability
   b) Loss of motor function; [1] for example, the inability to walk (or other appropriate movement impairments) [1]

Pages 181–183 **Psychological Problems**

An Introduction to Mental Health

1. Work; [1] satisfying interpersonal relations [1]
2. **Any three from**: positive attitude towards oneself; personal growth and development (or self-actualisation); feelings of independence (or autonomy); resisting stress; an accurate perception of reality; being able to cope with life and the changing environment (environmental mastery)
3. **Any two from**: appropriate public behaviour; control of aggression; politeness; control of socially and culturally offensive language
4. a) Geographical isolation (or other appropriate answer)
   b) **Any one from**: increased use of technology; pressure at school; pressure at work
5. The high suicide rate amongst men

Effects of Mental Health Problems on Individuals and Society

1. a) They might not socialise as much as they used to; [1] for example, seeing friends and other couples. [1]
   b) **Any one from**: Not engaging in activities once thought of as enjoyable; neglecting personal hygiene; not looking after oneself generally
   c) Can reduce the functioning of the immune system, [1] making physical illness more likely [1]
2. **Any one from**: social workers and/ or social care professionals (e.g. carers); mental health workers; health professionals (e.g. doctors, psychologists, mental health nurses)
3. Any appropriate answer, such as: people suffering from addiction might turn to theft to buy the addictive substance.
4. Increased rates of absenteeism

Characteristics of Clinical Depression

1. A type of clinical depression that occurs without mania
2. Duration (how long the episodes last)

---

3. Someone with a great deal of energy. [1] They rush around [1] but never get anything done. [1] They lack a sense of purpose in their actions [1] and survive on very little sleep. [1]
4. Men with depression are usually less likely to seek help.
5. a) **Any two from**: persistent sadness or low mood; loss of interest or pleasure; fatigue or low energy
   b) **Any three from**: disturbed sleep; poor concentration; low self-confidence; poor or increased appetite; suicidal thoughts/acts; agitation; guilt/self-blame.

Theories of Depression and Interventions

1. a) i) People with depression have lower levels of serotonin in the brain
      ii) A gene has been identified that reduces levels of serotonin. [1] This gene is more likely to be found in people with depression. [1]
   b) They assume that depression has an internal cause [1] when other factors such as upbringing or home life might be leading to the depression. [1]
2. Depressed people have a negative schema, [1] which is a pessimistic blueprint of the world that shapes their outlook. [1]
3. Stable
4. Tricyclic antidepressants block the transporter mechanism that absorbs serotonin and noradrenaline. [1] SSRIs mainly block serotonin only. [1]
5. Drug therapy involves taking pills to regulate brain chemicals, [1] while psychotherapy involves talking about your problems with a specially trained therapist. [1]
6. CBT, in conjunction with antidepressants

Characteristics of Addiction

1. Addiction refers to a behaviour that leads to dependency. [1] Abuse doesn't necessarily lead to dependence/addiction. [1]
2. a) At least one month
   b) **Any three from**: a strong desire or sense of compulsion to take the substance despite harmful consequences; impaired capacity to control substance-taking behaviour; pre-occupation with substance use and the giving up of activities once deemed important; a physiological withdrawal state when the substance is reduced or ceased
3. Any appropriate answer, such as shopping, gambling, gaming, internet use
4. Preoccupation (with activity); [1] persistence [1]
5. Reverting to earlier patterns of addiction soon after giving up

---

Theories of Addiction and Interventions

1. Family studies [1] and twin studies [1]
2. a) Rates of alcohol abuse [1] in identical and fraternal twins [1]
   b) Two-thirds
3. They might try to conform to the norms of the reference group/peers whom they admire
4. a) A drug could be used/a pill taken [1] that would cause the smoker to feel nauseous when they smoked a cigarette. [1] They would learn to associate the sick feeling with smoking [1]; they would stop smoking so that they didn't feel nauseous. [1]
   b) **Any one from**: negative visualisation; focusing on an unpleasant feeling
5. Acceptance of the addiction

Practice Exam Papers

Pages 184–202 **Practice Exam Paper 1 Cognition and Behaviour**

A Memory

01 D
02 A
03 D
04.1 **Duration**: approximately 30 seconds, or 18–30s. [1] **Encoding**: acoustic/sound-based. [1] Explanation should refer to the example: one feature of STM is that it has a limited duration – this means that Amina forgot the phrase in the time that the teacher was explaining it, because she didn't write it down immediately; [1] acoustic encoding means that we can retain exact words/sounds for a short time even if we do not fully understand them. [1]
04.2 A normal distribution shows a variable where central values are common and extreme ones are progressively rarer. [1] It has certain mathematical characteristics – its features include: a bell-shaped curve, mean/median/mode in the centre of the distribution, equal amounts of values below and above the mean. **[2 points for naming 2 of the 3 features; a sketch could also be credited for 1 mark]**
05.1 Atkinson and Shiffrin **[1 mark only if both are stated]**
05.2 Attention is the main means of transfer of information from sensory memory (SM) to STM. [1] Information is rapidly forgotten in SM, [1] and only items which are attended to enter the limited capacity short-term store. [1] Rehearsal keeps information in STM but also serves to encode items to LTM, according to the model. [1] So information which is rehearsed for a long period of time/maintained in STM for longer, or repeated more frequently, will enter LTM. [1] Could also discuss

---

information moving from LTM to STM by processes of retrieval or give an example. [1]

05.3 **Strengths**: It shows STM and LTM as separate stores of memory, a distinction supported by evidence from brain-damaged patients (or similar point). [1] The model also explains how sensory memory connects to the other stores of memory, emphasising that new sensory information can only be transferred from sensory to short-term memory if we pay attention to it. [1] The model is supported by Murdock's (1962) serial position (primacy and recency) curve/effect. According to the model, the primacy effect occurs because items at the start of a list are easier to rehearse and therefore get encoded into long-term memory, but by the middle of the list there are too many to rehearse. [1] The recency effect occurs because the last few items are in short-term memory, but because of its limited capacity, the middle items are pushed out from short-term memory in a process known as displacement. [1]
Weaknesses: According to the model, rehearsal is the only way that information can be permanently memorised. However, many things which are rehearsed are forgotten, and people appear to be able to take in information without rehearsing it. [1] This feature also neglects the importance of other factors in memorisation such as retrieval practice, spacing, visualisation and meaning/depth of processing. [1] The model does not account for the use of visual encoding in either short-term or long-term memory, but clearly people are able to take in and store visual information such as faces and maps. [1] The model is over-simplistic – it doesn't show the different types of LTM, such as episodic and procedural memory. [1]

B Perception

06 Sensation is the initial processing of external cues such as light and sound by specialist receptor cells in the body. [1] Perception is the brain building up a picture of the world using information from the senses and interpreting them/combining them with information from memory. [1]

07 A

08 C

09 It is a form of illusion. [1] There are two possible interpretations (in terms of an individual trying to make sense of an ambiguous 2D figure) or two ways to distinguish the 'figure' from the background. [1] Example: Rubin's vase or the Necker cube. [1]

10 **Depth cues**: occlusion, linear perspective, or any other appropriate answers. [2] The way that the bicycle occludes the street/building shows

that it is closer. [1] The linear perspective of the street edges [1] as well as the increasing height in plane of the street [1] shows that it is getting further away towards the top of the image. [1]

11.1 Refer to at least two factors associated with the perceptual set, e.g. emotions and expectations. In the case of Duncan, expectations made him think that he heard the doorbell when he didn't, [1] and emotions/feelings (hunger) made him find the crisps more appealing than usual. [1] Refer to the constructivist theory of perception, with examples such as the hollow face illusion showing the role of expectations/interpretation, or mention errors in perception such as hallucinations, illusions. [2]

11.2 **Describe** Bruner and Minturn, or Gilchrist and Nesberg. Also accept studies that link to factors in perception, e.g. Hudson's research into culture. Features will depend on the study chosen, but will typically include aim, procedure, findings. [4] **Evaluation**: include features of the research method used, such the artificiality of a lab-based experiment. Some research, e.g. Bruner and Minturn, is dated and hard to generalise to other situations. Could also feature positive points, such as the high level of control in lab studies or useful cross-cultural perspective. Useful in terms of understanding the perceptual set or helps to support one theory of perception (constructivist) rather than the other. [4]

C Development

12.1 B

12.2 D

13.1 **Any two areas from**: cerebrum/cerebral cortex, cerebellum, brain stem, thalamus should be named and accurately identified on Figure 4. [2] **Two functions from**: cerebrum – thinking and memory; cerebellum – controls precise physical movement and helps to coordinate actions; brain stem – essential basic functions such as breathing; thalamus – sensory relay. [2] Visual cortex could be described; 'a neuron' is not an acceptable answer.

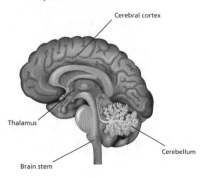

Cerebral cortex

Thalamus

Cerebellum

Brain stem

13.2 Brain development begins to develop around the third week after a new

baby is conceived/inside 10 weeks/embryonic stage of pregnancy. Begins with stem cells, which later transform into neurons. [1] True neurons begin to form on day 42 of a pregnancy, and major structures are present by day 56. [1] Baby's brain areas are largely complete by half-way through pregnancy. [1]

13.3 A newborn baby has a more complex level of neural interconnections than an adult, and development occurs by pruning unnecessary connections. [1] Other connections are strengthened as the child learns. A stimulating environment boosts successful development; a deprived one is harmful but can largely be overcome. [1] Most development is complete by adolescence but brain plasticity plays a role later in life. [1]

14 The theory is used in education, but there is no evidence that being taught according to a particular 'style' helps learning. [1] So-called styles may be just preferences, e.g. verbalisers. [1] Using multiple types of encoding is beneficial (e.g. dual coding) rather than a single one/best to use modality that suits the material to be learned (Willingham). [1]

15.1 Involved a physical model of three mountains and a set of photographs. [1] A child was shown the model; each mountain had something different at the top. [1] A doll was placed on the model at a different position from the child. [1] The child was then shown several photographs and asked to identify what the doll would be able to see. [1] Alternatively, can credit a brief statement of findings, e.g. older children tended to succeed, but those in the pre-operational stage chose a picture which was similar to what they themselves could see.

15.2 The study findings supported the idea that younger children are egocentric – they can't picture the world from another person's point of view. [1] This was considered to be normal at a young age of development – a child in the pre-operational stage. [1] However, other researchers have disagreed. [1] In particular, Hughes (1975) suggested that younger children only failed the three mountains problem because it was too difficult. [1] He created a simpler version of the experiment called the policeman doll study. In this version, a policeman doll was placed on the mountains model, and the child was asked to place a second doll where the policeman couldn't see it. 90% of four year olds succeeded. [1] The policeman doll study suggests that young children are able to take another person's point of view, and are therefore less egocentric than Piaget believed. [1]

D Research Methods

16.1 Examples – **any two from**: interview answers, IQ scores, language test scores, diary entries. **[2]** For each example, identify whether it is primary or secondary data, and quantitative or qualitative. For example, interview data is usually qualitative primary data. **[2]**

16.2 **Confidentiality**: researcher must avoid disclosing the man's identity in any publication/could use initials rather than his full name **or invasion of privacy**: participant's rights could be violated by reading his diary entries **or informed consent**: participant must understand fully what they are consenting to, but the man's brain damage could limit his understanding and therefore family consent may be needed. **[1 for issue; 1 for explanation]**

17.1 Independent groups design

17.2 **Random allocation**: used to avoid bias **[1]** in the selection of participants for the different conditions. **[1]**
A control condition: needed as a baseline, **[1]** to compare the experimental conditions to. **[1]**

17.3 Control involves keeping extraneous variables constant and minimised, **[1]** in order to determine whether the IV has an effect on the DV. **[1]** Example: the use of the same passages for all participants/the use of a lab environment to minimise distractions. **[1]**

17.4 Bar chart. **[1]** Chart does not need to show a particular pattern of results, but all three conditions must be displayed and labelled, as should the DV (e.g. percentage response, score on recall test or similar), like the following. **[2]**

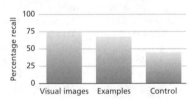

18.1 Stress/score on stress questionnaire; **[1]** percentage score on the maths activity **[1]**

18.2

18.3 B

18.4 Better sampling technique, e.g. random/using a larger sample.

18.5 It's not possible to conclude a cause and effect connection between the two co-variables in a correlation study. **[1]** There could be a reverse causation, i.e. poorer revision could lead to higher levels of stress. Or a third variable could cause both variables to change. **[1]**

Pages 203–217 **Practice Exam Paper 2 Social Context and Behaviour**

A Social Influence

01 B

02.1 How a person acts when they witness an emergency

02.2 **Any three factors from**: similarity of David to the lady (e.g. in terms of race/not gender in this case), number of other people present, the cost of helping, perceived expertise, pluralistic ignorance

03.1 75%

03.2 A description of how to select participants (e.g. random sampling, opportunity sampling, volunteer sampling). **[2]** Description of a feature of the study (e.g. estimating the number of sweets in a jar). **[1]**

04.1 64%

04.2 People were more likely to pick up litter if the actor was wearing a uniform. **[1]** A uniform suggests legitimate authority. **[1]**

04.3 Ethics: the researchers used deception. **[1]** Participants didn't know that they were part of an experiment and that the person asking them to pick up litter was an actor. **[1]** The study was conducted in a natural setting (a park) **[1]** so was high in ecological validity. **[1]**

05 Most likely study is Zimbardo's (1969) replication of Milgram's study. Could also cite Diener *et al.*'s (1976) study on anonymity of trick or treaters. Evaluation could include ethical issues or sampling methods. **[9]**

B Language, Thought and Communication

06 Verbal: Ria shouting "Pass!", Katie shouting "Yes!"; **[2]** non-verbal: Ria raising her hand, Ria jumping up and down

07 Animals only communicate to pass messages about survival/reproduction/territory/obtaining food/whereabouts. **[1]** Any appropriate example, e.g. rabbit thumping, waggle dance of the honeybee. **[1]** Humans communicate information about their lives and their plans for the future. **[1]**

08 Piaget indicated that development takes place in a number of stages and that language development is the result of cognitive (or thought) development. **[1]** According to Piaget, a child must first be able to use ideas and concepts before being able to use language. **[1]** However, a child might use and repeat words before understanding the concepts behind these words. Piaget called this egocentric speech. **[1]**

09 **Evaluation could include the following**: lack of ecological validity because Yuki used computer-generated faces to test participants and not real faces; **[1]** therefore findings cannot be generalised to real-life situations. **[1]** Demand characteristics: participants were aware that they were taking part in a study so may not have given true responses. **[1]** Findings cannot be generalised because the study only looked at one element of emotion (happy/sad) and not any other emotions. **[1]** Yuki used students to test the hypothesis. **[1]** Results might have been different if the study used older or younger participants. **[1]**

10.1 Hereditary/inherited/inborn/from genetics rather than being learned through experience/something that you are born with

10.2 The non-verbal behaviour in the study is the smiling of the babies, which was counted as number of smiles. **[1]** The results for both conditions can be described as similar **[1]** because there is only a difference of 7. **[1]** However, they can be described as different because the sighted babies smiled more. **[1]** The study can conclude that babies do not have to be able to see in order to smile. **[1]** Therefore, smiling is innate. **[1]**

10.3 D

10.4 Observation

C Brain and Neuropsychology

11 D

12 They carry messages from one part of the central nervous system to another. **[1]** They connect motor and sensory neurons. **[1]**

13 In the first stage, the hypothalamus recognises that there is a threat **[1]** and sends a message to the adrenal gland. **[1]** The adrenal medulla then triggers the release of adrenaline to the endocrine system and noradrenaline to the brain. **[1]** These stages then lead to a number of bodily changes, including: increased heart rate, muscular tension, faster breathing rate, pupil dilation, and reduced function of the digestive and immune system. **[3 marks for at least three bodily changes]**

14.1 **A:** temporal, **B:** parietal, **C:** occipital

14.2 **A:** somatosensory, **B:** auditory

14.3 The view that particular areas of the brain are responsible for specific functions, **[1]** such as vision and language. **[1]**

15 Modern scanning techniques such as fMRI scans rely on matching behavioural actions with physiological activity. **[1]** Because the person being scanned is usually conscious, they can be directed to produce particular actions (e.g. remembering a life event). **[1]** The blood flow patterns highlighted on the scan show the researcher how the areas of the brain are functioning during the activity. **[1]** Also, normal scans can be compared with scans of people with brain damage so that explanations for the damage can be discovered. **[1]** Tulving's study identified locations within the brain that are used for specific memory functions. **[1]** Researchers are then able to make inferences about areas of damage and their impact on behaviour. **[1]**

16 D

17 The motor neuron carries an electrical signal to a muscle, **[1]** which will cause muscles to either contract or relax. **[1]**

D Psychological Problems

18 **Any two from:** persistent sadness/ low mood, fatigue/low energy, poor concentration, suicidal thoughts/ acts, decrease in activity, change in sleep pattern, reduced self-esteem or self-confidence, ideas of guilt or worthlessness, loss of pleasurable feelings, agitation, loss or increase in appetite

19 Mania is characterised by periods of excitement or euphoria. **[1]** A person with bipolar depression might rush around and appear to be doing lots of things but never get anything done. **[1]** They would rarely sleep during manic episodes and have no real direction. **[1]**

20 C

21.1 Medication = 6
Medication and CBT = 8 **[2 marks for each correct answer]**

21.2 **Strength:** uses data from all participants; **[1] weakness:** sensitive to outliers **[1]**

21.3 Opportunity sampling (accept volunteer sampling)

21.4 **Strength:** relatively easy to create **[1]** because it uses people who are readily available. **[1]** **Weakness:** unrepresentative; **[1]** the sample is likely to be biased because only a particular type of person is likely to volunteer. **[1]**

21.5 Random. **[1] Weakness:** impractical and not representative. **[1] or** Stratified sampling. **[1] Weakness:** cannot be used for every study/ problems with sorting people into a single stratum **[1]**

21.6 Using both medication and CBT is more effective than using medication alone. **[1]** This is because people who received medication only as a form of treatment had a lower mean rating than those who received the combined treatment. **[1]**

22 Kaij (1960) **[1]** studied the rates of alcohol abuse in identical and fraternal twins. **[1]** He found that the concordance rate for identical twins was 54% and that for fraternal twins it was only 28%. **[1]** Kaij concluded that there are genetic and hereditary factors involved in alcohol addiction. **[1]**

Collins GCSE Revision

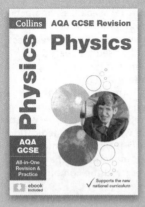
Collins AQA GCSE Revision
Physics
AQA GCSE
All-in-One Revision & Practice
✓ Supports the new national curriculum
ebook included

Collins GCSE Revision
Geography
GCSE
All-in-One Revision & Practice
✓ Supports the new national curriculum
ebook included

Collins GCSE Revision
History
British
GCSE
All-in-One Revision & Practice
✓ Supports the new national curriculum
ebook included

Collins AQA GCSE Revision
English
Language & Literature
AQA GCSE
All-in-One Revision & Practice
✓ Supports the new national curriculum
ebook included

Collins Edexcel GCSE Revision
Physical Education
Edexcel GCSE
All-in-One Revision & Practice
✓ Supports the new national curriculum
ebook included

Collins Edexcel GCSE Revision
Maths
Foundation
Edexcel GCSE
All-in-One Revision & Practice
✓ Supports the new national curriculum
ebook included

Collins OCR GCSE Revision
Chemistry
OCR Gateway GCSE
All-in-One Revision & Practice
✓ Supports the new national curriculum
ebook included

Collins AQA GCSE Revision
French
with Audio
AQA GCSE
All-in-One Revision & Practice
✓ Supports the new national curriculum
ebook included

Collins GCSE Revision
Religious Studies
GCSE
All-in-One Revision & Practice
✓ Supports the new national curriculum
ebook included

Collins AQA GCSE Revision
Spanish
with Audio
AQA GCSE
All-in-One Revision & Practice
✓ Supports the new national curriculum
ebook included

Collins AQA GCSE Revision
Food Preparation and Nutrition
AQA GCSE
All-in-One Revision & Practice
✓ Supports the new national curriculum
ebook included

Collins OCR GCSE Revision
Biology
OCR Gateway GCSE
All-in-One Revision & Practice
✓ Supports the new national curriculum
ebook included

Visit the website to view the complete range and place an order:
www.collins.co.uk/collinsGCSErevision

ACKNOWLEDGEMENTS

The author and publisher are grateful to the copyright holders for permission to use quoted materials and images.

Cover, p.1, p.153 © conrado/Shutterstock.com,
© Omelchenko/Shutterstock.com,
© Triff/Shutterstock.com
p.24 © ANIMATED HEALTHCARE LTD/SCIENCE PHOTO LIBRARY
p.25 © SCIENCE SOURCE/SCIENCE PHOTO LIBRARY
p.38 © Granger Historical Picture Archive/Alamy Stock Photo; © Marmaduke St. John/Alamy Stock Photo
p.190 © www.wikipedia.org/wiki/File:ID-Scenic-3.svg
All other images © Shutterstock.com

Every effort has been made to trace copyright holders and obtain their permission for the use of copyright material. The author and publisher will gladly receive information enabling them to rectify any error or omission in subsequent editions. All facts are correct at time of going to press.

Published by Collins

An imprint of HarperCollins*Publishers* Ltd

1 London Bridge Street,
London, SE1 9GF

© HarperCollins*Publishers* Limited

9780008227449

First published 2017

10 9 8 7 6 5 4 3 2 1

British Library Cataloguing in Publication Data.

A CIP record of this book is available from the British Library.

Authored by: Jonathan Firth and Marc Smith
Commissioning Editors: Katherine Wilkinson and Charlotte Christensen
Editor: Charlotte Christensen
Project Manager: Tracey Cowell
Cover Design: Sarah Duxbury and Paul Oates
Inside Concept Design: Sarah Duxbury and Paul Oates
Text Design and Layout: Jouve India Private Limited
Production: Natalia Rebow
Printed in the UK by Bell and Bain Ltd, Glasgow

HarperCollins PUBLISHERS
Since 1817

6 EASY WAYS TO ORDER

1. Available from www.collins.co.uk
2. Fax your order to 01484 665736
3. Phone us on 0844 576 8126
4. Email us at education@harpercollins.co.uk
5. Post your order to: Collins Education, FREEPOST RTKB-SGZT-ZYJL, Honley HD9 6QZ
6. Or visit your local bookshop.